R E V I

THE STORY OF THE WORKMAN AND TEMPLE FAMILIES PARALLELS THE GROWTH OF LOS ANGELES ITSELF. FROM 1830 TO 1930, THE TWO FAMILIES WERE INVOLVED IN EVERY FEATURE OF THE DEVELOPMENT OF SOUTHERN CALIFORNIA: CATTLE RAISING, AGRICULTURE, MINING AND OIL, BANKING, POLITICS, BUSINESS ENTERPRISES, AND CIVIC AFFAIRS. IN ALL OF THESE AREAS THE READER WILL FIND WORKMAN AND TEMPLE WOMEN AND MEN, OFTEN IN PROMINENT ROLES.

THIS ENGAGING STORY REVEALS SIGNIFICANT PEOPLE INVOLVED IN THE CREATION OF ONE OF THE WORLD'S GREAT CITIES. WITH CLARITY AND INSIGHT, PAUL SPITZZERI EXPLAINS HOW TWO FAMILIES CONTRIBUTED SO MUCH OVER AN EXTENDED PERIOD TO THE BUILDING OF SOUTHERN CALIFORNIA.

MICHAEL E. ENGH, DEAN OF BELLARMINE COLLEGE OF LIBERAL ARTS, LOYOLA MARYMOUNT UNIVERSITY, LOS ANGELES

THIS OUTSTANDING WORK PUTS THE WORKMAN AND TEMPLE FAMILIES IN THE RICH CONTEXT OF EARLY CALIFORNIA, EXPLAINS THEIR HISTORICAL TRAJECTORY, AND TELLS US MUCH OF THEIR CONTRIBUTIONS TO CULTURE AND ECONOMICS IN NINETEENTH-CENTURY CALIFORNIA. IMPORTANTLY, THIS BOOK ALSO EXAMINES THE CONTRIBUTIONS OF FAMILY MEMBERS WELL INTO THE TWENTIETH CENTURY. IT IS AN IMPORTANT CONTRIBUTION TO CALIFORNIA HISTORY.

GORDON MORRIS BAKKEN, PROFESSOR OF HISTORY CALIFORNIA STATE UNIVERSITY, FULLERTON

The Workman and Temple Families
of Southern California

THE WORKMAN &
TEMPLE FAMILIES
OF
SOUTHERN CALIFORNIA,

1830-1930

by

PAUL R. SPITZZERI

SELIGSON PUBLISHING INCORPORATED
DALLAS, TEXAS 2008

Book Cover:
photos courtesy of
the Seaver Center—see page 273
the Fell Types are digitally reproduced
by Igino Marini. www.iginomarini.com
concept—Dara Jones
design—Chris Flynn

Seligson Publishing Incorporated
660 Preston Forest Center
Suite 392
Dallas, Texas 75230
(888) 597-5758
seligson.publishing@gmail.com

❧ *Table of Contents* ❧

❧ P R E F A C E ❧

When I started working at the Workman and Temple Family Homestead Museum in 1988, it became immediately obvious that, though the museum had been open for seven years, surprisingly little research was conducted on the families and the museum site. Three years later, when the museum celebrated its tenth anniversary as well as the sesquicentennial of the arrival of the Rowland and Workman expedition, the guest speaker was David J. Weber, the eminent historian of the United States-Mexico borderlands. Yet it was striking that Dr. Weber, who gave an entertaining and informative presentation, had done his work on William Workman and John Rowland over twenty-five years before. The fact that updated research on the Workman and Temple families was badly needed was not just obvious to me. A family descendant, Donald Rowland, was likewise stirred to begin his own investigations, which yielded the book *John Rowland and William Workman: Southern California Pioneers of 1841* (Historical Society of Southern California and Arthur H. Clark Company, 1999).

Two weeks after Dr. Weber's presentation, I went on my first research trip, spending a couple of days at the Bancroft Library at the University of California, Berkeley. Soon, I was ensnared in the addictive habit of intense research, spending my days off in archives, libraries, historical societies, and other repositories, great and small, throughout the Los Angeles area and elsewhere in California. The list of places and staff members who assisted me are too numerous to mention, but anyone who does historical research is greatly indebted to those people, paid and volunteer, who do the decidedly unglamorous, little appreciated and underfunded work of preserving our material heritage.

I also was fortunate to have access to many family documents, letters, photographs, and other items and want to express my deep appreciation to those members of the Workman and Temple families who shared them with me, including Ruth Ann Michaelis, Betty Temple Miner, Douglas Neilson, Gary Temple, Josette Temple, Thomas Temple, David Workman, and the late Gabriela Quiroz Temple Sutter, F. P. F. Temple III and Walter P. Temple, Junior. I also want to single out the great deal of help I received from Don

ix

Rowland, particularly from sources he found in New Mexico, and from John Sharpe, who unearthed a great deal of valuable material on the Workman family in England.

Because I lacked a decent personal computer, I received the permission of my supervisor, Max van Balgooy, now of the National Trust for Historic Preservation, to use his computer, conveniently located adjacent to the rapidly-growing research files, where copies of my research and that of others was located, to write the manuscript. Virtually every evening, five days a week, after Max left for the day, I settled in at his desk and hammered away, starting the work in the fall of 1994 and completing it in the late spring of 1995. I also want to acknowledge Karen Graham Wade, Director of the Homestead Museum, and Alexandra Rasic, the museum's Public Programs Manager, for their support over the years.

I was also extremely fortunate to have the benefit of well-regarded scholars to read all of or portions of the manuscript, including Dr. Gloria Ricci Lothrop, who read the first chapter, and Dr. Michael Engh, Dean of the Bellarmine College of the Liberal Arts at Loyola Marymount University and Dr. Doyce B. Nunis, Jr., emeritus professor of the University of Southern California and long-time editor of the Southern California Quarterly, both of whom read the entire manuscript and offered many invaluable suggestions for improvement. For a greenhorn historian to have their guidance and assistance was more than I could have asked for.

This book flirted with publication after I completed it and again earlier this decade, but seemed destined for perpetual inertia. Thanks to the unflagging support and tireless energy of Dara Jones, proprietor of Seligson Publishing, and the advent of new technology, the project was revived again early in 2007. By then, new information had come to light, particularly some valuable letters and documents loaned by Josette Temple. While these were incorporated into the manuscript, I made no effort at any considerable revision, it seeming to me that it held up all right as it was. I sure hope I'm right about that!

Paul
14 August 2007

❧ CHAPTER ONE ❧

Extranjeros en California[1]

✺ 1830–1841 ✺

Jonathan Temple: Early California Mercantilist

When the brig *Waverly* landed at San Diego sometime in July 1827, it probably appeared to be one of the many trading ships arriving in the far-flung Mexican province of California seeking hides and tallow in return for manufactured goods. Trade between American ships like the *Waverly* and the ports of Mexican California had only been legally initiated five years before with Mexican independence from Spain, although illicit trade had existed during the twilight days of the Spanish period. This increased trade with Americans and Europeans brought greater foreign influence into the region, which was too distant from Mexico City to be effectively under the government's control. Beginning in the late 1820s, economic power yielded by non-Mexicans soon led to social and political clout when foreigners slowly trickled into California to settle and prosper.

The arrival of the *Waverly* was, therefore, notable because aboard the brig was a thirty-one-year-old New England native named Jonathan Temple, just arrived from Hawaii and intending to settle in southern California. Soon, Temple was living in Los Angeles, becoming the second American or European resident in the pueblo.[2]

Temple was born in Reading, Massachusetts in 1796 to Captain Jonathan Temple who earned his title by serving in a local militia, and his first wife, Lydia Pratt. The Temples were descended from English immigrants, the first of whom, Abraham Temple, had come to New England by 1636.[3] The family had been in Reading since at least the 1680s and was prominent there.[4] It

---

1   Foreigners
2   The first was Joseph Chapman, a shipwreck victim who arrived in Los Angeles in 1821.
3   Levi Daniel Temple, *Some Temple Pedigrees: A Genealogy of the Known Descendants of Abraham Temple* (Boston: David Clapp and Son, 1900), p. 9.
4   Ibid., p. 213; Lilley Eaton, *Genealogical History of the Town of Reading, Massachusetts* (Bowie, MD: Heritage Books, Inc., 1994), pp. 117–19.

JONATHAN TEMPLE, CIRCA 1855

SECURITY PACIFIC COLLECTION/
LOS ANGELES PUBLIC LIBRARY

is likely that Jonathan was the first of his family to leave New England, evidently around 1820.[5]

Temple did what many young Yankees, lured by adventure, the dollar, or missionary fervor, were doing in that period; he headed to Hawaii to seek his livelihood. American merchants had been trading there since the 1790s and their increasing presence brought them the kind of influence that they would later hold in California. As news of the island kingdom and its pagan culture traveled back to New England and a few Hawaiians were exhibited there, something like circus curiosities, bands of Protestant missionaries began to sail to the islands. They were inspired during this age of religious revivalism to preach the Gospel, as was being done in Spanish and Mexican California by Franciscan friars. Americans had only months before the arrival of the first missionaries contributed to the overthrow of the Hawaiian religious and social taboo systems shortly after the death of King Kamehameha I in 1819. The upheaval of the basic systems of social order among the natives opened the path to further foreign dominance of the islands. This was the atmosphere when Jonathan Temple arrived early in the 1820s.

Unfortunately, little direct evidence has been located about his years on the islands. During his stay, he owned his own sailing vessel and imported American goods for sale or trade with such items as the internationally cov-

---

5   Jonathan Temple did make occasional visits back to Reading, such as in 1857–58, when his daughter, Francisca, and her family were living in New York, but also traveling to Paris, where they moved to in the early 1860s. John H. Bancroft to F.P.F. Temple, 2 March 1858, courtesy of Josette Temple.

eted sandalwood.[6] Trade was fast and furious in those days and competition extremely keen. While tensions with the natives were to be expected, disputes existing between missionaries and traders also contributed to the difficult and dangerous atmosphere of 1820s Hawaii. One such incident involving Temple concerned the prerogative of the kingdom's authorities to seize the property of foreigners resident in the islands. An American missionary wrote in September 1823 that

> notice has been received today that Karaimoku [Kalanimoku, governor of Oahu, where Temple lived] and Boke [Boki, governor of Maui] have ordered Marine, Mr. Warren, Mr. Navarro and Mr. Temple to be stripped of their property. A large number of kanakas [native Hawaiians] entered Mr. Marine's house this morning to put the order into effect.[7]

Although it is unknown what precipitated the order and seizure, it is obvious that Temple, either individually or, more likely, in conjunction with the others named, had committed an act that infuriated local authorities. It may have been one of many possibilities, including selling liquor outside of the restrictions then in force, smuggling merchandise to avoid customs, or some action involving politics.

Still, it was three and a half years before Temple made the decision to move to California. The event was recorded in a surviving letter Temple wrote on 20 February 1827 from Oahu to a ship captain named John B. R. Cooper, residing at the time in Monterey. Mainly concerned with business, the letter documented the shipment of "one pipe [of] brandy & one Qr. cask [of] wine" Temple was sending in proxy by another captain. Temple's statement of going to California, however, was terse enough: "I expect we shall sail for California in the course [of] six weeks."[8]

---

6   John Steven McGroarty, *Los Angeles: From the Mountains to the Sea* (Chicago: The American Historical Society, 1921), p. 916, based upon information provided by Temple's nephew, John Harrison Temple. A draft of the younger Temple's sketch, written in August 1918, is kept in the Homestead Museum Archives, City of Industry, California, and provided courtesy of his granddaughter, Betty Temple Miner.

7   Ralph S. Kuykendall, *The Hawaiian Kingdom, Volume One: 1778–1854, Foundation and Transformation* (5th ed., Honolulu: University of Hawaii Press, 1976), p. 73.

8   Jonathan Temple to John R.B. Cooper, 20 February 1827, from a copy of the original in the Thomas Workman Temple II Collection. Courtesy of Ruth Ann Temple Michaelis and Gabriela Quiroz Temple Sutter.

California, like Hawaii, was a place relatively new to foreign incursion and like the islands soon subjected to American domination. However, in the 1820s, it was not nearly as vulnerable to foreign influence and power. Mexican independence in 1821 had opened the door for foreign trade with California and a gradual trickle of foreign ships began to dock at the territory's few harbors to conduct business. It was common for such ships to sail to Hawaii and California on the same trip, taking Hawaiian sandalwood and California hides back to the United States. The Richard Henry Dana narrative, *Two Years Before the Mast*, describes the many ships, often with large crews of Hawaiians, plying the coast of California.[9] Temple's vessel may have participated in this triangular trade network and from that experience given him the idea to relocate to an area with less competition and considerably less tension. By the summer of 1827, Temple was in San Diego. He remained there for some undetermined time and was baptized a Roman Catholic on 30 July 1827, which suggests his interest in permanent residency and in identifying with the local society.[10] We may wonder, however, about the sincerity of Temple's religious intentions and assume that his transformation from a Protestant to a Catholic was motivated by more earthly concerns. While it is thought that Temple did become a naturalized Mexican citizen, a letter written by him in the summer of 1839 to Thomas O. Larkin, American businessman and later United States consul based in Monterey, noted,

> By the last mail I wrote him [Jose Sepulveda] my reasons
> for not taking my letters of Naturalization, some of which
> were that I had doubts under the new Constitution whether
> the Governors had authority to grant them, but at the same
> time told him I did not pretend to interpret the Laws and
> that if the Government here was of the opinion that they
> had powers to grant them I would gladly receive my letter
> of Naturalization.[11]

---

9   In a 22 August 1859 letter written on Dana's return voyage to California, he said "of the people of Los Angeles of 1835,6, see John Temple, Stearns, and Warner. The former become immensely rich." Richard Henry Dana, *Two Years Before the Mast*, John H. Kemble, ed. (2 vols., Los Angeles: The Ward Ritchie Press, 1964), II, p. 421.

10 Marco R. Newmark, "The Life of Jonathan (John) Temple," *Historical Society of Southern California Quarterly*, XXXVI, 1 (March 1954): 46.

11 Jonathan Temple to Thomas O. Larkin, 23 August 1839, in George P. Hammond, ed., *The Larkin Papers* (10 vols, Berkeley: University of California Press, 1951) I: p.25.

Most sources indicate that Temple moved to Los Angeles later in 1827, but, in testimony for his brother, F.P.F. Temple, in a land claims commission hearing in 1856, Temple stated that he had settled in Los Angeles in 1828.[12] Sometime after his arrival, Temple obtained an adobe at the junction of what were later named Spring and Main streets and opened Los Angeles' first American-style store.[13]

The opening of the business had a great many implications for the *Californios* (native Californians of primarily Spanish/Mexican descent) of the pueblo. Prior to this, American goods were usually obtainable by going to San Pedro, where ships were anchored like floating markets, ready to barter hides for goods, or by getting them from those who had been to the ships. Temple could profit from this presence of desired American goods as a middleman, either by buying goods from the ships himself or arranging for his own shipments, and then selling them in his store, which was much more convenient to town dwellers and residents of inland ranchos.

In September 1830, Temple married nineteen-year old Rafaela Cota, a native of Santa Barbara who was related to the Dominguez family, owners of the enormous Rancho San Pedro south of Los Angeles. Marriage by someone like Temple to a member of the elite, or *gente de razon*, such as Rafaela, certainly made him a member of southern California's privileged class. Perhaps the two met through her Dominguez relations or maybe she was an occasional patron of his store when visiting her relatives. In the autumn of 1831 their only child, Francisca, was born.[14]

Temple's move towards integrating himself into the Californio society probably enhanced his business. Whether the marriage was for love or social acceptance is a matter of conjecture. Regardless, Temple built a successful business with the steady patronage of the Californios as well as from the slowly growing foreign community. Americans and Europeans were not only growing in numbers but were also gaining in economic, political, and social influ-

---

12 California Land Claims Case No. 217, Rancho La Merced (F.P.F. Temple and Juan Matias Sanchez), p. 62, Bancroft Library, University of California, Berkeley.

13 Main and Spring streets were rerouted to run parallel in the mid 1920s, when the Temple Block of buildings, descendant of Jonathan Temple's adobe store, was razed to make room for Los Angeles' current city hall.

14 The Temples appeared in the 1836 census of the Los Angeles district. Temple, age 40, gave his occupation as *commerciante* (merchant). Rafaela Cota was 24 and Francisca, 6 years old. J. Gregg Layne, "First Census of the Los Angeles District," *Historical Society of Southern California Quarterly*, XVIII (Sep.-Dec. 1936), 3: 81.

ence quite disproportionate to their size in the town. Still, amid the scarcity of information about Temple's business in this period is a documented incident from 1839 that indicates some tension at hand. Temple was transporting hides to San Pedro from Los Angeles for trade with Americans. Vents, or brands to indicate trade or sale, were needed before any transaction was allowed. According to this account, "some of the Lugo boys intercepted one of his creaking carretas piled high with *cueros* [hides] and demanded to see the bill of lading and the vents on the hides." Having found four unmarked hides, the Lugos departed with them. Temple's official complaint, probably to the pueblo's common council, "filled up some twelve pages of testimony."[15] Despite an incident like this, Temple would hardly have been able to operate a thriving mercantile house for thirty years without maintaining friendly terms, if not strong personal relationships, with the Californios. George Rice, like Temple a native of Massachusetts, settled in Los Angeles soon after and became his partner. According to Hubert H. Bancroft, the partnership lasted until 1832, after which Rice ran a saloon for three years before returning to New England.[16] During these early years, Temple was not limited to trade in Los Angeles. By at least 1840, he engaged in the traffic of hides, tallow, crops, wine and brandy throughout California. Also, two tangential pieces of information have survived pointing to Temple's involvement in trade in Baja California. One is a brief mention of Temple's shipping of goods there in early 1838, as noted by an employee of a Santa Barbara merchant, who wrote on a visit to Los Angeles that he and Abel Stearns, "met 'Old Sam' with a lot of goods belonging to Tempole [*sic*] which was going [to] embark" for the south.[17] An 1842 letter from Temple, then in the Baja California port city of San Blas, to Cesar Lataillade, a Tepic merchant mentioned that he was calling off his trading of nails because it would not fetch a suitable price in Alta California.[18]

15 Thomas W. Temple II, "Cattle Brands", unpublished MS, Thomas W. Temple II Collection, courtesy of Ruth Ann Michaelis Temple. Copy in the Homestead Museum Research Archives.

16 Hubert H. Bancroft, *History of California* (Reprint ed., Santa Barbara, CA: Wallace Hebberd, 1966), V: 635.

17 Doyce B. Nunis, Jr., ed., *The California Diary of Faxon Dean Atherton, 1836–1839* (San Francisco: California Historical Society, 1964), p. 90 (entry for 30 March 1838). Atherton also related an interesting story of how Temple's neighbor, J.J. Warner, came to him for assistance after drinking water laced with a poison. Temple administered zinc sulfate, which allowed Warner to vomit the poison out of his stomach.

18 Jonathan Temple to Cesario Lataillado, 15 April 1842 (in Spanish, translated by the author), from a copy of the original. Thomas Workman Temple II Collection, courtesy of Ruth Ann Temple Michaelis and Gabriela Quiroz Temple Sutter.

There are surviving letters, however, written to Thomas O. Larkin, which provide greater detail about Temple's business activities, including the frequency of rather contentious negotiations. In May 1839, for example, Temple wrote Larkin:

> I shipped the Aguar[dien]te [brandy] and consign'd it to Mr. [Thomas] Park, with orders to sell it on my account, but provided he did not dispose of it all to leave the ballance [sic] with you, as you had wrote me, that what you wanted for your own use you would allow me $60 pr bbl [barrel] in hides.
>
> There was 17 bbls in barriles [sic] and 10 bbls or 180 Galls. [gallons] in the casks—making 27 bbls. You say that Aguarte is selling on board vessel for 450 in hides. I have sold a number of bbls. here for $50 in hides without any expence [sic], and the probability is that it will fetch $50 in cash before there is any more made.[19]

A little more than two weeks afterward, Temple complained that, regarding a load of flour sent by Larkin, "I am afraid you have sent it to a bad market. I cannot get an offer for it. I may probably work off some of it at retail, but I am afraid it will sour as soon as hot weather comes." Temple noted that wheat sold much better than flour, although he also added, "I have not had a single call for wheat, corn or beans this year...in fact the people have nothing to buy with." Things had gotten so bad, he continued, that "Business is at almost a compleat [sic] stand, I have not done half as much as I did last year by this time."[20]

Larkin's reply to these two letters pledged that "I will take your Brandy at 27 bbls—at $50 providing Capt. Penhallow or you make good two Bbbs that appeared to be lost or unaccounted for." Larkin also proposed selling flour at a lower price than previously offered, noting that Eulogio Celis, a prominent Los Angeles resident, was selling wine at $25 cash and brandy at $40.[21] Temple's next letter claimed he knew nothing of the two missing barrels of

19   Jonathan Temple to Thomas O. Larkin, 5 May 1839, Hammond, *The Larkin Papers*, I: p.9.
20   Temple to Larkin, 23 May 1839, Ibid., I, p. 11.
21   Larkin to Temple, 4 June 1839, Ibid., I, pp.12–13.

brandy, noting that the receipt showed no missing amount and that, "I shall hold you responsable [*sic*] to me for $60 pr bbl—for what you use yourself, as I have your signature to that effect. As regards the flour I should not like to take it on my a/c [account], but will do the best I can with it—as yet I have made no sales, nor do I know how much there is of it."[22]

In his rejoinder, Larkin's frustration with the arrangement was revealed as he wrote that,

> It was my expectation that you would close with my offer when I agreed to take so much of the leaking out on my own hands—and you to take the flour. But, no, it appears not. You say at $50 per Bbb & the Bbb returned, you are the losser [sic]. Brandy must command a different price your way, from what every one tells me.
>
> You say if I can prove that one Bbb was taken on board *you* have no doubt that Mr. P[ark] will make it good to me. *I* shall not put myself to that trouble; if *you* wish for prove [sic], I will enquire for you. As far as I am concerned, you might just as well call it 37 Bbbs as 27. I only agreed in my letter to you on the leakage, because the Brandy was consigned to me, and I did not want the owner to lose by it, but when I am called on to pay for what I never had nor no one pretends that it leaked out, I must decline trading on such terms.
>
> You need not *repeat*, that you have my signature for payment of $60 Etc. I also know you have. I thought you would be willing to take good flour at a fair price, in order to continue trade between us. It seams not! You will only sell it if you can, and give me cr. *as you sell it.* [I] Don't like the mode.
>
> If you have lost on this Brandy, you will not blame me. It was sent to me any how and without any letters i.e. deliverd to me. The offer of leakage, I would not have made to you had you been *here*, yourself.

22   Temple to Larkin, 20 June 1839, Ibid., I, pp.13–14.

Should you still hold the flour I shall consider it paid to you.[23]

In the face of Larkin's rebuke, Temple's response was somewhat conciliatory, as he wrote to the consul,

> You may rest assured that could I have disposed of the flour, I would gladly have done it & pass'd it to your account, so that we could continue our traffic, so desireable in exchange of articles of the two places, but I perceive that it will be impractible at present, as wheat is nearly as cheap here as in monterrey...and no purchasers at that on account of there being no demand in the market.
>
> I never call'd on you to pay for more than you rec'd but as circumstances were such, I offer'd you the lot as you rec'd it.

Temple concluded wryly by noting, "It appears that we both are going to make bad business in our shipments. Business remains dull."[24] His next letter showed that Temple accepted Larkin's terms, noting "I shall make a dead loss of more than $150." Further correspondence echoes the common complaint of both men about debtors who were slow in making their payments. Regarding one such man, Temple wrote, "[T]ell him that he had better not come down this way, for if he does I shall not be as lenient as I have been... I may fall in with him some time."[25] The summer of 1840 was no better than the one of the year prior and it is noteworthy that no known business dealings or correspondence passed between these two prominent figures of early California after this period.

With Temple's foothold established in Mexican-era Los Angeles, it is interesting to contemplate his views of and involvement in the political arena. The earliest glimpse of this comes in a 2 January 1832 letter by Temple to Captain John B. R. Cooper in Monterey. Just the day before, Los Angeles

---

23 Larkin to Temple, 22 July 1839, Ibid., I, pp.17–19.
24 Temple to Larkin, 8 August 1839, Ibid., I, pp.22–23.
25 Temple to Larkin, 10 January 1840, Ibid., I, pp.31–32.

resident Pío Pico had taken over the reins of government in California after a coup unseated Governor Manuel Victoria. Writing about the resolution of a debt owed him by Juan Bautista Alvarado, who would later become California's governor, Temple told Cooper to send him the one hundred dollars "by the first opportunity as I wish to circumscribe my accounts in as small a compass as possible in these times of revolution." Unfortunately, no other known record indicates how much difficulty Temple may have experienced in this first Californio revolt against a Mexican-appointed government.[26]

A more direct participation in political matters by Temple occurred during what has become an infamous episode in Los Angeles history and a difficult one to interpret– the creation of California's first vigilance committee. The formation of the organization was motivated by the murder in March 1836 of Domingo Feliz by Gervasio Alipas, the suspected lover of Feliz' wife, María del Rosario Villa. The *alcalde* (mayor) and pueblo *ayuntamiento* (city council) had mediated the dispute between Feliz and his wife and had arranged for their reconciliation. As the two left the pueblo for their home, however, Feliz was ambushed and stabbed. On 7 April, a week after the body was found, a group of fifty-five prominent Los Angeles residents, including fourteen Americans and Europeans, met at Temple's adobe store and house and formed a *junta defensora de la seguridad publica* (committee for public safety). Victor Prudhomme was chosen president, Manuel Arzaga, secretary, and Francisco Araujo, commander of an armed force. By inference from his role as host, Temple was, undoubtedly, a member of this committee. At two in the afternoon a resolution, drafted by Prudhomme, was presented to the pueblo officials and reveal the reasons for the formation of the committee:

> *Salus populi suprema lex est.* The subscribing citizens, at the invitation of the rest, justly indignant at the horrible crime committed against Domingo Felix, bearing in mind the frequency of similar crimes in this city, and deeming the principal cause thereof to be the delay in criminal cases through having to await the confirmation of sentences from Mexico, fearing for this unhappy country a state of anarchy

---

26 Jonathan Temple to John B. R. Cooper, 2 January 1832, from a copy of the original, Thomas Workman Temple II Collection. Courtesy of Ruth Ann Temple Michaelis and Gabriela Quiroz Temple Sutter.

where the right of the strongest shall be the only law, and finally believing that immorality has reached such an extreme that public security is menaced and will be lost if the dike of solemn example is not opposed to the torrent of atrocious perfidy—demand the execution or the delivery to us for immediate execution of the assassin Gervasio Alipas and the faithless Maria del R. Villa, that abominable monster who cruelly immolated her importunate husband in order to give herself up without fear to her frantic passions, and to pluck by homicide from the slime of turpitude the filthy laurel of her execrable treason...[27]

Many intriguing ideas leap out of this violent denunciation. First is the Latin phrase at the beginning, translated as "The welfare of the people is the highest law," calculated to lend juridical authenticity by precedent as well as to locate the demand in the hands of "the people" rather than that of the author. Then there is the plain statement that the ineffectual judicial system in the province, subject to the approval of officials in Mexico City, warranted the action of the vigilantes.[28] Another interesting feature of the statement was the simple identification of the killer, while María Villa was vilified and excoriated according to the stereotype of the wanton woman.

What this document reveals is that, even though three-quarters of committee members were Californios and Mexicans, it was the imposition of legal principles by an American and European minority that drove the work of the vigilantes. Even at a quarter of the number comprising the committee, the American and European contingent was represented far out of proportion to its ratio in the pueblo's population. No doubt, the Californio members of the group justified the creation of the committee, believing that it would have a mitigating effect on crime in the town, but at what cost? This is what makes the events surrounding the vigilance committee a vital landmark in the history of Los Angeles during the Mexican era: an early, concrete example of emerging foreign influence in the region.

---

27 Bancroft, *History of California*, III: pp. 418–419.
28 In 1836 the Californios also revolted against the governor appointed by the federalist regime in Mexico City, so there was a contextual aspect to the vigilante episode to consider, as well.

Pueblo leaders showed a great deal of courage by refusing to accede to the committee's demands, even though they had to contend with the mob outside the adobe in which the prisoners were jailed. The announcement of this decision provoked the crowd to storm the building, seize Alipas and Villa and shoot them. Their bodies were displayed at the adobe entrance for two days as a warning to future criminals. Temple's role as a member of the committee, however, did not appear to affect his prosperous business, which continued for another twenty years, or his standing in the community. Still, the vigilante committee affair prefigured much of the dynamic change that would transform California in the subsequent decade.

"To A Good Advantage"—William Workman in New Mexico

Immigrating to Mexican territory, becoming a Mexican citizen and marrying a native woman, operating as a merchant, and getting involved in controversial local affairs—this itinerary established by Jonathan Temple in Los Angeles was mirrored in northern New Mexico by an Englishman named William Workman.

Workman was born in November of 1799 in Temple Sowerby, a village in northwestern England, not far from the Scottish border and near the main road leading from London to Edinburgh. The region of Workman's childhood was then known as Westmorland County, but today is encompassed within the larger county of Cumbria. The area was and still is very rural, sparsely populated, and somewhat severe in its topography and climate, although it is renowned for the famed Lake District national park, home to poet laureate William Wordsworth and inspiration to other Romantic-era poets, such as Samuel Taylor Coleridge. Workman's parents, Thomas and Lucy Cook, had eight children, of whom William was the fifth. Thomas Workman, whose family had long lived in the region, was a glazier who seemed to specialize in stained and painted glass and was the owner of a fairly large amount of property in the village of Clifton, not far from William's birthplace. Due to the inheritance of this land from a childless aunt and uncle and the income derived from it, the Workman family appeared to have what may be called, by today's standards, an upper middle-class existence.[29] The family's home, an

---

29 This is based upon evidence researched recently by Clifton resident John Sharpe, including the nature of the bequest of the Clifton property made to Thomas Workman by his uncle David

impressive Georgian-era house, still stands out in Clifton, which today is only 100 persons larger than it was two centuries ago. As with Jonathan Temple, there is a relative paucity of documentable information on Workman's early years in England, although we do know he had some education and was likely apprenticed to the saddlers trade.

Of the eight Workman children, three left for the United States, in part, perhaps, because of the same lure of economic opportunity and relative political, religious, economic and social freedom that drew others from Europe. It may also be that the remoteness of the Westmorland area may have influenced their decisions. There were also national conditions that were likely factors for their migration to America. England's biggest problem was war—on two fronts. The most significant was the ongoing struggle in Europe with Napoleon which continued for some fifteen years. A continental blockade introduced by the French emperor was so effective that, by 1811, the British economy was in difficult straits. English fortitude and Napoleon's fatal decision to invade Russia in 1812 turned the tide of the war and led to British victory at Waterloo in 1815. The other conflict was the war of 1812 with the United States which, though the British managed to set fire to Washington, D.C., ended with a truce and England greatly relieved to end both wars at nearly the same time. Perhaps a more immediate personal reason, however, was a December 1814 settlement made by Thomas and Lucy Workman to their children that allotted enough money to underwrite trips to the United States.[30]

The aftermath of the Treaty of Paris in 1815 brought a renewal of English immigration to American shores. One of those Britons who came across in the latter half of the decade was William's older brother, David. According to his son, William Henry, later one of Los Angeles' most powerful citizens, David came to America in 1817, worked at the saddler's trade in New York for the next two years and then, perhaps because of the debilitating depression of 1819, headed west. The recent discovery of a document in England, however, shows that Thomas and Lucy Workman signed an agreement with their eldest surviving son, granting him half of a bequest or settlement of cash in 1818.

Harrison in 1788 and a settlement made by Thomas Workman to his children in December 1814 (see note 30 below). From a 9 January 1996 letter to the author by Mr. Sharpe. This information is also supplemented by a list of bequests made to the Workman children in Thomas Workman's will, a typescript copy of which is kept in the Homestead Museum Research Archives.

30 *Notes from Deeds of Castleton Cottage [Brackenbank], Clitfon, England*, copy provided to the author by John Sharpe, the owner of Brackenbank/Castleton Cottage.

David then used this money to emigrate to America.[31] In 1819, David was in Missouri, soon to be the union's newest state and situated at the edge of the American frontier. He settled in Franklin, founded in 1816 on the Missouri River, along which an important transportation network was developing and the significance of the town, which had a population of 1,200 by 1820, would become much more marked.[32]

This was the year that Mexico obtained its independence from Spain and opened up trade to the United States and other countries. Just as California experienced increased activity, so did the northern provinces of New Mexico and Texas. In 1821, Stephen F. Austin obtained trading and colonization privileges from the Mexican government in the latter and William Becknell in the former. Becknell lived in Franklin, Missouri from 1817 and operated a ferry at nearby Arrow Rock. Perhaps it was the same economic panic at decade's end that may have provided the impetus for David Workman's relocation to Franklin which also spurred Becknell, facing creditors' lawsuits, to seek out better opportunities in New Mexico. In September 1821, Becknell and his party opened the now-legendary Santa Fe Trail, returning to Franklin early the next year. His initiative had profound implications for not only the local scene in Missouri but in the more immediate context of regional trade and, eventually, national Mexican and American politics.[33] David Workman's new home then took on great importance as the trailhead to a burgeoning route of trade with a new market for enterprising Americans and others. Perhaps David recognized the potential Franklin now showed through this development. He dissolved his saddlery partnership, assumed sole proprietorship and returned to England in 1822, probably to inform the family of his success and to entice brother William into returning to Missouri with him.[34] Certainly, if the new trail were to prove successful, David would find his business increased and would need assistance. He may have envisioned himself getting involved

---

31 William Henry Workman, "Reminiscences of My Coming to California", *Annual Report of the Pioneers of Los Angeles County, 1908–09* (Los Angeles: Pioneers of Los Angeles County, 1909), p. 1. Copy in Homestead Museum Research Archives courtesy of David A. Workman, David Workman's great-grandson; Thomas and Lucy Cook Workman to David Workman, Cash Advance from Trust Settlement Agreement, 18 July 1818, copy in the Homestead Museum Research Archives courtesy of John Sharpe.

32 David A. White, comp. *News of the Plains and Rockies, 1803–1865* (9 vols., Spokane: The Arthur H. Clark Company, 1996–2001), I1: 19.

33 White, *News of the Plains and Rockies, 1803–1865*, I: pp. 50–51.

34 Franklin *Missouri Intelligencer*, 4 June 1821, as cited in David Weber, "William Workman," in LeRoy and Ann Hafen, ed., *The Mountain Men and the Fur Trade of the Far West* (10 vols., Glendale, CA: The Arthur H. Clark Company, 1965–1972), VII: 381, note 3.

in trade, as indeed he did in later years. Whatever the purpose, David was successful in his enticements and William agreed to go to America with him. In June 1822, William signed an agreement with his parents to withdraw his entire settlement and David cashed out his remaining half of his bequest.[35]

Meanwhile, Agnes, the eldest Workman child, had left England for the United States in the summer of 1820, arriving in Philadelphia.[36] Although listed by her maiden name, she married John Vickers, who was known to her family in England, and the two lived in Baltimore, where she died in 1848.[37] Only these three Workman children married and raised families, so the English branch of the family died out in Clifton in 1884, with the death of Thomas Workman, Junior.[38] There are, however, distant relations of the Workmans living in northern England today.

David and William landed, as their sister had, in Philadelphia and on the same packet, the *Liverpool*, in September 1822. They were listed on the cargo manifest as saddlers and it is interesting to note the goods the brothers brought with them: "1 Trunk, 1 Box of wearing apparel-one Case of Carpenter's tools, Bed & Bedding."[39] It is probable that the brothers spent the winter with their

---

35 Thomas and Lucy Cook Workman to William Workman, Cash Advance from Trust Settlement Agreement, 3 June 1822 and Thomas and Lucy Cook Workman to David Workman, Cash Advance from Trust Settlement Agreement, 3 June 1822, copies in Homestead Museum Research Archives courtesy of John Sharpe.

36 Manifest of the packet *Liverpool* from Liverpool, England to Philadelphia, 23 August 1820, National Archives and Records Administration, Washington, D.C. Copy in Homestead Museum Research Archives. Agnes Workman was listed as age 27 with no occupation. Because her maiden name was given, it is presumed she married after her arrival in America.

37 See, for instance, Thomas Workman, Sr., to David and William Workman, 21 December 1835, where Vickers is referred to as "a gloomy, sulky hound"! An earlier letter, Mary Workman to David Workman, 1 January 1829, noted that Thomas was "as bitter as ever" about Vickers, although "Agness assures us that Vickers, since his abode in America has borne the unimpeachable character, holds a respectable and lucrative situation and seen near to all her wants so that he leaves her as one with [nothing] ungratified. With such a person how can we think her faulty in selecting him?" Typescript copies of both letters in the Homestead Museum Research Archives, courtesy of the Conrad Krebs Family Collection and David A. Workman. Agnes Vickers also housed William's son Joseph in Baltimore during the 1840s, undoubtedly to provide him with a better education, see F.P.F. Temple to Abraham Temple, 8 February 1847 and 2 May 1848, Thomas Workman Temple II Collection, courtesy of Ruth Ann Temple Michaelis and Gabriela Temple Sutter, which mention William Workman's request of Abraham Temple to send money to his son. The last request came just a few months before Agnes Vickers' death in August 1848.

38 David's son, Elijah, journeyed to England to close the family estate, since he was, by the law of primogeniture, the oldest male living heir. Several family heirlooms brought back on that trip survive in family hands today, including a book of religious meditations written in intricate calligraphy and drawing by Mary Workman, sister of William and David and now owned by Mary Regina Workman.

39 Cargo manifest for the packet *Liverpool* from Liverpool, England to Philadelphia, 5 September 1822, National Archives and Records Administration, Washington, D.C. Copy in Homestead Museum Research Archives.

sister in Baltimore and then arrived in Franklin in March of 1823.[40] For the next two years, William worked in his brother's employ.

It was undoubtedly at the saddlery, as traders and trappers stopped to have their horses reshoed, saddles repaired and wagons and carts fixed, that Workman heard exciting information about the opportunities that existed in points west and southwest. Whatever the proximate cause, William decided to join a caravan on the Sante Fe Trail to New Mexico in the spring of 1825 and to seek his fortunes there. It is probable that Workman was on the caravan captained by Augustus Storrs, which left for Santa Fe with 105 men, 34 wagons, and 240 mules and horses in mid-May and arrived in New Mexico in early July.[41] What was somewhat unusual about William's intentions, though, was his decision to settle in New Mexico, whereas most American and European traders and trappers would journey to the region in the spring and summer, engage in their vocation, and then return to their homes in the United States for the winter, before repeating the cycle again.

David, meanwhile, remained in Franklin, until a flood in 1828 wiped out the town. He then stayed on in the new town that was constructed and later lived in nearby Boonville. He married Mary Hook (a descendant of a well-known Revolutionary War officer) in 1825, although she and their only child died in childbirth. He then married Mary's sister, Nancy, and the couple had three children: Thomas, Elijah, and William. David also engaged in various trading expeditions that would, in later years, take him as far south as Chihuahua and west to California.[42]

William's arrival at Santa Fe is documented by his registration at the customs house there in July 1825.[43] Shortly afterward, he ventured north to Taos, now renowned for its ancient Indian pueblo and as an artist's colony, but in the mid-1820s known for its colony of fur trappers and traders.

Incidentally, William Workman was not the only employee of his brother's establishment to leave for New Mexico and settle in Taos. A young apprentice to the saddlery told his story in an 1856 dictation:

40 Franklin *Missouri Intelligencer*, 1 April 1823 as cited in Weber, "William Workman", p. 381, note 4.
41 White, *News of the Plains and Rockies, 1803–1865*, II: 20, 78
42 William H. Workman, "Reminiscences," p. 2.
43 Weber, "William Workman," p. 382.

I was apprenticed to David Workman to learn the saddler's trade. I remained with him two years. The business did not suit me and, having heard so many tales of life in the mountains of the West, I concluded to leave him. He was a good man, and I often recall to my mind the kind treatment I received from his hands, but taking into consideration that if I remained with him and served my apprenticeship, I would have to pass my life in labor that was distasteful to me and, being anxious to travel for the purpose of seeing different countries, I concluded to join the first party for the Rocky Mountains.

In August 1826, I had the fortune to hear of a party bound for that country. I made application to join this party, and, without any difficulty, I was permitted to join them.

The young man, whose name was Christopher (Kit) Carson, neglected to mention that he had run away from the saddlery.[44] David Workman did not seem to be too angered by his apprentice's departure, because he waited a month before notifying the authorities, gave false directions as to where Carson was believed to have headed and offered little incentive, in fact the minimum reward, for his return. This can be seen in the advertisement in the *Missouri Intelligencer*, that he was, by law, required to place:

> To whom it may concern: That Christopher Carson, a
> boy about sixteen years old, small of his age, but thick set,
> light hair, ran away from the subscriber, living in Franklin,
> Howard Co., Missouri, to whom he had been bound to learn
> the saddler's trade, on or about the first day of September
> last. He is supposed to have made his way toward the up-
> per part of the state. All persons are notified not to harbor,
> support, or subsist said boy under penalty of the law. One
> cent reward will be given to any person who will bring back
> the said boy.

---

44 Blanche C. Grant, ed., *Kit Carson's Own Story of His Life* (Taos: Blanche C. Grant, 1926), pp. 9–10.

David Workman
Franklin, Oct. 6, 1826.[45]

Although Carson built part of his legendary career as a fur trapper, the main vocation of foreigners in the northern Mexican territories, the sheer number of trappers had, by the 1830s, led to the extinction of beaver in an increasingly wider region. Some new arrivals like Workman, therefore, soon found other pursuits.

An important artifact survives that provides a fascinating glimpse of one of William's intended activities, as well as the conditions of those foreigners that settled and traded in New Mexico in the mid 1820s. A letter, written from William to David on 13 February 1826 from Taos, while containing very little fraternal content and focusing more on business matters, gave this little aside (spelling and grammar as written):

> You will think it is a long time befor you hear from me but their has not been a company gone in expect [except] one and at that time I was not able to moove in bed I have had a severe spell of sickness morso that I ever had in my life and if it had not a been for Mr Stanly I should have died for they was no Doctor hear and not much medison, and it is one of the meenest Country to be sick in the world for their no nurishments to be got...

This also reveals evidence of William's limited education, although this is not surprising because it was common for English boys to receive only a rudimentary education. These youngsters were often taught enough reading and writing to get them to the important phase of their schooling, which was learning a trade.

From this opening, the letter abruptly turns to the matter at hand, namely the request of William to have David send him supplies needed for William's planned enterprise: the manufacture of liquor. He wrote: "David I have sent you in a draft of two hundred dollors...we [Workman and partners Matthew Kinkead and Samuel Chambers] have want you to get of Aberham Barns eighty gallon stills and some other articles which I will give you a list of..." The

---

45 Franklin *Missouri Intelligencer*, 6 October 1826.

list included brass cocks, tools (such as axes, hoes, a chisel, augers, picks, and a hammer), a water crane, and other items.

There is, however, one note of further interest regarding the request for some of the materials, since William wrote, "[B]e shoor never to name it to any person for they are countraband Articles"; liquor manufacture was forbidden to non-Mexicans for the obvious concern the influence these manufacturers might have over the residents. Noted Mexican borderlands historian David Weber, who edited the letter, which is the earliest surviving epistle from a non-Mexican in New Mexico, observed that, if the still was indeed delivered, it represented the first known and documentable existence of American-made stills in the region. In a postscript, William let David know that he had not done well his first winter in making an income: "Mr. Patton and myself tried our work in St ta Fee this winter and could sell nothing as for trunks I can Barter them of to a good advantage but their is very little money in Country..."[46]

The letter firmly establishes William's intention to enter the distilling business, from which he made the beverage known as "Taos Lightning," which leaves no doubt as to its potency! Workman also sought to make money in a variety of other ways, including the unsuccessful bartering he and Patton had done the winter of 1825–26.

It is fortunate that this correspondence and a number of others between the family in England and David and William survives. In these communications we get a rare glimpse of the personal nature of our subjects, as well as a welcome opportunity to learn about the Workman women, of whom we know little. Mary, the youngest sibling of the brothers, seemed to have been better educated than her brothers, which is somewhat of a surprise given the resistance women encountered in education. Her letters and those of the two Thomases, father and son, are about the only surviving primary sources that reveal familial feelings. Frequently tender, sometimes chiding and often frustrated by the brothers being remiss in answering letters or in delaying a return voyage (after 1822, David never returned home and William's one journey back was in 1851–52) Mary's letters give a sense of the effects that time and distance had on the separation of the family across an ocean and half a continent. For instance, a letter from New Year's Day 1829 begs William to "know

---

46   William Workman, "A Letter From Taos, 1826," David J. Weber, ed., *New Mexico Historical Review*, XLI (April 1966): 155–164.

by an English pen the state of his Mother's health, and her great wish to see him, but not only him, but you all once more."[47]

In another missive, of December 1835, she implores: "[F]or the future let me entreat of you not to write such a distance to friends without tenderness. Come William my bonny boy you have lived in the world a little longer than I have (though you may not explore the minds of men so much as the outside of the globe), yet you cannot be without the experience that tenderness begets tenderness...give us the trial another time and you will find the difference."

Later, Mary wondered why William was so willing to visit David at Franklin, but not return to the family nest and concluded, "Business, not brotherly love, leads you undoubtedly to David." She entreated him to come to England, adding, "If brotherly love alone will not bring you to England, let business attend..." Finally, a curious query from Mary about a trip William was evidently considering asked, "But is it dangerous to ask, Mister, what motive carries you to the Sandwich Islands [Falkland Islands?] in Anarctic Seas [sic]? Is it love, riches, or curiosity? Oh! give us the preference."[48]

Other letters include notes from the two Thomases, father and son. The elder Workman displayed the spirit that had led him to travel to faraway London as a young man and which must have infused his sons. He even dreamed of joining them in the Americas at the spry age of seventy-nine, declaiming, "You would have been a welcome guest this Winter without staying at Franklin & I would have returned with you not doubting I would have made it pay."[49]

William Workman's contact with his family seems to have been much less frequent in later years. The only known source is a draft letter dated 8 February 1847 from William to his sister Agnes Vickers, who lived in Baltimore. In it, he refers to the fact that he had not heard from his family since his father's death in 1843. He referred briefly to his good health, to the quantity of fruit grown in the Los Angeles area, and wished to be remembered to his son, Joseph, who at an unknown date was sent East to live with his aunt and attend school.[50] Agnes Vickers died in 1848, at which point it is unclear if Joseph stayed in Maryland. However, he is said to have resided with his uncle

47 Mary Workman to David Workman, 1 January 1829, Conrad Krebs Family Collection. Krebs was a grandson of Elijah H. Workman, son of David Workman.
48 Mary Workman to David and William Workman, 21 December 1835, Ibid.
49 Thomas Workman, Sr. to David and William Workman, 21 December 1835, Ibid.
50 Draft of a letter from William Workman to Agnes Workman Vickers, 8 February 1847, courtesy of Josette Temple.

David in Missouri, joining David and his family for their overland migration to California in 1854 as well as a reunion with Joseph's own family.

Regarding pay, fur trapping was earlier mentioned as being the most prevalent occupation in the borderlands region. While it is thought that Workman did not actually do a great deal of trapping, it is believed he was an agent of the American Fur Company.[51] Additionally, there was the 1827 expedition referred to earlier that took him to the Colorado River. This journey was described in three different accounts. One was written in 1865 by J.J. Warner, a prominent southern California resident, who explained that:

> In the fall of 1827 a party of about fifteen men, under [James Ohio] Pattie [a famed trapper and explorer], was made up in Taos, to trap the Gila river from its sources down to the Colorado. In this party were Mr. William Workman, a young Englishman, then and until 1841, living in New Mexico, and now of La Puente rancho, in this [Los Angeles] county, and Mr. [George] Yount, of Napa [another well-known mountain man.] Before reaching the mouth of the Gila, a majority of the men became so dissatisfied with their leader [Pattie] that a separation took place. A majority withdrew, and elected Mr. Workman as their leader. The two parties continued on down the Gila until they reached the Colorado, trapping beaver upon it for some distance above the mouth of the Gila, and down stream to tide-water. The party commanded by Mr. Workman returned to New Mexico.[52]

In the spring of 1828, the Pattie contingent continued into California, where, while in San Diego, they met young Pío Pico, who became godfather to James Pattie's father at his baptism as a Catholic and later figured prominently in California history and in the lives of the Workman and Temple families.

Pattie, meanwhile, in his reminiscences, made no mention of any dissatisfaction with his leadership and, instead, attributed the reluctance of Workman and the others to the "too long and tedious" route along the Gila and Colorado

---

51 See, for example, Boyle Workman, *The City That Grew* (Los Angeles: The Southland Publishing Company, 1935), pp. 7–8.

52 J.J. Warner, "An Episode in the History of California," San Francisco *Daily Alta California*, 2 July 1865.

rivers and claimed that, upon the separation of the group, the members were, "all expressing the same regret at the separation, and heartily wishing each other all manner of prosperity, we shook hands and parted!"[53]

George Yount gave his version of the party in which he claimed he and a man named Allen were the leaders of the group. He did relate an incident, however, in which a Mojave chief, thought to have treacherous designs on the expedition members, was threatened with a cocked rifle by Workman, one of several known volatile expressions of temperament on his part. Because beaver skins were subject to importation duties, Yount said that the furs were cached outside Taos until a night smuggling operation could be conducted and that a still house in the pueblo "had been converted into a recepticle of smuggled goods, and an underground passage led to the grand subterranean cache." It has been suggested that this still house, doubling as a smuggler's den, belonged to Workman.[54]

Despite these activities, fur trapping was not Workman's main occupation. Sometime after his arrival in Taos, he became friends with John Rowland, who is believed to have been in the pueblo two years prior to Workman. Born about 1791 either in Maryland or Pennsylvania and of Welsh descent, Rowland had lived in Pennsylvania (which, in fact, was listed as his birthplace in the 1850 census) and Ohio before venturing to Mexican territory. The two men became business partners and operated a distillery together, while Rowland also ran a flour mill and Workman owned a store. Their friendship spanned nearly fifty years, although surprisingly little is known about their relationship. Nor is there much in the way of information about how successful their businesses were, although Workman later told a friend in California, Stephen C. Foster, that he had lost $4,000 in 1833 when a trappers' expedition that he had supplied was massacred by Apaches, whose chief had been killed by Americans.[55] George Nidever, a trapper of some note, also recalled, "Workman had a store in San Fernando. He sold clothing, provisions, &c. We did most of our trading with him."[56]

53 Richard Batman, *The Personal Narrative of James Ohio Pattie* (Reprint ed., Missoula: Mountain Press Publishing Company, 1988), pp. 99–102.
54 Weber, "William Workman," p. 384, quoting Charles L. Camp, ed., *George C. Yount and His Chronicles of the West* (Denver: Old West Publishing, 1966), pp. 43–45, 51–53, 62.
55 Stephen C. Foster, "Los Angeles from 1847-1849," MS, Bancroft Library
56 William H. Ellison, ed., *The Life and Adventures of George Nidever* (Berkeley: University of California Press , 1937), 21. Weber's article on Workman also cited an 1839 manifesto of Workman's merchandise, "William Workman", p. 384, note 13.

WILLIAM WORKMAN &
HIS DAUGHTER,
ANTONIA MARGARITA
WORKMAN DE
TEMPLE,
CIRCA 1852
*PHOTO COURTESY OF THE
HOMESTEAD MUSEUM,
CITY OF INDUSTRY, CA*

Not long after Workman returned from the Gila trapping expedition in June 1828, he was baptized into the Roman Catholic Church.[57] Possibly this had something to do with a recently passed amendment by the Mexican Congress to the Naturalization Act of 1824 and was the fulfillment of one of the conditions of Mexican citizenship. Although the actual documentation of citizenship has not been located, Workman was identified in records in New Mexico and California as a *naturalizado* or naturalized citizen. As in the case of Jonathan Temple, it is possible to assume that Workman, an Episcopalian, converted for the boon to his business and social connections rather than for any spiritual benefits it might have conferred upon him. This is perhaps supported by the fact that later, in California, Workman was initiated into the Masonic fraternity, which held beliefs quite alien to Roman Catholicism. Other indications of his citizenship and his growing involvement in the Taos community included his service as secretary for a district electoral *junta* in 1832 and petitions for land grants in 1834 and 1835 (the results of which are not known.)[58]

---

57 Baptism of William Workman, 4 June 1828, Book B-47, Taos Baptisms, Archives of the Archdiocese of Santa Fe, New Mexico State Archives.
58 Weber, "William Workman," p. 385.

Finally, there was Workman's union with Taos native Nicolasa Urioste (sometimes given as Uriarte), sometime around 1829. "Union" is used because there are no indications in New Mexico yet found that reveal a marriage record. The Workmans' great-grandson, historian and genealogist, Thomas Workman Temple II, however, located a record of a marriage between the two, held at the Mission San Gabriel in February 1844 and the couple's copy of the official Church investigation into their marriage from the preceding winter survives.[59] It may well be that they were married by a civil official or that they lived common-law in New Mexico, not unusual occurrences.[60] As it was, the Workmans remained together for nearly fifty years and raised two children, daughter Antonia Margarita, known commonly by her second name and born in July 1830, and son Jose Manuel, born about 1832.[61]

Unfortunately, though not surprisingly, given the absence of most women in the public records of the period, little is known about Mrs. Workman, aside from her birth date of 19 April 1802 and her death date of 4 February 1892.[62] Years later, Mary Julia Workman, David Workman's granddaughter, wrote to a friend:

> William Workman had married a Pueblo Indian woman
> in Santa Fe, that is, without benefit of clergy. The Indian
> woman's name was Nicolasa. [S]he spoke no English and

---

59 Notes from Thomas Workman Temple II, based upon marriage registers for the Mission San Gabriel. The ceremony on 19 February 1844 was a double wedding, the other involved Workman's friend Benjamin Wilson, who had come to California with Workman and Rowland in 1841. A marriage investigation, a process to investigate betrothed couples with testimony of witnesses as to their knowledge of the intended, for William Workman and Nicolasa Urioste from late 1843 survives. Thomas Workman Temple II Collection, Homestead Museum Research Archives, courtesy of Ruth Ann Temple Michaelis and Gabriela Quiroz Temple Sutter.

60 Rebecca McDowell Craver in *The Impact of Intimacy: Mexican-Anglo Intermarriage in New Mexico, 1821–1846* (El Paso: Texas Western Press, 1982) surveyed the conditions of unions between American and European men and New Mexican women in the period the Workmans began living together, concluding that common law marriages were not only common between foreign men and New Mexican women, but between New Mexicans generally. One given factor was the excessive fees charged by the clergy for performing ceremonies. Craver mentions Workman and John Rowland in the context of the Rowland and Workman expedition of 1841, pp. 140–141.

61 The baptismal records of the Workman children list them as "hija natural" or "hijo natural", indicating that they were illegitimate, at least in the eyes of the Catholic Church, which would not list William Workman's name as father, presumably, because he had not married Nicolasa Urioste in a church-sanctioned marriage. New Mexico State Records Center and Archives, Book 1: 363, 409. Joseph Workman's birth date is not known with certainty. His grave marker reads June 19, 1831, but the census listings for 1870, 1880, and 1900; the Los Angeles Great Register of Voters; his death certificate; and other sources vary, with the commonest years being 1832 and 1833.

62 The above mentioned baptismal records of the Workman children show the mother's name as both Nicolasa Urioste and Nicolasa Valencia. The maternal grandmother's name in both listings, however, read Valencia as the surname.

he spoke very poor Spanish...He was anxious to do what
was right, but Nicolasa was not acquainted, naturally, with
English ways of living.

While it is certainly plausible that Nicolasa Workman was a Pueblo and it
seems the marriage may not have been church-sanctioned (until, that is, 1844),
the idea of a language barrier seems unthinkable. Even if Nicolasa knew no
English, William Workman could hardly have survived in business and personal contacts in his many years of living in Mexican territory without a fac-
ile command of Spanish. There also seems to be a hint of provincialism in the
last sentence of the letter, in which Mary Julia wrote that her grandmother,
Nancy Hook Workman, "cooked some dishes that pleased the poor old man
and gave him some of the former comforts," as if Mrs. Workman was lacking
essential qualities as a wife because of her ethnic background.[63]

Ethnicity was, in fact, often at the center of conflicts which, in the mid
1830s, brought sweeping changes in both New Mexico and California. The
Mexican government in tipping the scale between federalism, where states
exercised more local control, and centralism, in which decisions mainly ema-
nated from Mexico City, inclined most often toward the latter. Much of this
was due to increasing concern over foreign influence in Mexico proper as well
as in the border provinces of California, New Mexico, and Texas. A new
constitution was promulgated in 1836, instituting centralist policy and in
the northern territories, appointing centralist governors when the locals were
largely used to rule from amongst their own ranks. Another decision of the
Mexican government in this period, the Secularization Act of 1833, was designed to deflate some of the immense power and draw out some of the great
wealth of the Roman Catholic Church. A sweeping piece of legislation, the
act mandated the dismantling of the mission system and called for the release
of neophyte Native Americans, who were to receive the larger share of mission
lands. Although the act read as a noble, populist document, the reality was
that mission lands were taken over instead by the land-owning elite, who followed by incorporating Native Americans into peonage. Many of these landowners were Americans and Europeans who had worked their way into the
gente de razon by marriage, citizenship, or both.

---

63 Mary Julia Workman to Mary Gibson, 16 April 1929, Sarah Bixby Smith MSS, Rancho Los Cerritos
Historic Site, Long Beach, California. Copy in Homestead Museum Research Archives.

The tension in the northern territories then increased with the onset of centralism, although the problems in Texas had been brewing long before, when the hostility of the growing American and European population towards the Mexican government led to occasional armed skirmishes. The response in Mexico City was the reactionary institution of a heavily centralized system of rule which only served to further heighten tensions. War broke out between the territorial administration and foreign-led rebels in the autumn of 1835 and culminated in such myth-making events as the Battle of the Alamo. The final defeat of the Mexican army in the spring of 1836 led to the creation of an independent republic in Texas.

Meanwhile, centralist policy implemented in California and New Mexico also contributed to a growing unrest. In the former, the residents developed such a strong sense of separate identity, because of their isolation, that they did not identify themselves as Mexicans, but rather as Californios. Accustomed to having their own governors, the Californios reacted bitterly to the announcement of a centralist appointee, Mariano Chico, who took office in April 1836, just as Texas was falling to the Americans, and precipitated a second revolt. The rebels wanted to restore the federalist Constitution of 1824 and be left to their own version of self-rule. Chico decided not to confront the opposition and fled the region in July leaving the governorship to another centralist, Nicolás Gutierrez. After an armed force, including some fifty Americans and Europeans, marched towards Monterey, Gutierrez surrendered, leaving the governorship to native Californio Juan Bautista Alvarado, who presided over the legislature's call for a return to the 1824 Constitution. In contrast to events on the coast, the centralist appointee in New Mexico in 1837, Albino Perez decided to stand up to the rebels. In August Perez' troops were routed and the governor captured and executed the next day. The rebels appointed a governor named José Angél Gonzales, who hailed from Taos. In September supporters of the rebels in that pueblo moved to take revenge on those thought sympathetic to Gonzales. Meanwhile, the *Franklin Missouri Intelligencer* newspaper reported in November that Workman and Rowland "were forced by the rebels to take sides with them; and apprehensions were entertained for their lives."[64] Workman and Rowland had just embroiled themselves in problems a month before the revolt erupted, when the two were accused of

---

64 *Franklin Missouri Intelligencer*, 15 November 1837, quoted in Weber, "William Workman," p. 386.

smuggling merchandise in two stills, and Workman alleged to have been trying to bribe customs officials to let him pass.[65] In the south of the province, a new group arose, led by ex-Governor Manuel Armijo, claiming loyalty to the centralists and which marched north to unseat the new Gonzales administration. By early 1838, Armijo had captured Gonzales and the other rebel leaders, executed them, and consolidated power in his hands. Armijo's rule in New Mexico would often be leery of foreigners and resulting events served to reinforce his feelings.[66]

This was due to activity emanating from Texas in the spring of 1840. The republic had been claiming for some time that its natural western border was the Rio Grande River, which was obviously more than irritating for the New Mexicans, most of whom lived east of the river in communities like Santa Fe, Albuquerque, and Taos. On 14 April Texas President Mirabeau Lamar issued a proclamation "To the Citizens of Santa Fe", in which he announced,

> The great River of the North [Rio Grande] which you inhabit, is the natural and convenient boundary of our territory, and we shall take great pleasure in hailing you as fellow citizens, members of our young Republic, and co-aspirants with us for all the glory of establishing a new happy and free nation...
> I shall despatch...about the month of September proximo, one, or more, Commissioners...to explain more minutely the condition of our country. Until the arrival of these Commissioners, I have empowered some of your own citizens, Capt. W.G. Dryden, Mr. W.H. Workman [sic], and Mr. Rowland (to whom the views and feelings of the Government have been communicated) to confer with you upon the subject matter of this communication.[67]

---

65 *Judicial Proceedings in the Arraignment of Julian Workman*, 20–24 July 1837, MANM R-23, F 963 and *Judicial Proceedings in the Arraignment of Juan Roland*, 18–22 July 1837, MANM R-23, F951, New Mexico State Archives. Copy made available to the author courtesy of Don Rowland.

66 The principal source for this section is gleaned from David Weber's fine study of the Mexican-American borderlands, *The Mexican Frontier, 1821–1846: The American Southwest Under Mexico* (Albuquerque: University of New Mexico Press, 1982).

67 Charles Adams Gulick, Jr., ed., *The Papers of Mirabeau Bonaparte Lamar* (6 vols., Austin, Tx: Texas State Library, 1968), III: pp. 370–71.

Although Lamar stated that Workman and Rowland had been apprised of "the views and feelings" of Texas in the regard to the proposed enterprise, no documentation is known as to why the two were chosen for the posts or the level of activity in which they were engaged.[68] There are two other accounts, however, that bear on Workman's possible involvement in the Texan affair. Juan B. Vigil, a lawyer in Taos, accused him and Charles Bent of complicity with the Texans, to which the two confronted Vigil and charged him to recant or prove his claims. Vigil's answer is not recorded, but Workman's answer is, because he beat the barrister with a whip and then with his fists until Bent pulled him away. Bent's account was that: "the word was hardly out of his [Vigil's] mouth, when Workman struk him with his whip, after whipping him a while with this he droped it and beate him with his fist untill I thought he had given him enough, whareupon I pulled him off."[69] Bent noted to Manuel Alvarez, United States consul in New Mexico, that if Vigil were not convinced of Workman's seriousness, the latter "would be right glad to setle the affair, in the maner, thare was a similar affair setled in Sonoro, onse."[70] The second was a claim by a man only known as Bustamente that there were several conspiracies against the New Mexican government, and "the one in August was led by the American Julian Werkman [sic], whom the Texans had empowered in this department, with the sole purpose to form the revolution, which is the reason he came from Taos to Santa Fe, accompanied by some of his countrymen intent on assassinating governor Armijo."[71] Without corroboration from other sources, it is impossible to determine whether Workman did indeed lead such an attempt and, if he did, why was he not arrested and prevented from leaving New Mexico? In any case, Workman clearly was not a man to be trifled with and his tendency to embroil himself in political matters continued later in the decade in southern California.

Lamar took ill later in the year and the expedition was postponed until 1841. When it was reconstituted, Workman and Rowland were not reap-

68 Weber, "William Workman", p. 387, Given that Dryden settled in Los Angeles after 1850 and continued his friendship with Rowland and Workman, it may have been he who recruited the others to join him as temporary commissioners.
69 Thomas E. Chavez, *Manuel Alvarez, 1794–1856: A Southwestern Biography* (Niwot, Co: University Press of Colorado, 1990), p. 73. and Weber, "William Workman", p. 387.
70 Charles Bent to Manuel Alvarez, 19 February 1841, as quoted in Weber, "William Workman", p. 387.
71 Hubert Howe Bancroft, *The History of Arizona and New Mexico, 1530–1888* (San Francisco: The History Company, Publishers, 1889), XVII: 321–22, note 21. The author thanks Donald Rowland for alerting him to this item and Sylvia Hohenshelt for translating the passage.

pointed commissioners. In the atmosphere of the time, however, and with a governor in Santa Fe hostile to non-Mexicans, it may not have mattered that the two were no longer associated at least directly to the expedition.[72] Not surprisingly, then, Rowland and Workman prepared to leave the province as 1841 dawned.

---

72 Background information on the Texas-Santa Fe Expedition was obtained from primary source documents regarding the arrest of William G. Dryden and his interrogation in Chihuahua City in the fall of 1841 as well as the Lamar Papers. "Interrogation of William G. Dryden," *Archivo de Guerra* (Mexico), *Frac. 1, Leg. 1*, 1841 and 1842: 47, Bancroft Library.

🌿 C H A P T E R   T W O 🌿

A Beginning and an End

⌘ 1841–1848 ⌘

Journeys to California

While William Workman and John Rowland planned their exodus to California, nineteen-year old Pliny Fisk Temple, something a little like Richard Henry Dana seven years before, embarked on his own ocean-bound journey to California. Temple was born in February 1822 at Reading, Massachusetts as the last child of Captain Jonathan Temple and his second wife, Rebecca Parker. He probably had just completed his schooling when he left for Los Angeles to see his half-brother, Jonathan. Thirty-five years later, in an interview for Hubert H. Bancroft, Pliny told of his journey:

> I left Boston on the Am[erican] Bark Tasso on the 18[th] of Jan[uar]y 1841. [The] ship came to this coast on a trading expedition from the house of Bryant & Sturgis of Boston. I was a passenger on board. [I] arrived at [the] port of Monterey in 156 days —ab[ou]t [the] 26[th] of June.[I] remained in Mont[erey] a few days —from there came to Santa Barbara on a Sch[oone]r commanded by Capt. Leidesdorff...From there [I] came here by land —on arriving at this place I found my brother John, whom I had never seen before, he being the oldest & I the youngest of our family —he had left home before I was born. [H]e was engaged in [the] mercantile business. [I] remained with my brother till 1849.[1]

Pliny Temple arrived in Los Angeles sometime around early July and it may be that he only intended to visit, as letters from his brother, Abraham and

---

1   Francis Pliny Fisk Temple, "Recollections of Francis Pliny Fisk Temple," 1877, p.2., MS, Bancroft Library. The *Tasso* was a ship that traded in California from 1841 to 1848, according to Dana, *Two Years Before the Mast*, p. 480 (appendix A.)

sisters Cynthia Temple and Clarinda Bancroft, written in January 1842 hint. These letters, which are rare examples of correspondence in Mexican-era Los Angeles, provide great insight into the concern the New England Temples felt for their kindred in exotic, far-flung California. Abraham, for example, opened his letter with a particularly exuberant expression of sibling affection: "Another year has flown since we last met and is none numbered with those that have been enjoyed by us in <u>harmony</u> together, and notwithstanding the wildness—may moan between us, and ocean lashes its foaming sides, still the <u>chord of affection</u> is not broken, ay it is <u>strengthened</u>, and I trust no <u>time</u> or <u>distance</u>, or any unforeseen circumstance will ever <u>lessen</u> or <u>diminish</u> the <u>af-fections</u> that bind us together as <u>brothers."</u> After expressing some guilt, "fear-ing lest my influence has led you to take a step which ere this you may have requited," and then following with a request concerning "under what <u>circum-stances</u> whether you think there is a good opportunity of investing money in the section," Abraham concluded by offering "If you are desirous of return-ing home and have not the means, come and will defray the expense now or at any time."[2]

Sister Clarinda, meanwhile, offered similar sentiments in her missive, opening with this remarkable passage:

> More than a year has elapsed since you left the shores of happy New England, since you left the maternal roof, where you left one of the kindest and best of <u>mothers</u>, and who feels <u>deeply</u> for your welfare, where <u>we enjoyed</u> the pleasures of childhood, love, health, peace, and competence, blessed our dwellings, and all the allurements of the world. Although time and distance has seperated [sic] us from each other, you are not <u>effaced</u> from my memory, a kind and <u>affectionate brother</u>, it was with unspeakable joy that I heard you were wafted safely across the mighty deep. Dear P, reflect on the unbounded goodness of <u>God</u> is preserving your life, while many have found a watery grave.

---

2   Abraham Temple to Pliny Fisk Temple, 24 January 1842. Courtesy of Josette Temple.

Further, she pointedly inquired, "I feel *extremely anxious* to know...how long you think of remaining on the coast."[3]

Cynthia, too, opened with a passage deep with feeling for her brother.

> Neither time, nor distance, effase [sic] the memory of those we love, although one year has passed since we parted although the vast waters of the Ocean separate us yet my affection for you has not in the least abated, my mind often unconsciously reverts to the happy scenes of childhood through which we have passed, then we bounded over hill and dale as light as the rock over the mountain, of youth when we gathered around the paternal hearth participating in each others joys and sorrows, and now we have arrived to years of manhood we are seperated [sic] where we can no longer enjoy each others society, but may I not be permited [sic] to hope that this shall not always be the case! Can it be that we shall never again meet this side of eternity! God only knows, but if not, may we be prepared through sanctifying grace to meet in Heaven where parting is not known.

More than her brother and sister, Cynthia then offered Pliny a lengthy digest of news and gossip from home. She also added an interesting passage in which she wrote, "I hope you will curtail the period of your <u>tarrying and you and brother J return to happy New England</u>. I want you to write what your prospects are, what length of time you think of remaining on the Coast, how you like it, how you got from the ship to J, whether you have <u>suffered</u> on <u>account</u> of the <u>drought</u>, how you found your clothes when you come to get ashore, and how you got your clothes washed, and tell me whether you think there is any place like <u>home</u>, like our <u>own native land</u>."[4]

Indeed, this reference to the familiar comforts of their New England home was a recurring theme in these letters, as well as periodic concerns about Pliny living a moral, upright life in a place that, to them, must have seemed far removed from the civilization they knew. In December 1843, for example, brother Abraham implored his brother to "be watchful of your morals and

---

3   Clarinda Temple Bancroft to Pliny Fisk Temple, 30 January 1842, Courtesy of Josette Temple.
4   Cynthia Temple to Pliny F. Temple, 28 October 1842. Courtesy of Josette Temple.

health for on those depend your usefulness, and success in life, be honest, be virtuous, avoid the cups, avoid her whose step takes hold on hell, in fine avoid all vices that tend to degrade."[5] In a corollary vein, Pliny's sister Cynthia wondered, "Have you not often sighed for the comforts of home, which you are deprived, of the various means of intellectual and moral improvement which happy New England affords? Here every facility for intellectual improvement is introduced, here internal improvements are continually going forward, here we enjoy every comfort, and almost every luxury which every climate affords and here everyone can worship God after the dictates of their own conscience."[6] This passage clearly expressed a view of a backward and religiously intolerant California.

Despite the earnest exhortations of his New England siblings, Pliny prospered in California and stayed the rest of his life, allowing himself just one return visit in 1870. Still, he remained in regular contact with his siblings in Massachusetts and a number of Pliny's drafts and copies as well as original letters from his siblings survive, with much of interest about life in California, and rare windows into Pliny's personality as well. For example, an interesting letter to Abraham in December 1843 refers briefly to the newly-appointed governor of Alta California, Manuel Micheltorena, the effects of a drought on the hide-and-tallow industry ("Business remains dull on the coast owing to the scarcity of rain the year past, there not being grass sufficient to fatten the cattle. We have not received even one bag of tallow this year, so you can judge more or less the condition of the country at present"), and the arrival of gold seekers in a placer discovered in the spring of 1842 north of Los Angeles.[7] Another letter to Abraham in 1844, was enclosed with ten ounces of gold from the Placerita Canyon field, with instructions to give three ounces to their mother, and then providing a laundry list of sundry goods that Pliny needed his brother to purchase with the remainder of the gold.[8]

In an 1848 letter to his brother Abraham, he expressed a typical concern for his mother, "I feel very anxious to hear from you & all our friends & particularly our beloved Mother. I hope she is in the enjoyment of comfortable

---

5   Abraham Temple to Pliny F. Temple, 10 September 1843. Courtesy of Josette Temple.
6   Cynthia Temple to Pliny F. Temple, 28 January 1842.
7   Pliny F. Temple to Abraham Temple, 10 December 1843. From a transcription by Pliny's son, John H. Temple, now in the Homestead Museum Collection.
8   Pliny F. Temple to Abraham Temple, 30 June 1844. Courtesy of Josette Temple.

health. I trust everything that lays in your power will be done to promote her happiness."[9]

Eight years later, Pliny wrote to his sister Cynthia from his home in Springfield, California in the Sierra Nevada gold country where he was expanding his interests. Responding to the death of his mother, Lucinda, Pliny wrote,

> I received the sad tidings of the sickness & death of our kind and affectionate Mother. I am now deprived of the pleasure of ever seeing her again here on earth, but trust we may meet in a happier clime, where
>
> Eternal day excludes the night
> And pleasure banish pain
>
> I regret that my arrangements have been such that I could not leave to have made you all a visit before the spirit of our kind Mother took its flight to another & happier world.

Cynthia, who was ill and died six months later, was exhorted by her brother in another tender moment to join him in California:

> I am sorry to hear that your health still continues feeble. If you think you can stand the trip out here, I will make arrangement for you to come. If you could get here I think it would be the means of prolonging your days, we could sit under our own vine & fig here & none to molest or make us afraid. Margaret would be very much pleased if you were here & should you get able you would instruct the little boys.

At the end of the letter, Pliny, who enclosed $500 for a cemetery tombstone for his parents, added in a postscript, "lamenting with you all the loss of our Dear Mother, who watched over us in the happy days of our childhood & taught us to tread the paths of virtue."[10]

---

9   F.P.F. Temple to Abraham Temple, 20 September 1848. Courtesy of Josette Temple.
10 F.P.F. Temple to Cynthia Temple, 2 July 1856. Courtesy of Josette Temple.

When Pliny arrived in Los Angeles, John Rowland and William Workman were preparing to depart for California in increasingly greater earnest. Meanwhile, the administration of Governor Armijo was closely watching the movements of foreigners in Mexico and even preventing them, for a time, from leaving their towns. Workman and Rowland, though, were able to secure passports for their emigration west. In Workman's case, the permit to travel and invoice of effects that he obtained in July 1841 listed "40 Bales of Domestic Serapes, 8 Pack loads of Household furniture and utensils, [and] 1 load of effects for expenses of my family and pay of the servants on the way."[11]

Meanwhile, the partners were disposing of their inventory of merchandise at their enterprises at Taos, which made at least one of their competitors none too pleased with the effect on his business. Simeon Turley, a distiller in Taos, wrote to his brother in April: "I have done bad business this year. Cold not Colect the Money I have Credited and Roland and Workman is Selling whiskey at half price to Sell out to gowe to Califorene and untill they Sell out I shall have to Lay Silent and Sell noe."[12]

Although their motivations were not as urgent or political as those of Rowland and Workman, another emigrant party, the Bidwell and Bartleson, had formed at Sapling Grove, Missouri in the spring for a journey to northern California. This group left Missouri on 6 May taking a route that later emigrants would roughly parallel two years later when the Oregon Trail was opened. A few days after the expedition had left, some men arrived hoping to join that group, but finding themselves too late, made their way on a caravan to Santa Fe, where they learned of the plans of Rowland and Workman.

By September as the members of Texas-Santa Fe Expedition neared New Mexico, the members of the Rowland and Workman Expedition massed together to depart for the coast. The exact number of members is not known because the list given by Rowland to the authorities in Los Angeles only indicated the head of the household for the families that were traveling as well as the names of individuals. There were at least twenty-five, though, who started from Santa

---

11 Administration of Customs for the Department of New Mexico to William Workman, *Permit and Invoice of Goods*, 13 and 14 July 1841, in the possession of Josette Temple. Rowland's passport is kept at the Huntington Library (item HM 40485). Written on the reverse of the passport are two statements from Ygnacio Palomares, half-owner of Rancho San Jose and future neighbor of Workman and Temple, dated 6 December 1841 and Santiago Arguello, dated 28 February 1842, recognizing Rowland and Workman's arrival and the former's request to go to Monterey.
12 LeRoy and Ann Hafen, *The Old Santa Fe Trail* (Lincoln: University of Nebraska Press, 1993), p. 210.

Fe. Northwest of the capital, at Abiquiu, a party of New Mexicans, who may have numbered fifteen or more, asked to join on and were welcomed. The list presented by Rowland to the authorities in Los Angeles included: William Workman and family; William Gordon and family; John Rowland; James D. Mead (listed as Doctor; he was an Episcopalian clergyman); Benjamin D. Wilson; William Knight; Jacob Frankfort (tailor); William Gambel [sometimes misspelled Gamble] (naturalist); Thomas Lindsay (mineralogist); Hiram Taylor (musician); Wade Hampton (gunsmith); Isaac Given [usually given erroneously as Givens] (engineer); John McClure; James Doke; Jonathan Lyman (physician); Daniel Sexton (carpenter); Albert J. Tibeau; Albert G. Toomes (carpenter); William Moore (cooper); Fred Batchelor (cooper); Frank Bidebey (carpenter); Frank Quinn (blacksmith); Michael White; Manuel Vaca and family; Lorenzo Trujillo and family and Ignacio Salazar and servant.

The expedition followed the Old Spanish Trail, which had been opened in 1829, and was in fact neither old nor Spanish. Prior to the Rowland and Workman expedition, however, it had never been used by a large group of immigrants, but was traveled by regular caravans of traders between New Mexico and California. The path of the trail was somewhat circuitous, moving northwest from New Mexico, through a corner of modern Colorado, and into central Utah, before running southwest roughly along present-day Interstate 15 through lower Nevada, passing an encampment called "Las Vegas" and through the Mojave Desert and Cajon Pass to Los Angeles. Some writers have thought the expedition went along the Gila River route (used by the trapping expedition of 1827 of which Workman was a member), but accounts of those in the group that wrote of their experiences clearly indicated the Old Spanish Trail. Nor was the expedition a "wagon train," an assumption based on the fact that 1840s overland caravans universally consisted of wagons. The route's difficult terrain, in fact, precluded the use of anything but pack mules and horses. Ahead of the expedition was a trading caravan led by New Mexican Esteban Vigil, which arrived in Los Angeles in late October. Vigil made a report of his caravan to the authorities and added, "I give you notice that a party of American merchants are coming and with them are others who have the intention of residing in this country."[13]

---

13 Eleanor Lawrence, "Mexican Trade between Santa Fe and Los Angeles, 1830–1848," *California Historical Society Quarterly*, 10 (March 1931): 34.

Descriptions of the trip in later years were provided by six members of the expedition: William Gambel, Isaac Given, Jonathan Lyman, Albert Toomes, Michael White and Benjamin D. Wilson.[14] There are, not surprisingly, some notable differences among these accounts. Unfortunately, Rowland and Workman, the leaders of the group, left no surviving reminiscence or mention of the expedition, except for Rowland's passport and list of passengers and Workman's passport and invoice of goods.[15]

Gambel, a native of Philadelphia who studied ornithology under famed naturalist James Nuttall, was barely eighteen when he made the journey to California. Though his description given in a letter to his mother in January, 1842 from Los Angeles was brief, he observed:

> [T]hough it was a long and dangerous journey, I have got through without sickness or accident. We left Santa Fe the 1st of September and arrived here the last of November going three months travelling over Rocky mountains, barren deserts, worse than those of Arabia, sometimes having to do without water 2 & 3 days at a time, and towards the last almost starving in want of provisions, suffering also innumerable other difficulties...but am glad I have got through them safe.[16]

Given and Toomes, along with Hampton and McClure, were among those who had missed the Bidwell-Bartleson party and, consequently, arrived in New

---

14 John McClure, who traveled with Given and Toomes from Missouri to Santa Fe, wrote an anonymous account, dated 23 July 1841, of that trip to the Evansville (Indiana) *Journal*, which was also published in Baltimore later that year. He, evidently, wrote nothing of the trip to Los Angeles. White, *News of the Plains and Rockies, 1803–1865*, II: pp. 135–143. See also *Santa Fe and the Far West* (Los Angeles: Glen Dawson,) 1949.

15 Although he did not evidently write of the 1841 trip, Rowland did write to United States consul in Santa Fe, Manuel Alvarez, about his return trip in the fall of 1842, noting, "safe arrival here [Los Angeles] on the 12th of December last, after a very tedious and disagreeable journey; on the road we had nearly all the time very cold unpleasant weather in which our women and little ones suffered very much...I shall always feel grateful to the Divine Ruler of the destinies of us mortals for having delivered me from the bondage of the Taosanios and Apaches to which I was always doomed whilst in New Mexico." Rowland's trip was his third in two years (quite an accomplishment for a man in his fifties), was a month later than the 1841 trip, and he had the consideration of his wife and children. John Rowland to Manuel Alvarez, 23 February 1843, no. 315, Benjamin Read Collection, New Mexico State Archives. Copy provided courtesy of Don Rowland.

16 William Gambel to Elizabeth Richardson Gambel, 14 January 1842, MS, Historical Society of Pennsylvania and Bancroft Library.

Mexico about the first of July. Given recalled the expedition as if he and his compatriots were the organizers:

> Among the new recruits to our party obtained at Santa Fe
> were John Rowland, formerly of Ohio, William Workman,
> a native of England [and the others above listed]... We sup-
> plied ourselves at Santa Fe with an abundance of provisions,
> consisting of groceries, flour, hardtack, dried beef, and buffalo
> meat, prepared after the manner of the trappers... When we
> reached the Mexican village of Abiquiu, at the crossing of
> the Rio Grande, we purchased 150 head of sheep to furnish
> a supply of fresh meat on the journey, hiring native herders
> to drive them. Some of the company also employed Mexi-
> cans as servants... We were overtaken shortly after leaving
> Santa Fe by a party of New Mexicans...who asked and were
> granted the privilege of travelling with us. Being but scant-
> ily supplied with provisions, they were necessarily obliged
> to live off our bounty, but fortunately for all parties, we had
> enough to spare. In as much as one of this party had previ-
> ously made the trip to California, we employed him as our
> pilot, and he proved an intelligent guide... In order to avoid
> meeting the roving bands of hostile Indians, infesting the
> most direct line of travel, the route selected by our guide was
> a somewhat circuitous one. Entering through the Cajon Pass,
> we reached the settlements, not far south of Los Angeles on
> November 5th.[17]

Because Workman and Rowland had clearly planned their journey months ahead and were joined by many others in New Mexico, it is interesting that Given and his companions could be so self-serving in attempting to claim credit for recruiting the larger party.

Toomes' version, meanwhile, appeared in the San Francisco *Evening Bulletin* of 27 July 1868 and mentions nothing like Given's assertion of au-thority, though he gives another interesting spin to the dynamics of both the Bidwell-Bartleson and Rowland and Workman groups. He wrote:

---

17 Isaac Given, "A Pioneer of '41", MS, pp. 10–12, Bancroft Library.

I claim that we were the first emigrants who ever started from the States to California... Our party was divided into two companies, who left Independence on the 6th of May 1841, and we got into California on the 10th November of the same year. The first company was headed by Robert H. Thomes[18], who crossed over by way of Salt Lake, and the second was headed by William Workman, who went by way of Santa Fe and the middle route to Los Angeles; and both got into the country at nearly the same time. We were all armed with rifles, and mounted on horseback...but we arrived all safe and hearty, and nearly every one of the immigrants mentioned have either died in the State or still reside here. But I never want to cross those hard deserts and big mountains again, except on the railroad... We suffered great hardships, and got into very tight pinches for food and water, but we made up for it when we got among the fat beef and venison of California.[19]

Of course the statement that the two companies left Missouri in May is mistaken, though the real issue was that Toomes thought that linking the two groups gave them greater impact in this history of Western American emigration.

Hoping to recover his health, Lyman, who was in New Mexico on his way to Chihuahua before being diverted to California, gave an account which dealt more with the topography he encountered along the trip than the other surviving reminiscences. His version was quoted in an 1849 book which was one of the many works that fed the curious fascination of eastern Americans with remote California. Lyman also provided more detail of the route than those of any of the other accounts noting that it:

[L]ay northwesterly, up the head waters of the Rio Bravo del Norte —over the dividing ridge between those waters and

---

18 Because Thomes was a business partner of Toomes, it was natural for the latter to credit the for-mer instead of Bidwell and Bartleson.
19 Albert G. Toomes, "The Pioneer Overlanders of 1841," San Francisco *Evening Bulletin*, 27 July 1868.

the upper branches of the San Juan, and northwardly across
these to the Rio Colorado of the West —down the northern
bank to the Californian Mountains —and through these to
El Pueblo de Los Angelos, near the coast of the Pacific.

Lyman also described the somewhat forbidding territory from central
and southern Utah through a "place of encampment called las Vegas" and
through the harsh Mojave desert, which "has no equal on this continent for
barrenness." He further claimed to have seen some ancient city, and Thomas
J. Farnham, whose book contained Lyman's recollections, wondered, "Was not
this the Cibola of the early explorers; the land visited by the Jesuits —filled
with people and wealth...?" The account mentioned that Lyman "suffered so
many hardships and privations...that he, as well as his animals, barely lived to
reach the green fields and pure waters of the Californian Mountains."[20]

Michael White had first settled in Los Angeles in 1828 before going to
New Mexico about a decade later. In an 1877 dictation for Bancroft, he remembered that, "most of the time I was in the store of Mr. Wm. Workman
of Taos."[21] His account demonstrates, however, the pitfalls of a seventy-five-
year-old man looking back thirty-five years:

> In the fall of 1840...we formed a party of 94 or 95 all for-
> eigners, started from Taos in September for California,
> and arrived here in December at the Cajon. We celebrated
> Christmas day at the Cajon. We met with no adventures on
> the road. Indians would occasionally come to our camp and
> beg for something to eat, which we gave them.[22]

Aside from being a year off in his reckoning, White seemed to greatly
overestimate the number of those present, and his date of arrival is much later
than that given by other accounts.

Finally, there was Benjamin Wilson, a native of Tennessee and resident of
New Mexico since 1833, who, in his Bancroft narrative, noted the effects of
the Texas-Santa Fe Expedition on the formation of the expedition:

---

20 Thomas Jefferson Farnham, *Life, Adventures, and Travels in California* (New York: Nafis and
    Cornish, 1849), pp. 312–318.
21 Michael White, *California All The Way Back to '28* (Los Angeles: Glen Dawson, 1956), p. 43.
22 Ibid., p. 47–48.

Under the circumstances, Rowland, Workman, and myself, together with about twenty other Americans, including William Gordon and William Knight, concluded it was not safe for us to remain longer in New Mexico. We formed a party and were joined by a large number of New Mexicans. In the first week of September 1841, we started from our rendezvous in the most western part of New Mexico, a place called Abiqui, for California, we met no accidents on the journey, drove sheep with us, which served us as food, and arrived in Los Angeles early in November of the same year.[23]

There are three notable points to be made regarding these accounts: first, the claim of Given that he, Toomes, Hampton and McClure "recruited" the rest of the group, while Toomes himself, although lumping the Bidwell-Bartleson and Rowland-Workman groups together, said Workman was the leader of the latter. It was Rowland, however, who carried the letter of introduction to California officials from the United States consul in Santa Fe, Manuel Alvarez, and presented the list of expedition members to the authorities in Los Angeles. If a role of primacy in the leadership of the expedition must be assigned, and perhaps it is purely an academic point, it appears that Rowland is the obvious choice. Secondly, in terms of the difficulty of the trip, descriptions range from Given and Wilson's comparative silence to the hardships enumerated by Gambel, Toomes, and Lyman. Finally, regarding the plans of the expedition members once they arrived in California, the accounts again vary. Rowland's member list presented to the authorities in Los Angeles stated:

> "Those with families came with the intention of relocating in this Department and also those with an occupation looking for employment. and some of the others to examine and look over this department with the object of relocating now or coming back later after returning to their Country."[24]

23 Benjamin D. Wilson, "The Narrative of Benjamin D. Wilson" (dictation for H.H. Bancroft, 1877) in Robert G. Cleland, *Pathfinders* (Los Angeles: Powell Publishing Company, 1929), pp. 382–83.
24 John Rowland to Second District Prefect Manuel Dominguez, *List of Expedition Members*, 6 February 1842, from copy in Homestead Museum Research Archives.

Toomes, as was noted earlier, stated that many of them had lived in California, though he does not explicitly say what the members planned. Given, however, observed that

> Rowland and Workman, about the only members of our party who had reached middle age, were the only ones of our number who had come to the country with the intention of remaining, the remainder were young men, who had made this long journey, mainly through motives of curiosity and love of adventure, having no definite object in view.[25]

Yet, Wilson's comments are very different from Given's, though he seemed to be one of those who was covered by Given's assertion:

> As far as I am able to judge, Rowland, Workman, Gordon, and Knight, and most of the foreigners of our party came here with the intention of settling. I had no such idea; my plan was to go to China and from thence return home [Tennessee]. But after three different journeys to San Francisco, in search of a ship to go to China, I arrived at the conclusion that there would be no chance for carrying out my original intention.[26]

Wilson remained in southern California, where he became more well-known perhaps than any other member of the expedition. Among his activities were stints as the first American-era county clerk and mayor of Los Angeles, two terms as state senator, federal Indian agent and well-regarded writer on the region's native Americans, and a career as a major wine-maker. His name has passed down in posterity through the naming of Mount Wilson in his honor.[27]

Many of the members of the expedition eventually decided to remain in California or to return in later years. Aside from Rowland, Workman and

---

25 Toomes, "The Pioneer Overlanders of 1841."
26 Wilson, "Narrative," p. 383.
27 Wilson also was involved in a subdivision of his Lake Vineyard ranch property in present San Marino with F.P.F. Temple and others in 1875 (see Chapter Four). Material on Wilson can be found in Midge Sherwood, *Days of Vintage, Years of Vision* (San Marino: Orizaba Publications, 1982.)

Wilson, those who settled in southern California included Sexton, who lived near San Bernardino and then near the Mission San Gabriel; White, whose adobe stands on the grounds of San Marino High School; Frankfort, who deserves remembrance as the first Jew to settle in the region and Trujillo, who became a leader of the New Mexican settlement of Agua Mansa (also known as San Salvador) on land donated by Juan Bandini on the Rancho Jurupa near present-day Riverside.[28]

Among those who chose to emigrate to northern California were Given; Toomes; Gordon, the first American or European to settle in today's Yolo County; Knight, remembered by the place names of Knight's Landing and Knight's Ferry; Lindsay, believed to be the first resident of Tuleburg, now Stockton; and Vaca, for whose family Vacaville was named. Many of the expedition members either stayed very briefly or left immediately; a couple went to Oregon to settle; Mead headed for Hawaii before returning to Boston; and Gambel who stayed briefly in California as secretary to Thomas Ap Catesby Jones, known for his improvident seizure of Monterey in 1842. Gambel did return to his Philadelphia home for a few years, but the lure of gold brought him back to California in 1848. Soon after his arrival, however, in the gold fields he died of typhoid fever.[29]

The arrival date of the expedition was significant for Englishman Workman because it was Guy Fawkes Day. To commemorate the event, Workman later placed a glass plaque on his office door at his home which read in gilt letters:

Puente
William Workman

28 Surveys of the Agua Mansa/San Salvador community may be found in Joyce Vickery's *Defending Eden* (Riverside: History Department, University of California, Riverside, 1977); Harold A. Whelan's "Eden in Jurupa Valley: The Story of Agua Mansa", *Southern California Quarterly*, LV (June 1973): 113–130; and R. Bruce Harley, *The Story of Agua Mansa: Its Settlement, Churches and People, First Community in San Bernardino Valley, 1842–1893* (San Bernardino: Diocese of San Bernardino Archives,) 1998 and "Lorenzo Trujillo: Founder of Agua Mansa, 1795–1855," unpublished manuscript, 1999. Regarding Jacob Frankfort's distinction as the first Jewish resident of southern Califonia, see Max Vorspan and Lloyd P. Gartner, *History of the Jews of Los Angeles* (San Marino: The Huntington Library, 1970), p. 4.

29 Wilson, Givens, and Toomes related the whereabouts in the late 1870s of many of the expedition members, while Bancroft's *California Pioneer Register and Index, 1542–1848* (Baltimore: Regional Publishing Company, 1964,) provides information on almost every member. Also, "William Gamble, M.D.U. of Pa., 1848, Ornithologist" by John Middleton, pp. 2–4, MS, Historical Society of Pennsylvania/Bancroft Library. See also Briton Cooper Busch, ed., *Alta California, 1840–42: The Journal and Observations of William Dane Phelps* (Glendale: Arthur H. Clark Co., 1983), pp. 266, 304–306 for Gambel's journey on Phelps' ship, *Alert*, from Los Angeles to Monterey.

Arrived Nov. 5, Guy Fawkes Day, 1841[30]

As mentioned above, Workman left no account of the trip, though he did leave a postscript of sorts regarding his position in New Mexico, in the form of a letter to Manuel Alvarez dated 23 February 1843. In it he wrote, "I...heartily sympathize with you in the persecutions which you have had from the Barbarians amongst whom you are" and roundly lambasted an acquaintance named John Scolly, whose signature was on the permit and effects invoice issued for Workman's departure to California, for his "base and doublefaced conduct" and "his character for falseness and duplicity" in an unknown incident. In calling Scolly "an undeserving old hypocrite," Workman further revealed his aptitude for dealing squarely with his enemies and added, "I should be glad that you would take the trouble to let him know that such are my opinions respecting him."[31]

Meanwhile, in a similar vein, New Mexican Governor Armijo left little doubt what he thought of the departure of Workman and Rowland. According to official documents, Armijo believed that the two were going to California on a mission from President Lamar of Texas and fired off this parting shot concerning:

> ...the naturalized foreigners Juan Rooland and William Workman, traitors who have gone to California to seduce and confuse its inhabitants, whose exemplary punishment would be the only dike to the torrent of evils that they have committed in this department under my command, and will be the ones which undoubtedly they will commit in the Californias.[32]

Such seduction and confusion was more appropriate, however, regarding the Texas-Santa Fe Expedition, which reached New Mexico in October.

---

30 The plate is now owned by Workman's great-great-granddaughter, Josette Temple. Temple's uncle, historian and genealogist, Thomas W. Temple II, presented it to the new Workman Elementary School in La Puente in 1941 as part of the observance of the 100th anniversary of the Workman and Rowland expedition. It was dropped, however, as it was being handed to the school principal and was broken into three pieces, which were glued back together!
31 William Workman to Manuel Alvarez, 23 February 1843.
32 New Mexico Governor Manuel Armijo to the Mexican Ministry of War and Navy, 22 September 1841, as quoted in Hafen and Hafen, *Old Spanish Trail*, p. 207.

It suffered from poor planning and leadership and the difficult journey from Austin. Armijo and his soldiery had little difficulty in dispersing the ragtag force and in seizing main agent William G. Dryden and his commissioners. Dryden was interrogated in Chihuahua City and, when asked why Rowland and Workman had gone to California, replied, "it was convenient for them to leave Santa Fe so that they would not be compromised."[33] Eight years later, in 1850, Dryden relocated to Los Angeles. Serving as a lawyer, justice of the peace, and long-time county judge, he was known for his questionable judicial qualifications and colorful courtroom conduct. He represented Rowland and Workman in land claims during the 1850s, and it can be assumed that the three often commiserated on their adventures in New Mexico. Dryden died in Los Angeles in 1869.

Chroniclers of California history have pointed to the Bidwell-Bartleson party as the archetype of overland pioneers. Because the party consisted entirely of Americans and Europeans, had a unified purpose of immigration, and departed from the United States to Mexican California, some have considered it as a precursor of American domination and annexation of the province. Consequently, the Rowland-Workman expedition has been relegated to footnote status because it was a group consisting of Americans, Europeans, and New Mexicans (most part or full Indian), without a unifying purpose going from one part of Mexico to another. A rather useless point of contention over the years centered around which of the groups reached California first, because Bidwell and Bartleson reached Marsh's ranch at the foot of Mount Diablo in present-day Contra Costa County on the 4th of November while Workman and Rowland arrived at the Mission San Gabriel the next day. Instead of being seen as competitors for the dubious distinction of who was first in striking California soil (for what were, after all, the boundaries of the province in 1841?), these expeditions ought to be recognized together as the precursors to the amazing transcontinental migration west that characterized the 1840s and afterward. The question of which was first or which was more important bears little significance to the more important meaning of what their arrival signifies in the history of California.[34]

---

33 "Interrogation of William G. Dryden," *Archivo de Guerra* (Mexico), *Frac.* 1, *Leg.* 1, 1841 and 1842: 47, Bancroft Library. Translation by the author from a copy in the Homestead Museum archives provided by Steven Born.

34 The Bidwell-Bartleson expedition's 150th anniversary was marked by the publication of a book edited by Doyce B. Nunis, Jr. called *The Bidwell-Bartleson Party: 1841 California Emigrant Adventure* (Santa Cruz: Western Tanager Press, 1991.) The Rowland and Workman expedition

The Rancho La Puente

After the dissolution of the expedition and rest from the journey, John Rowland traveled to Monterey and petitioned Governor Juan Bautista Alvarado for the Rancho La Puente, twenty miles east of Los Angeles. In pre-European years, the area contained a significant native American settlement called, by chronicler Hugo Reid, *Awig-na*, which was located on San Jose Creek between what became the Rowland and Workman homesteads.[35] The region was first seen by Europeans in 1769 when the Portolá expedition crossed the Puente Hills on the southern end of the San Gabriel Valley and descended into the broad plain below. Both Father Juan Crespí and engineer Miguel Costansó noted that the group had to build a bridge (or *puente*) over a creek (named San Jose) in order to move on to the northwest, hence the name given to the local area in later years, though Portolá bestowed the name San Miguel on it.[36]

Two years later, when the Mission San Gabriel was founded at its original site along the west bank of the San Gabriel River (now the Rio Hondo channel) at Whittier Narrows as the first permanent European settlement in southern California, the La Puente region became mission property and in years following was valuable for stock grazing and such agricultural pursuits as wheat raising. As early as 1792, the Rancho La Puente was a designated name for the area and four years later, a report by a priest stated that La Puente had 3,000 cattle, over 4,000 sheep, and horses pastured upon it.[37] La Puente was also distinguished because of an adobe granary built as part of the successful raising

anniversary was largely unnoticed, except for a lecture by prominent U.S./Mexican borderlands historian and early Workman and Rowland biographer David J. Weber at the Workman and Temple Family Homestead Museum.

35 Bernice Eastman Johnston, *California's Gabrieliño Indians* (Los Angeles: Southwest Museum, 1962), pp. 142–143.

36 Juan Crespí, *A Description of Distant Roads: Original Journals of the First Expedition into California, 1769–1770*, Alan K. Brown, editor and translator (San Diego: San Diego State University Press, 2001), 325–29; Thomas W. Temple II's explanation in Lenore Rowland, *The Romance of La Puente Rancho* (Covina: Neilson Press, 1958), pp. 23–24. See also John Rowland to Governor Juan Bautista Alvarado, *Petition for a grant to the Rancho La Puente*, no date, General Land Office Docket No. 160, California Private Land Claims [Microfilm C-I 100:160], pp. 31–32, Bancroft Library. Miguel Costansó, "The Portolá Expedition of 1769-1770, Diary of Miguel Constansó," Publications of the Academy of Pacific Coast History, Vol. 2, No. 4 (August 1911), University of California, Berkeley; Gaspar de Portolá, "Diary of Gaspar de Portolá During the California Expedition of 1769-1770, "Publications of the Academy of Pacific Coast History, Vol. 1, No. 3 (October 1909), University of California, Berkeley.

37 Zephyrin Engelhardt, *San Gabriel Mission and the Beginning of Los Angeles* (San Gabriel: Mission San Gabriel, 1927), pp. 201–202.

of wheat by Indians supervised by the Mission priests. Eventually, maps such as those produced to document the progress of surveys under the California land claims process and others denoted the site as "Mission Graneros."[38] One undocumented source claims that the rancho was granted in 1820 to a Ramon F. Aguilar, a Spaniard, who, during the resulting independence of Mexico from Spain, abandoned his holdings and fled California.[39] Otherwise, the La Puente region remained unowned for the first few years after secularization of the missions took place in the mid-1830s.

In his undated petition to Governor Alvarado sometime in early January 1842, Rowland wrote:

> [D]esiring the repose of my family and their well being...
> I need a tract of land on which to put my property, and
> which I can cultivate for the support of my said family, and
> as there is in the Ex-Mission of San Gabriel a vacant place
> at La Puente...being in the East bounded by El Chino and
> San Jose, and on the West by the River San Gabriel, on the
> North by the land of Don Luis Arenas [Rancho Azusa], and
> on the South by the land of Senor Perez of the Nietos and
> Los Coyotes, wherefore I beseech your Excy that you will
> grant me in property the land which I solicit which *may be
> four leagues a little more or less* [author's italics].[40]

The italicized portion is important, because, although it gives the figure of four square leagues, a little less than 18,000 acres, Rowland described the neighboring ranchos, the borders of which enclosed an area that was about eleven square leagues, or some 49,000 acres. This vagary regarding the size of the rancho would come to haunt Rowland and Workman. Curiously, Workman is not even mentioned in Rowland's petition.

---

38 Several editions of the "Map of Public Surveys in California" between 1856 and 1861 show the "Mission Graneros" and are in the Homestead Museum Collections.
39 Dan and Janet Powell, *La Puente Valley-Past and Present* (La Puente: La Puente Chamber of Commerce, 1958), p. 33. This WPA history written in 1937 did not provide sources for this alleged transaction to Aguilar.
40 John Rowland, *Petition for a Grant to the Rancho La Puente*, undated [probably early January 1842], G.L.O. Docket No. 160, p. 31, California Private Land Claims.

Benjamin Wilson, who was probably making his first trip north to seek passage to Asia, later recalled that he had accompanied Rowland to Monterey and gave this account:

> Mr. Rowland had obtained from the priest at San Gabriel, and from the Prefect of the Second District, certificates stating that there was no objection to the granting of Messrs. Rowland and Workman, the Ranch of La Puente, which they had petitioned for, as such grant would not be prejudicial to the Neophytes.
>
> Upon the presentation of the documents to the Governor the grant was made to the petitioners.[41]

Actually, Alvarado had made a preliminary grant on 14 January which required permission of the Second (or Southern) District Prefect and mission superintendent, as well as "an exact map" since Rowland had no way of "knowing the Extent it [the rancho] has."[42] Perhaps Wilson was mistaken in what Rowland's "certificates" consisted of, because writings of the friars at San Gabriel clearly belie his claim that Rowland had any agreement with the mission fathers.

Possibly based upon hearsay, Isaac Given's account appears colorfully embellished with this little tidbit that would indicate a contradiction to the established convention that land grants were given without monetary consideration:

> For the consideration of $1000.00 paid in hand, this obliging official [Governor Alvarado], without hesitation, granted all the applicants asked. By way of quieting any adverse criticism of his official act or reconciling any charge of partiality against him, he would modestly reply, 'Why gentlemen, you never offered me anything.'"[43]

---

41 Wilson, "Narrative," p. 383.
42 Governor Juan Bautista Alvarado, *Preliminary Grant to the Rancho La Puente*, 14 January 1842, G.L.O. Docket No. 160, p. 32, California Private Land Claims.
43 Given, "A Pioneer of 1841," p. 13.

Given undoubtedly viewed the payment as little more than a bribe, assuming there was any such transaction, though he correctly noted the "adverse criticism" of the clergy at Mission San Gabriel, who strongly disputed the grant to Rowland. Father Tomás Esténega, when asked by Second District Prefect Santiago Argüello to report on mission claims to La Puente, answered: "The land of La Puente belongs to this community of San Gabriel, which occupies it with more than five hundred head of large cattle, and in no manner does this community consent that the land should be alienated since it is the only place which the Mission has for sowing and to support its cattle."[44]

Five days earlier, on 21 February 1842, Father Narciso Duran wrote to the Mexican Minister of the Interior and Public Instruction a protest over the petition of Rowland and Workman:

> [T]he Reverend Missionary Father of the Mission of San Gabriel communicates [on 13 February] that this departmental government, following its plan and system of alienating or selling the ranchos which are the property of the unfortunate neophytes of these Missions, just sold a rancho belonging to the Mission of San Gabriel called La Puente, where the Mission has more than a thousand head of cattle and horses, in order to adjudge it to an Anglo-American named Juan Roldan, recently arrived in this territorial department, and that he has ordered the Mission to vacate the site which is distant less than two leagues from it.
>
> I solemnly protest in the name of the neophytes of the Mission of San Gabriel, once, twice, and three times as may be customary in law, against the sale or alienation of said Rancho of La Puente...and particularly not to said Juan Roldan...[45]

Nevertheless, it is wondered why Duran had such a particular aversion to granting the rancho to Rowland. Prefect Argüello dismissed the claims of the padres by reporting to Alvarado that, "notwithstanding the Revd. Minister

---

44 Father Tomás Esténega to Prefect Santiago Argüello, 26 February 1842, from the G. L. O. Docket No. 160, p. 35, California Private Land Claims.
45 Zephyrin Engelhardt, *San Gabriel Mission and the Beginning of Los Angeles*, pp. 201–202.

DAVID ALEXANDER & WILLIAM WORKMAN, 1851

PHOTOGRAPH ATTRIBUTED TO MATHEW B. BRADY,
COURTESY OF THOMAS E. TEMPLE

of said Mission maintaining its right of property, I believe that it is not so much covered with stock...because at present it is rented by the Minister to a citizen of this place."[46] This said, Alvarado soon issued permanent title of the rancho to Rowland. This was not done, however, without a sharp reaction by the governor to a letter Duran sent to Esténega, criticizing Alvarado for his grant of La Puente to Rowland. In his 5 February 1842 letter, the governor reproached Duran for his letter to Esténega "which is full of contemptuous reproaches and insults against my person." Referring specifically to an accu-

---

46 Prefect Santiago Argüello to Governor Juan Bautista Alvarado, 28 February 1842, G. L. O. Docket No. 160, pp. 35–36, California Private Land Claims.

sation that Alvarado's reliance on the support of foreigners would make him "one of the first victims in case the foreigners take possession of the country," the governor replied "O Narciso! I have a large spy-glass with which I can see what is going on at a distance ...[t]reat me with the respect which the dignity of the post I occupy deserves ... I must never be made to figure as a toy or puppet of your caprice and cavils." In an April reply, Duran stated that his letter to Esténega was misconstrued and that Arguello "acted tracherously by substituting [what the letter actually said] and stating what is not true."

In his comments to Esténega about La Puente, Duran questioned whether Arugello "and some others had invesigated whether or not said Roldan [Rowland] was or was not the one styled traitor by General Armijo in his report to the Government." This, of course, referred to the comments of Armijo cited at the end of the last chapter about Rowland and Workman going to California "to seduce and confuse its inhabitants."[47]

As part of the process of acquiring final title, the new owners' next step was to meet one of the conditions of the preliminary grant by having the rancho surveyed. This responsibility fell to Isaac Given, listed as an engineer in the membership roster of the expedition. Given's account reveals the characteristics of surveying in Mexican California:

> After providing a rope of 4 poles in length and the necessary number of stakes, each about 3 feet long, setting the compass at the north-west corner of the tract, which was to be run around and calculate the area of, sighting a tree in line something like a mile distant, the object was pointed out to the chain carriers, who were directed to go to it in a straight line and further instructed on how to keep tally —mounting my horse, I sallied forth at old time California speed for the line tree, dismounting to set the compass, and sight another object in line, expecting to lay off in the shade until the chain carriers should come up. I was not a little astonished to see those assistants, close at hand on horseback and running at full canter.

---

47 Mary Elizabeth Harris, "John Rowland and William Workman, Pioneers of Southern California," Thesis, University of California, Berkeley, pp. 110–15.

Remonstrating against the loose mode of carrying chain, Workman rather churlishly remarked that to have the men do that work on foot, would cost more than the land was worth. In consequence of this original procedure, the survey failed to close by a mile, which inaccuracy doubtless in after years caused the parties no little trouble and increased expense. A map was made, which with the accompanying field notes, were submitted to the governor, who thereupon made out the promised title.[48]

This last section undoubtedly refers to the permanent title issued by Alvarado on 9 March 1842, so probably the survey was completed in late February or early March. Whether Given's mention of the error causing grief to the owners was reflected in the American land claims proceedings of a decade and more later is not known. However, there were certainly problems aplenty due to a long-standing dispute over the size of the rancho. Relative to this, the permanent title specified that the grant was for four leagues with "the surplus thereof to remain to the Nation for the convenient uses."[49] This amounted, then, to seven additional square leagues within the recognized boundaries of the rancho.

With title to a portion of La Puente secured, Rowland traveled in April to New Mexico, where he left his family, and returned in December 1842 with them and other immigrants. During his absence, Workman had established residence on the rancho. Benjamin Wilson in land claims testimony in 1854 recalled, "It was first occupied in 1842 by Julian Workman, who raised a crop of corn and beans on it. He had a shanty there in the spring and he commenced an Adobe house in which he moved and he resided in it the ensuing winter and has continued living in it ever since."[50] David W. Alexander testified in a separate land claims interview that "Workman had cattle and Horses on the land in December of 1842," which was when Alexander came to California, accom-

---

48   Given, "A Pioneer of 1841," pp. 13–14.
49   Governor Juan Bautista Alvarado, *Permanent Title to the Rancho La Puente*, 9 March 1842, G. L. O. Docket No. 160, pp. 36–37, California Private Land Claims.
50   Benjamin Wilson, *Deposition in the Land Claim to Rancho La Puente*, 21 October 1852, Board of Land Commissioners Docket No. 127, pp. 7–8 California Private Land Claims.

panying Rowland. Concluding his testimony, Alexander further corroborated Benjamin Wilson's recollection of Workman's farming enterprises.[51]

The Workman adobe was situated on a little knoll a few hundred yards north of San Jose Creek, the same watercourse that the Portolá expedition spanned with that *puente* that gave the area its name and which generally provided a year-round source of water for agricultural uses around the home. The house, believed to have been a three-room, flat-roofed, whitewashed adobe, was distinguished by a basement. Whether this was a continuation of the pit from which the adobe bricks used to build the house were made or not, the presence of a basement was highly unusual, if not unique, in southern California. Though evidently not one to commit to paper his thoughts, Workman did leave a couple of brief notes regarding his settlement on the rancho. In April 1842, after Rowland had left for New Mexico to retrieve his family, Workman wrote his partner, "I am hear [sic] on the little River at work and am well pleased with the situation."[52] A little less than a year later, he wrote Manuel Alvarez, United States consul in New Mexico, stating, "Mr. Roland and myself are busily employed in establishing our farms all your acquaintances here are well and I believe pretty well satisfied with this country."[53]

Cattle and Commerce in Mexican California

In 1843, a year and a half after William Workman settled on La Puente, Jonathan Temple obtained his own rancho when he purchased the Rancho Los Cerritos from his wife's relatives in the Dominguez family.[54] This 27,000 acre parcel, which encompassed most of present-day Long Beach and portions of neighboring cities, was one of five ranchos that, in 1834, was carved out of the enormous Nieto grant of 1784 for the family heirs. The following summer near the Los Angeles River, Temple constructed a large two-story adobe home, one of the first multi-level structures in southern California. He kept his main residence, however, in Los Angeles and used the adobe at Los Cerritos

51 David W. Alexander, *Deposition in the Land Claim for Rancho La Puente*, 21 October 1852, Board of Land Commissioners Docket No. 127, p. 6, California Private Land Claims. Alexander, who came to California with Rowland in the 1842 expedition was a close friend of Workman and Jonathan Temple.

52 William Workman to John Rowland, 14 April 1842. Original owned by the Historical Society of the La Puente Valley. Copy in Homestead Museum Research Archives.

53 William Workman to Manuel Alvarez, 23 February 1843.

54 Guillermo Cota, Manuel Dominguez, and Rafael Gallardo, *et. al.*, to John Temple, *Deed to the Rancho Los Cerritos*, 16 December 1843, Book 1: 169, Los Angeles County Archives.

as a country home, raising livestock to supplement his significant merchandising and trading income. Writing home to their brother Abraham on 27 November 1844, Pliny Temple made mention of Jonathan's latest holding: "Brother John purchased a tract of land last spring containing about 20,000 acres sufficiently large to maintain 6 or 8 thousand head of cattle and horses. He has built a house on the Ranch the past season and got on 700 of cattle besides sheep, horses, etc."[55]

Like all rancheros in southern California, William Workman, Jonathan Temple and Pliny Temple engaged in cattle raising, though little direct information survives from the era about their specific activities. Workman received his cattle brand from *alcalde* José Dominguez in May 1842, Jonathan Temple was given his in January 1844, and Pliny Temple was registered in August 1847. Each had subsequent brands and counter brands re-registered.[56] This was the time in which cattle were raised for their hides and tallow, because beef was of no use commercially. San Pedro was the main anchorage in the region, as poor a natural harbor as it was. Richard Henry Dana, for example, had no kind words for the primitive port and the awkward method of transporting hides from land to ship. For Jonathan Temple, the transport of hides to San Pedro was a matter of only several miles, while for his brother and for Workman such shipments may well have required an overnight journey. Data is quite scarce about the extent of their wealth in this era, though hard cash was often lacking and barter was a method frequently employed in the region. Perhaps the number of cattle and the amount of acreage the men owned served as a better barometer of their success in those days. There was also a great deal of uncertainty regarding economic enterprise, particularly in an industry that was so dependent on water in a semi-arid environment.

---

55 Pliny Fisk Temple to Abraham Temple, 27 November 1844. Copy of the original in the Homestead Museum Research Archives.

56 *Certificate of Registration for a Cattle Brand to William Workman, 23 April 1842, Walter P. Temple, Jr. Collection; Certificate of Registration for a Cattle Brand to F.P.F. Temple, 18 August 1847, Thomas W. Temple II Collection; Certificate of Registration of a Counterbrand of William Workman, 19 May 1855, Book 2: 136; Certificate of Registration for a Cattle Brand to Jonathan Temple, 15 May 1852, Book 2: 14; Certificate of Registration for a Cattle Brand for F.P.F. Temple, 8 April 1846, Book 1: 80; Certificate of Registration for a Cattle Brand for F.P.F. Temple, 21 July 1851, Book 2: 2; Certificate of Registration for a Cattle Ear Mark to F.P.F. Temple, 21 July 1851; Book 1: 138; Certificate of Registration for a Counterbrand to F.P.F. Temple, 7 May 1861, Book 3: 165, Los Angeles County Recorder, Seaver Center for Western History Research, Natural History Museum of Los Angeles County; Ana Begue de Packman, "California's Cattle Brands and Earmarks", Historical Society of Southern California Quarterly 27 (December 1945): 130, 149.*

Indeed, there is a great deal of mythology associated with the "days of the don." Images of dandied rancheros parading about on caparisoned horses and alluring senoritas with flashing eyes captivating their men while dancing the fandango at the ever-present fiesta implied, to Americans and Europeans, that the Californios were more interested in play than work. Ideas of an unfettered, carefree existence, as if money were of no concern, do not mesh with the reality that, as much as the Californios enjoyed their amusements, life on southern California's ranchos had its disconcerting aspects.

Not all of the activities of the Workman and Temple families were based on cattle. Jonathan Temple had his store in Los Angeles with brother Pliny in his employ and Ygnacio García as manager. In June 1845, he and David W. Alexander purchased from Abel Stearns the *Casa de San Pedro*, a store and warehouse at the harbor in San Pedro, where for some seven years, they conducted a profitable enterprise in the sale of hides and tallow to incoming ships.[57] He also formed a partnership on 1 January 1843 with John Paty, James McKinley and Henry D. Fitch known as Paty, McKinley and Company. The four used Paty's bark and, as the shipowner wrote, "We opened a store in San Francisco and traded up and down the coast. We left Mr. Wm H. Davis in charge of our store and McKinley opened another store in Los Angeles in company with C. Fluyge [Charles Flugge]." This association lasted only two years, however, before Paty bought out his partners' interests in the company in February 1845.[58] While not of any likely significance financially, it is of interest to note that Temple was also the Los Angeles agent of California's first newspaper, the *California Star*.[59]

Business pursuits also occasionally occupied the younger Temple, aside from his duties at his brother's store. An early example occurred on the heels of the discovery of gold in March 1842 by Francisco Lopez near present-day Newhall. This accidental act led to a significant mining effort for several years in the canyon that now bears his name. Historiographically, the gold rush in the north six years later has overshadowed the Lopez discovery, but the earlier find left its impression on Pliny Temple who wrote to his brother Abraham in May:

---

57 Doris Marion Wright, *A Yankee in Mexican California: Abel Stearns, 1798–1848* (Santa Barbara, Wallace Hebberd, 1977), pp. 47–48.
58 "The Journal of Captain John Paty, 1807–1868," *California Historical Society Quarterly*, 14 (December 1935): 324–325.
59 California *Star*, 18 December 1847.

There has been a gold mine discovered about 40 miles from the Pueblo, the gold is of a fine quality and some grains have been found worth nearly three dollars.

There are upwards of 50 men to work washing the earth and there are expected the coming fall a large number of Sonorans to work in the mines. Should this prove to be as rich in quantity as it is in quality, the country will in a very short time have a different aspect.[60]

A letter, written eighteen months later, reveals that Pliny went from being a mere observer to a participant in the little gold rush that struck the Los Angeles area:

There...arrived from Sonora a small party of miners to work in the mines of California. There has been at times nearly two hundred persons working at the Placer mine and a good quantity of gold taken out. I send you enclosed a sample and should like to have you take it to some Goldsmith, one experienced in the business to ascertain the real value. It can be bought here for cash at twelve dollars pr. ounce should it prove to be good as there is every appearance of it, it will bring at the mint eighteen to twenty dollars, and therefore be a source of speculation.[61]

Again in November 1844, Pliny sent off to his brother Abraham "10 ounces of fine gold which I wish you to sell," to purchase with the proceeds a number of goods. These included handkerchiefs, gloves, pen knives, pistols, a balance for weighing the gold Pliny was obtaining, a gross of pencils, 100 knitting needles, a gross of shirt buttons, tooth brushes, and note paper.[62] Some of this was intended for Pliny and Jonathan, but the larger quantity of items may have been to sell in the Temple store. Such accounts show Pliny's early

---

60 Pliny Fisk Temple to Abraham Temple, 11 May 1842. Original facsimile in Homestead Museum Research Archives.
61 Pliny Fisk Temple to Abraham Temple, 26 December 1843. Ibid.
62 Pliny Fisk Temple to Abraham Temple, 27 November 1844. Ibid.

start in business, his early contacts with the East, and the merchandise that was available in Los Angeles. Abraham's response came back in the following fall: "The gold sand you sent was good quality & I have disposed of it at $18 pr. ounce... I think you may do well to send on more if you can obtain it at $14 per ounce."[63] The Lopez Canyon gold discovery did not give the region the "different aspect" Pliny Temple referred to, but it remains a fascinating, if under-recognized event in southern California history.

Partisan Politics and the American Invasion

While Pliny Temple was engaged in projects to sell gold dust, William Workman found himself involved in political struggles in California, an ironic situation in light of his reasons to leave New Mexico to come to the coast. One of the many internecine political struggles that plagued the vulnerable territory involved Governor Manuel Micheltorena, an appointee in 1842 by the government in Mexico City, who was unpopular with his relatively independent constituents. The Californios, who were used to choosing their own administrators, also despised Micheltorena for his armed guard, which was said to consist mainly of recruited convicts. The division between the northern and southern regions of the province also entered into play here, as politicos in the south began to raise a challenge to Micheltorena. Chief amongst the southerners was Pío Pico, who was born at the San Gabriel Mission in 1801. He spent much of his early life in San Diego and styled himself a revolutionary, opposing the close-vested control of the central government in Mexico City. After a revolt unseated Manuel Victoria in late 1831, Pico assumed temporary governorship. Thirteen years later, Pico was one of the leaders opposing the administration of Micheltorena.

What made the revolt of 1844–45 different from previous uprisings was the significant presence of Americans and Europeans on both sides. Micheltorena enlisted the support of the Swiss-born entrepreneur, John Sutter, in leading a battalion of non-Mexicans against the southern rebels. For his part, Pico entrusted his foreign contingent to William Workman, who was commissioned a captain, and John Rowland, who was made a lieutenant. A number

---

63 Abraham Temple to Pliny Fisk Temple, 24 October 1845, courtesy of Josette Temple. While much of the letter was about selling gold dust from the Placerita Canyon gold placer in the East, there is an interesting query from Abraham about the potential of a steam-powered mill in Los Angeles!

of members of the Workman-Rowland expedition appeared on both sides of the conflict, including Thomas Lindsay and Isaac Given in the north and Benjamin Wilson, Michael White and Daniel Sexton in the south. White, in fact, in his dictation for Bancroft thirty years later, told how he was "recruited" by Workman to serve with him. Justice of the Peace Juan Sepulveda sent for White with the admonition that if he did not comply to the request he would be deemed traitorous. Upon arriving in Los Angeles, White saw Sepulveda. A curious incident ensued,

> Just then a fellow came and took my hat away and then brought it back with a red ribbon around it. Then Mr. Wm. Workman came out of the office and asked me to what party I belonged. I said, 'To the party of myself.' 'Then,' he said, 'you are one of my soldiers.' I told him I did not see it and he pointed to my hat, saying I had his ribbon. I did not want to have anything to do with the revolution, but Workman took me against my will to Cahuenga. Our captain was Workman and our lieutenant was Rowland. Our company had about 100 men.[64]

If true, White's story shows that Workman took his role seriously in the pending conflict and was not above clever deception to recruit members for his company.

Micheltorena marched towards Los Angeles in early 1845, and in February the rebels in Los Angeles advanced to Cahuenga Pass, several miles northwest of the town, to confront him. Given the scant supply of guns and powder, the "Battle of Cahuenga" amounted to little more than a staredown between Micheltorena and Pico. Later, Pico recalled that Workman and Jonathan Temple were among the southern California residents he brought together for the "defense of the liberty and interests." Forming his assembled troops into three companies, Pico entrusted command to Juan Gallardo, Juan Crispin Pérez, and Workman. After Pico, Workman, and four others scouted a favorable location from which to greet Micheltorena, a skirmish ensued, in which a horse was killed and "a man from Los Angeles had his hat blown off" —these

---

64 White, *California All The Way Back to 1828*, pp. 39–40.

MANUEL MICHELTORENA AND PÍO PICO
COURTESY OF THE BANCROFT LIBRARY,
UNIVERSITY OF CALIFORNIA, BERKELEY, CALIFORNIA

consisted of the casualties of the Battle of Cahuenga. Pico soon found cause to berate his compatriot when:

> I saw that Captain Workman and Don Santiago McKinley had dropped their arms and gone toward Micheltorena's forces, but they were fired upon and turned back.

> I then went to where Workman was and told him if I again saw him attempting contact with the enemy I would not consider him a friend of mine. He protested his great loyalty, assuring me he was incapable of betrayal.[65]

In his Bancroft dictation, Benjamin Wilson gave his version of events, making it sound as if there was a consensus among citizens to defend Los Angeles

---

65 Pío Pico, *Historical Narrative*, Arthur Botello, trans. and Martin Cole and Henry Welcome, eds. (Glendale: Arthur H. Clark Company, 1973), pp. 105–112; Wilson, "Narrative," pp. 391–94.

against Micheltorena and he specifically named Workman and Rowland as among those who "were armed and determined...to prevent Micheltorena and his scum from entering Los Angeles." Noting that Workman "had some Americans under him", Wilson described the march and positioning at Cahuenga. After the exchange of gunfire, Wilson , diverging from what Pico recalled, stated that

> Mr. Workman and myself, having learned that the Americans and other foreigners in the Micheltorena party were commanded by some of our old personal friends, and feeling convinced that they had engaged themselves on that side under misapprehension...we sent our native Californians to reconnoiter, and ascertain in what part of the field those foreigners were. It was at once decided between Mr. Workman and myself that I was to approach them if possible under a white flag.

At this point, claimed Wilson, James McKinley joined him and they approached the Micheltorena side, were fired upon, but were recognized with their flag by the Americans on the other side. After reassuring these men that Pico would guarantee their safety if they yielded the field, Wilson said he called Pico over to make this promise on his word "and that of Don Benito Wilson and Don Julian Workman." Obviously, Pico's account was structured to retain his sense of authority, while Wilson made it appear as if he, Workman and McKinley had engineered the outcome. This shows a possible dichotomy at work. Did the Californio leader have control of the situation leading to his ascension to power, or did his foreign subordinates portend the future by arranging for the denouement?

Just after he capitulated to Pico and his forces, which had cut off his access to the north and east, and surrendered authority to the former, Micheltorena made sure to remind his adversary that war between Mexico and the United States was imminent and he should prepare for that certainty.

Pliny Temple, in a letter to his brother Abraham ten months later, wrote about his impressions of the "battle":

> Last February the Californians with the assistance of
> foreigners sent General Micheltonen [sic] with his troops
> out of the country. The battle was fought about ten miles
> from this place [Los Angeles]. There was a great number of
> cannon fired, but without injury to either party, except the
> killing of a few horses which is not of much consequence in
> this country. Had the General gained the day the Pueblo
> probably would have been plundered by his troops...but they
> were not victorious, they were sent to San Pedro to embark
> on board an American ship for San Blas.[66]

In his 1877 Bancroft dictation, Temple remembered that Workman had "about 40 foreigners" under him and "when the two opposing parties faced each other there was a heavy cannonading which we could distinctly hear in town."[67] Temple's account otherwise agrees with Wilson's.

Micheltorena's warning to Pico about the probable declaration of war was probably no surprise and, within a year and half the latter presided tenuously over the last days of the Mexican era in California. In the meantime, perhaps in anticipation, Pico began granting or selling California real estate to Californios, Americans and Europeans alike on an unprecedented scale. One major transaction to Workman after the governor's accession may fall more appropriately under the category of a reward for services rendered. In July 1845, Pico confirmed a petition of Rowland and Workman to append the name of the latter as an owner of the Rancho La Puente. This petition claimed that Workman's name had inadvertantly been left off the petition of 1842, when Rowland clearly made it known that he was asking for La Puente for he and his family. Pico's new grant made no mention of leagues, but rather defined the rancho by the boundaries first applied in 1842, implying eleven square leagues. When the Assembly, which was led by Pico, met on 3 October to confirm the grant, however, it specified that the grant was for four leagues. Once again, confusion regarding the size of the rancho was created and would be brought up again in the American land claims process.[68]

---

66 F.P.F. Temple to Abraham Temple, 27 December 1845, Original facsimile in the Homestead
    Museum Research Archives.
67 F.P.F. Temple, "Recollections," p. 6.
68 Pío Pico to John Rowland and William Workman, Grant to Rancho La Puente, 22 July 1845;
    California *Asamblea* [Assembly], Order for Petition for Rancho La Puente Forwarded to Committee
    on Vacant Lands, 4 August 1845; Francisco de la Guerra and Narciso Botello, Committee on

Several other grants of land made by Pico to Workman during this period might additionally be classified as anticipatory to the American invasion. One, petitioned for by Workman in April 1846, was for "a small island named Alcatraz or Bird that is unoccupied." Workman, who undoubtedly realized its strategic location could benefit him, drew with his request the attention of officials in Yerba Buena (San Francisco), including Manuel Castro and Francisco Rico. The two noted in a late May letter to Pico that Alcatraz "can be of value for establishing on her some kind of lighthouse that provides light on dark nights for the protection of ships in course there." Pico took Castro and Rico's statement under consideration, although they no doubt would have preferred that Workman not receive the grant. Pico's *expediente,* or grant read:

> ...it has been granted to Don Guillermo Workman, naturalized Mexican citizen of the region of this city [Los Angeles], the little Island called Alcatraz or Bird that he has petitioned for...under the condition that he establishes, as soon as possible, a light that can give protection on dark nights to those ships navigating there.

Pico then instructed the customs house officer at Yerba Buena to ensure that this condition was met.[69] By July, however, the American navy had invaded the territory. Sometime in the latter half of the year, Workman deeded the island to Pliny Temple, mention of which was first made by Jonathan Temple in a letter to their brother Abraham in February 1847: "Pliny is well and doing well, he has an island in San Francisco which I think the Government [the United States] will purchase to fortify, it will probably bring 5 or 6000 [dollars]."[70]

On 2 March 1847, nearly two months after the Battle of Los Angeles ended hostilities in California, acting Governor John C. Frémont, who had a survey

---

Vacant Lands, Report on Rancho La Puente, 30 September 1845; California *Asamblea*, Approval of Report on Rancho La Puente, 3 October 1845, G. L. O. Docket 160, California Private Land Claims.

69 See the Jenkins Family Papers on Alcatraz, Bancroft Library, for the *expediente* and correspondence quoted here. William W. Jenkins was a friend of the Temple family who received a share of their interest in the island. His descendants donated the papers to the Bancroft in 1961. Copies of these materials used for this book were obtained by the author and David A. Workman.

70 Jonathan Temple to Abraham Temple, 6 February 1847. Original facsimile in the Homestead Museum Research Archives.

conducted of strategic sites in the San Francisco Bay area, executed an agreement with Temple to purchase Alcatraz. The document read,

> In consideration of Francis Temple [by then known as Francis Pliny Fisk or F.P.F. Temple] having conveyed to the United States of North America a certain island, commonly called White or Bird island, situated near the mouth of San Francisco bay, I, J.C. Frémont, governor of California, and in virtue of my office as aforesaid, hereby oblige myself as the legal representative of the United States, and my successors in office, to pay the said Francis Temple, his heirs or assigns, the sum of five thousand dollars, ($5,000), to be paid at as early a day as possible after the receipt of funds from the United States.[71]

Over a year later, Pliny wrote to Abraham regarding Alcatraz and the proposed purchase of the island: "I have endorsed in favor of Capt. W.D. Phelps a bond of Gov. Frémont for five thousand dollars it being for a small island I sold him situated in the Bay of San Francisco, which he takes with other documents of his over to the City of Washington to collect."[72]

Frémont's actions of authority during his brief tenure as governor of California upon American annexation were invalidated by court-martial, however, and the bond evidently was never paid. Later claiming that he had paid Temple out of personal funds, Frémont tried to claim the island as his own. But, in 1850, as a result of a report on strategic lands, President Millard Fillmore declared Alcatraz a military possession. At that point it probably seemed moot for Temple to file a claim for Alcatraz under the auspices of the California Land Claims Act. Never one to give up easily on something of potential benefit, Frémont, in 1856 attempted to sue for possession of the island. Temple, reading of Frémont's case in the newspaper, wrote to lawyer Volney

---

71 John C. Frémont to F.P.F. Temple, *Promissory Note for Alcatraz Island*, 2 March 1847, cited in *The Proceedings of the Court-Martial of Lieutenant Colonel John C. Frémont*, Senate Executive Document 33, 30th Congress, 1st Session, 1847, Los Angeles County Law Library. Copies of this document and other material on Alcatraz Island furnished by David A. Workman.

72 F.P.F. Temple to Abraham Temple, 22 April 1848, Thomas Temple Papers, Seaver Center. In September 1848, F.P.F. wrote to Abraham and added that "In case that bond of J.C. Frémont is paid I think it would be advisable for you to expend the balance after deducting two hundred dollars for Mother & pay yourself for any [expenses?]", F.P.F. Temple to Abraham Temple, 20 September 1848.

Howard, then practicing in San Francisco but later a well-known resident of Los Angeles, informing the attorney of his claim.[73] Nearly seventy-five years later, the status of Alcatraz was being contested by various members of the Temple family, although no formal proceedings were ever initiated and no sound foundation for a claim ever developed.[74]

Alcatraz was not the only island deeded over to Workman by Pico. San Clemente, off the coast near the present city of that name, was also granted to him and the governor's brother, Andrés. Like Alcatraz, the island was seized on behalf of the American military and recent efforts by the descendants of Workman to have the U.S. government acknowledge Workman's ownership of the island proved unsuccessful.[75]

Pico's final land transaction with Workman came on 8 June 1846 for the Mission San Gabriel, granted to Workman and Hugo Reid, owner of the adjoining Rancho Santa Anita. The grant to San Gabriel included the mission and associated buildings, as well as lands amounting to eleven square leagues (about 49,000 acres). The document specifically mentioned that Workman and Reid were being awarded the property because they "have rendered considerable services to the government and also lent good assistance for the better preservation and security of the department under guarantee of just recompense." Workman and Reid were to have paid "the debts outstanding against said Mission ...also to assign a proportional part or sum for the maintenance of the ministering Fathers who may live there, and for the preservation of divine worship." Specifically, the condition of paying Mission creditors within two years for debts incurred was included, and the sale was "of the principal and private edifices of other improvements, gardens, vineyards, and other real estate and cattle."[76] The claim won confirmation by the Board of Land Commissioners and the United States District Court in Los Angeles for the lands, but not the structures of the mission, before being invalidated in the spring of 1864 by the United States Supreme Court, mainly on the ground that Pico had no authority to grant the property.[77] Jonathan Temple, meanwhile, was sold the

73 Los Angeles *Star*, 23 February 1856; F.P.F. Temple to Volney Howard, 4 March 1856, Jenkins Family Papers, Bancroft Library.
74 The above information regarding Alcatraz Island was obtained from documents in the Jenkins Family Papers at the Bancroft Library and from papers from the descendants of John H. Temple.
75 Information on San Clemente Island was provided by David A. Workman.
76 Harris, "John Rowland and William Workman, Pioneers of Southern California," pp. 115–19.
77 Los Angeles *News*, 28 May and 9 June 1864. James F. Shunk, *Photographic Exhibits in California Land Cases from the Mexican Archives* (San Francisco: n.p., 1861), pp. 38–47; Los Angeles *Star*,

Mission La Purisima by Pico, near present Lompoc in 1845, although his hold on the property was also lost in the land claims process.[78]

Amongst all of the political intrigues and the maneuverings before the American invasion, two important personal events took place for the Workman and Temple families. The first, and more unusual, involved the ceremony performed at the Mission San Gabriel in February 1844 that included nuptials by William and Nicolasa Workman, a double ceremony with Benjamin Wilson and his first wife, Ramona Yorba. As was mentioned earlier, no marriage certificate was found in New Mexico and this ceremony in California seems to indicate that the union of the two had been, for some fifteen years, either civil or common-law marriage.[79]

Then in September of 1845, the link between the Workman and Temple families was established through the marriage of William and Nicolasa Workman's daughter, Margarita, to Pliny Temple. The event is significant in an ethnically changing Los Angeles, because it was the first nuptial in the city where both bride and groom had foreign last names. The event also included a Roman Catholic baptism for Temple, who took the baptismal name of Francisco, giving him the distinctive moniker of F.P.F., by which he was thereafter known. The couple lived at La Puente with the Workmans, where their first two children were born, Thomas (1846) and Francis (1848).

Less than a month after the marriage came a letter from F.P.F.'s brother Abraham, apprising him of a rumor that had been spreading throughout the eastern United States: "The attention of many Americans is directed to your coast. I have heard that 1000 men would start from the Western States early next spring. It seems to be a settled point in the minds of our country-men that California is destined to become a part [of the United States.]"[80]

23 October 1852 and 12 November 1870; *United States v. Workman et. al.*, 68 U. S. Reports (December term 1863), pp. 745–769.

78 Pío Pico's friendship with the Workman and Temple families seems to have been extensive. In addition to Workman's support of Pico's challenge to Micheltorena, the various land grants and sales of land made in 1845–46, and, later, the lease of space in Pico's 1868 building to the bank of Hellman, Temple and Company, Pico wrote an 1864 letter of recommendation for a Francisco Acosta to Workman. It has also been reported in undated Whittier, California newspaper accounts from about the 1960s that, when Pico lost his Ranchito to a blatant swindle in 1892, he moved in with Walter and Charles Temple for a brief time and left them a chair and a bench, the latter of which still exists at Pío Pico State Historic Park.

79 Thomas Workman Temple II, the Workmans' great-grandson and an historian and genealogist, found a record of the marriage ceremony. A copy of his notes are in the Homestead Museum Research Archives.

80 Abraham Temple to Pliny Fisk Temple, 24 October 1845, transcription by Pliny's son, John H. Temple, courtesy of Josette Temple.

By the spring of 1846, as Abraham Temple had heard, the American army had marched into California from New Mexico and was headed towards San Diego and Los Angeles. In August Abraham expressed his concern over the situation by writing F.P.F. that, "...it is with a degree of anxiety that I write to you at this time, considering the relation the U.S.A. sustain[s] towards Mexico & her territories, fearing lest you & brother J. may be involved in serious difficulties, touching Life, Liberty, and Property."

This concern was not so severe, though, as to inhibit Abraham from inquiring of his brother about "what inducements" there would be for him to settle in California. Abraham noted that, "Emigration is the order of the day from the Western states to California, and many will from New England."[81] F.P.F.'s answer, coming in late June 1847, after the American conquest, was in the form of a highly descriptive, three-page letter in which he wryly observed "that you have a slight touch of the California fever; the only remedy is to take a trip out here as I have told you before." Describing the climate, economy, natural resources of California and the preferred route of travel around the Horn, F.P.F. concluded, "if you can make up the sum of five thousand dollars or make arrangments with some one to go halves with you & expend them in suitable goods for the market, I am confident you could make a good thing out of it." He then listed several dozen items in demand for his brother to consider bringing.[82] Despite this lengthy inducement, there is no evidence Abraham Temple ever made a trip to California.

Meanwhile, the usual internal conflict amongst the Californios in Los Angeles made their already tenuous defense against the Americans even more difficult. José Castro, the political head in northern California, fought with Pío Pico about how to meet the invasion of the Americans, as well as how to deal with the Bear Flag revolt and the seizure of Sonoma by American residents of the department. Angelenos feared Castro would march from Monterey and seize control of the entire province. Uniting against another anticipated invasion from Californios in the north, a group of some eighty residents of Los Angeles met on 24 June 1846 and appointed William Workman commander of all forces to defend the pueblo. But American naval forces seized

---

81 Abraham Temple to F.P.F. Temple, 4 August 1846, Ibid. Abraham also congratulated his brother on his marriage, writing that it "gave Mother some surprise, she thinking it lessened the prospect of your return."
82 F.P.F. Temple to Abraham Temple, 28 June 1847. Original facsimile in the Homestead Museum Research Archives.

Monterey in early July and removed Castro from authority, so Workman's command was dissolved.[83]

ROBERT FIELD STOCKTON
COURTESY OF BANCROFT LIBRARY,
UNIVERSITY OF CALIFORNIA, BERKELEY, CALIFORNIA

While the Americans subjugated the north, John Frémont headed from San Diego towards Los Angeles at the end of July and Commodore Robert Stockton arrived at San Pedro from Monterey. Because it was said there was a large group of Californios at Abel Stearns' Rancho Los Alamitos, Stockton wrote Frémont to meet him at Jonathan Temple's adjacent Rancho Los Cerritos. While a guide was sent to show Frémont the way to Los Cerritos,

---

83 Bancroft, *History of California*, V: 51.

Stockton occupied himself by busily drilling his men on land maneuvers.[84] On 13 August their combined forces marched into Los Angeles without firing a shot and took over the town. After Frémont's departure for the north, Stockton proclaimed martial law, named Jonathan Temple alcalde, and left a garrison of fifty men under Marine Lieutenant Archibald Gillespie to govern the pueblo in his stead.[85] Stockton then returned to San Pedro and sailed to meet Frémont at Monterey.

The young and imperious Gillespie allowed his power of authority to go to his head, issuing unnecessary restrictions on local residents. In late September an initial band of fifty Californios invaded Gillespie's quarters and, after being repelled, grew to a force of several hundred. In his memoirs, prominent Angeleno Stephen C. Foster recalled an intriguing incident related to him by Enrique Avila. According to Avila, Jonathan Temple's wife Rafaela took ammunition from her husband's store and donated the armaments to the Californios in revolt. It is not known how significant this donation was to the cause. Nor is known how much Temple, who was alcalde of Los Angeles after the Americans seized it, was aware of Rafaela's assistance to the Californios.[86]

Meanwhile, to the east at the Rancho Chino of Isaac Williams, Americans began to band together for protection against Californios inflamed with the natural desire to defend their homes and land. By the first part of October Gillespie had surrendered his garrison and retired to San Pedro, where he and his men took ship and left the area. Monterey alcalde Walter Colton noted in his diary that as Gillespie fled Los Angeles, "He had a permit from the American alcalde [Temple] to [im]press horses wherever found."[87] In the meantime, Santa Barbara and San Diego were also briefly reclaimed by Californios. On the 8th of October a new force of Americans, just landed at San Pedro, met a force of Californios at the Rancho Dominguez, not far from Temple's rancho. The Californians continued to show their spirit by repelling an attack by the Americans, killing a few of the invaders, and evading injury to themselves. José María Flores, leader of the southern Californians, encamped his regiment at

---

84 Neal Harlow, *California Conquered: The Annexation of a Mexican Province, 1846–1850* (Berkeley: University of California Press, 1989 paperback ed.), p. 150.

85 J. Gregg Layne, "Annals of Los Angeles," *California Historical Society Quarterly*, 13 (December 1934): 302.

86 Stephen C. Foster, "Los Angeles From 1847 to 1849," p. 44, MS, Bancroft Library.

87 Walter Colton, *Three Years in California* (Reprint ed., New York: Arno Press, 1976), p. 64. Colton also recorded that Gillespie carried intelligence to Stockton via "a few words over the signature of the alcalde, rolled in a cigar, which was fastened in his hair.", Ibid., p. 65.

Los Cerritos and assumed general leadership because both Pío Pico and José Castro had fled the province for Mexico proper. On the 23rd, Stockton returned to San Pedro, learned of the recent battle with the Californios, and judged the Angeleno force to be far greater than it was. He then sailed to San Diego to seize that much smaller pueblo and to wait for reinforcements.

In the meantime, the scenario at Chino involving the Americans huddled in Isaac Williams' adobe and the surrounding Californios played itself out. Benjamin Wilson recalled that he had heard from David Alexander and John Rowland about the revolt against Gillespie, and he went to Chino, where, on 23 September the Williams adobe was surrounded by what Wilson estimated to be between eighty and one hundred men. Rather than fight, the Americans decided to surrender and were presently marched to Los Angeles and held as prisoner there. William Workman, possibly because he was English, was unmolested, though not inactive regarding the plight of his friend Rowland and others with whom he was well acquainted. Wilson recalled that Workman immediately contacted "leading Californians" including his neighbor, Ygnacio Palomares, half-owner of the Rancho San Jose in present-day Pomona. Workman evidently used the argument that any harm done to the prisoners held by Flores would be answerable to the Americans, who would inevitably be in charge. This persuasive line of thinking seemed to have impressed, for according to Wilson, "...one night Flores' headquarters was attacked, the Californians' side being led by Workman, Palomeres [sic], and other prominent Californians. At a late hour in the night, the firing ceased. Workman rushed into our prison bringing us the glad tidings that Flores was a prisoner..."[88]

Bancroft's history stated that Workman and Palomares took advantage of the Californios' feelings against Flores' autocracy to remove him from power.[89] But when Stockton returned towards Los Angeles, the opponents of Flores relented, and he reassumed control of the Californio forces. The prisoners had not been allowed to leave Los Angeles, since the Californians, even if they were against sending them to Mexico, were still united in defending the pueblo against the American army. Jonathan Temple's Los Cerritos rancho served as the prisoners' home for some time in November while the Angelenos awaited Stockton's renewed attack from San Diego. Wilson remembered that he and

---

88   Wilson, "Narrative," pp. 403–04.
89   Bancroft, *History of California*, V: 332–33.

John Rowland returned to their families in early January when Stockton's force approached from San Juan Capistrano.[90]

Michael White, another prisoner of the Californians, gave his version of the events of that period, recalling that "we were not especially well treated." In addition to Palomares, White also named José Antonio Carrillo and Palomares' partner, Ricardo Vejar, as those who assisted Workman in freeing the prisoners. In a rare glimpse into Workman's charitable side, White recalled,

> A day or two later, I came over to Workman's. I did not want to say I had nothing to eat, but he divined it, and asked if I had brought a sack. I said 'yes' and he gave me a sack of flour, and told me to send my ox cart next day and he would load it for me. I did so and got a good supply of grain and other things.[91]

As Stockton headed to Los Angeles from San Diego, he camped at San Juan Capistrano just after New Year's 1847. John S. Griffin, who would later be a prominent physician in southern California, was a member of Stockton's force and remembered that, on the morning of 4 January a flag of truce, borne by Workman and two others, was brought to the camp for the purpose of delivering to Stockton a letter from Flores, offering peace in exchange for a general amnesty. The next morning, Workman reappeared and, "after some talk with the Commodore —Commodore Stockton sent a proclamation to the Californians offering them peace."[92] Workman, having used his persuasive powers to help free the Chino prisoners, had thus negotiated an important agreement in the concluding days of the war in California.

The letter Griffin referred to was dated 1 January with Flores writing,

> it is probable at this time the differences which have altered the relations of friendship between the Mexican republic and that of the United States of America have ceased... A number of days have elapsed since the undersigned was invited.

---

90 Wilson, "Narrative," pp. 404–07.
91 White, "California All The Way Back to 1828," p. 64.
92 George Walcott Ames, ed., "A Doctor Comes to California —The Diary of John S. Griffin, 1846–47," *California Historical Society Quarterly*, 21 (December 1942): 348–349, published in book form as *A Doctor Comes to California* (San Francisco: California Historical Society,) 1943

. .to enter into a communication with you...to obtain an honorable adjustment for both forces...and for that reason has thought it opportune to direct to you this note, which will be placed in your hands by Messrs. Julian Workman and Charles Flug[g]e, who have voluntarily offered themselves to act as mediators.[93]

Having reached a satisfactory agreement with Stockton, Workman then left the camp, presumably returning to Los Angeles with Flugge to report the results to Flores.[94]

On the 9th, the Californios and Americans met near the San Gabriel River (the channel of today's Rio Hondo) and fought what would be the concluding battle of the Mexican-American War in California. As was the case with almost all of the conflicts in the territory during the war, the fatalities were few: one Californio killed and five Americans wounded. The Californians then retired and on the 10th, Workman, Eulogio Célis and Juan Avila brought a flag of truce to the American camp to ask protection from Stockton for the region's residents.[95]

With Flores and his men having fled, Stockton marched into Los Angeles and took control of the pueblo once again. Benjamin Wilson, meanwhile, recounted that on 9 January he went to La Puente to meet with Workman, who harbored two fleeing Californios. The fact that Workman was sequestering them, along with his role as negotiator between the Mexicans and Americans on the 4th, 5th, and 10th, adds to the suggestion that he maintained good relations with the Californians. Although Wilson claimed to have accompanied these men to Los Angeles on the 10th to intercede on their behalf with Stockton, he made no mention of Workman's meeting with Stockton to assure just treatment of local residents.[96]

In the aftermath of the battle of Los Angeles, a dispute arose between Frémont, Stockton, and General Stephen Kearney, who was to assume the duties

---

93 José María Flores to Robert F. Stockton, 1 January 1847, quoted from Edwin Bryant, *What I Saw in California* (Minneapolis: Ross & Haines, Inc., 1967), pp. 402–403.

94 Bancroft, *History of California*, V: 387.

95 Ibid., 396–7. See also an account from an unidentified member of Stockton's force in "The Battle of San Gabriel," Los Angeles *Star*, 23 March 1861. Interestingly, a draft of a letter written by Workman to his sister Agnes, dated 8 February only a month after the events mentioned here, he makes no reference at all to the war or his role in it. Draft letter from William Workman to Agnes Workman Vickers, 8 February 1847.

96 Wilson, "Narrative," pp. 408–10.

of governing the province in Frémont's stead. In the prosecution of conquest, Frémont and Stockton had incurred debts to many local residents for supplies to the army. One of the creditors was Jonathan Temple, who related in a letter to the family in Massachusetts a month after hostilities had ended that, "My losses in this affair I calculate at not less than $10,000, but am in hopes that the Govt. will remunerate me for them at some future time."[97] Temple rather underestimated the amount of money he was owed by Frémont. A decade passed before a resolution to the issue was reached. A schedule of claims filed against Frémont and heard and adjudicated by the military in 1856 revealed Temple's claims were for nearly $18,000 with all but some $2,300 disallowed or suspended by the ruling body.[98] Whether he was ever reimbursed for this fraction of his losses is not known. In this same letter, Temple also wrote that both he and F.P.F. had been taken prisoner and feared for their property (Rancho Los Cerritos being in the proximity of the theater of actions).

While the brothers were, obviously, not part of the group seized at Chino, F.P.F. may have joined his brother at Los Cerritos, when the prisoners were transferred there. When Frémont decided to go to Monterey in mid-March to talk with General Kearney about the issues at hand, many prominent citizens of Los Angeles, including the Temple brothers and Workman, sent him a letter requesting him to stay until the security of the region could be ensured. The Californios were still simmering with resentment, the letter stated, and because Frémont had the respect of many of the American and European residents of the Los Angeles area, his presence would maintain order. Frémont replied on the 20th, expressing his gratitude for the confidence of area residents, but that he had to settle the matter if he was to hand over the administration of government to Kearney.[99] Frémont's letter of that date to Workman suggests that the latter was a firm supporter of his:

> I had the pleasure to receive a few minutes since a letter from
> Mr. [Benjamin] Wilson, acquainting me with the regret felt
> by the people at my departure, —and the farther gratifica-
> tion to learn from him that you had been kind enough to

97 Jonathan Temple to Abraham Temple, 6 February 1847. Original facsimile in the Homestead Museum Research Archives.
98 *Statement of the Office of Board for Examination of Claims Contracted in California Under Lieutenant Colonel Frémont*, 18 April 1852, 5–19. Copy provided by David A. Workman.
99 Harlow, *California Conquered*, pp. 256–57.

express your entire approbation of my official conduct and
your confidence in the success of the measures which I had
adopted for the promotion of the public interest. Being much
pressed today by many engagements I can only delay to thank
you for your friendly disposition to me...

After explaining to Workman how he and Commodore Stockton had
"contracted extensive liabilities...which it will be difficult for new authorities
to support," Frémont detailed his plan to go to Monterey "with the view of requiring as an act of common justice and propriety...that this assumption of our
responsibilities be made by my successor." Frémont concluded by expressing
his wish that if his request were not granted, he would return to Los Angeles
to seek the advice and "concert" of his friends and supporters and expressed
to Workman the wish that, "I shall then receive your aid and countenance in
my efforts to support the integrity of my administration."[100] These are curious words that hint at something akin to *armed* support for Frémont if negotiations in Monterey were not satisfactory to him. In light of Frémont's other
actions of the period and the charges brought against him in his subsequent
court-martial, the letter stands as an interesting document of the period and
seems to indicate Workman's support or acquiesence of the American takeover,
even as he appears to have maintained the respect of Californios.

Yet, a July 1848 report by Colonel Jonathan D. Stevenson, Los Angeles
garrison commander, to Colonel Richard Mason, military governor of
California, provides another view. Stevenson wrote about the return of Pío
Pico to southern California from his self-imposed exile in Mexico and the alleged claim that he was seeking to reestablish his rights as governor. Stevenson
noted that on the 15th,

...he [Pico] reached the ranch of an Englishman named Workman, some eighteen miles from here. This man [Workman]
has ever been hostile to the American cause and interest,
and is just the man to advise Pico not to come in and report
to me... On Sunday and Monday I was advised that many
Californians had visited Pico at Workman's and that the

100 John C. Frémont to William Workman, 20 March 1847, a copy of a transcription from the Thomas
W. Temple II Collection, Homestead Museum Research Archives.

same story had been told them of his having returned to resume his governortorial functions, &c... I issued an order (copy inclosed) requiring him to report to me immediately in person. I sent my adjutant with a detachment of men to the ranch of Workman to deliver to Don Pío in person a copy of this order, with instructions to bring him in by force, in case he refused or even hesitated to obey.[101]

Pico subsequently left for San Fernando, when John Reed, son-in-law of John Rowland, arranged for Pico to meet with Stevenson and negotiate terms for the ex-Governor's return to residency. What is striking in the statement is Stevenson's use of the term "hostile" for Workman's attitude, a far different sense than Frémont's lauding of Workman's support.

It may be safely assumed, despite the ambiguities of the above statements regarding Workman's opinions, that he and Jonathan and F.P.F. Temple (their Latina wives remaining silent in their obscurity) welcomed American occupation as ensuring political, social and economic stability and the opportunities for a higher standard of living. It may be wondered, as well, having spent years living in Mexican California, how much identification and affinity they had for Mexican culture. Still, it cannot be ascertained from their own words, because they left so little behind as to their feelings regarding the conquest. Interestingly, William Workman wrote a short letter to his sister Agnes, then resident in Baltimore, that was enclosed with Jonathan Temple's letter in February 1847, but made no mention of the excitement in which he had so important a role. The Temple brothers, though they had more to say, confined themselves largely to matter-of-fact descriptions of the war's events. Jonathan Temple, as indicated, decried his treatment as a prisoner of the Californios and showed concern for himself and his possessions. In writing to brother Abraham the day after Jonathan's above letter, F.P.F. gave a mostly descriptive account of the events of the previous six months, though he did write that "the country has been for the most of the time in a horrible condition" and that the Bear Flag Revolt in Sonoma in June 1846, was "a bad tendency." Finally, he wrote that Commodore Sloat's seizure of Monterey in early July was "as he

---

101 John Frost, *Frost's Pictorial History of California* (Auburn: Derby and Miller, 1850), pp. 476–479 (Appendix J.)

ought to have done" in light of the chaos of the Bear Flag revolt.[102] This indicates that, though disapproving of filibustering schemes such as the Bear Flag fiasco, the Temples and Workman, by association, felt the conquest to be of benefit to them and their compatriots.

In the postwar period, the Workman and Temple families, like other southern Californians, resumed their daily activities. At first their situation was probably little changed from that under Mexican rule, at least in social and political terms. Though unknown to them, of course, the next decade would bring them unprecedented and inconceivable wealth as the events of the following year would begin a transformation in the society of southern California that, by and large, remained predominantly Mexican for another generation but gradually felt the influence of Americanization.

---

102 F.P.F. Temple to Abraham Temple, 7 February 1847. Original facsimile in the Homestead Museum Research Archives. An interesting sidelight was his mention of "great talk in the U.S. of a railroad being constructed across the mountains to this country. I hope when it is completed I shall have the pleasure of making you a visit."

CHAPTER THREE

Change of the Century in California

❧ 1848–1864 ❧

"A Very Rich, If Miserly, Man"

American occupation, although humiliating to many Californios, was endured without any appreciable amount of violence in protest against the conquest or a greatly noticeable change in immediate day-to-day activities. In fact, Mexican cultural lifestyles continued to predominate in southern California for nearly twenty more years, until the collapse of the pastoral cattle industry in the middle sixties, which was the result of severe drought, the end of the boom years of the Gold Rush, the importation of better cattle breeds, and other factors. There were occasional manifestations of tension and violence in the post-conquest period between *Californios*, Mexicans, on one hand, and Americans and Europeans on the other. This reflected the difficulties Los Angeles experienced as it moved from a frontier town to an emerging city. Another demographic dynamic came at the end of the Civil War when a surge of immigration, largely composed of southerners fleeing the devastated ruins of the Confederacy, infused the region. As southern California absorbed the new arrivals and communications increased with the East through, for example, the telegraph, the Americanization of Los Angeles grew correspondingly. Some of this process slowly entered the region much earlier, manifesting itself most directly through one of the landmark events in nineteenth-century American history, the California Gold Rush.

Ironically, on the morning of 24 January 1848, nine days before the Treaty of Guadalupe Hidalgo was signed formally ending the war, James Marshall, working on the construction of a mill for John Sutter on the banks of the American River at Coloma, discovered placer gold. Soon the famous rush was on. In letters to their brother Abraham the following September both Jonathan and F.P.F. Temple made mention of the sweeping changes taking place in California as a result of gold fever. F. P. F., for example, noted that, with the conclusion of the Mexican-American War, "Col. Stevenson, Regt of N.Y. volunteers are now disbanded and are making their way towards the gold mines which have been lately discovered on the rivers Sacramento & San Joaquin; they are immensely rich." Jonathan, meanwhile, noted that it would be quite some time before "good order" came to California "on account of the unequalled quantity of gold that has been found." Echoing the concerns of many a resident regarding the wholesale desertion of laborers, military personnel, servants and others to the mines, Jonathan also expressed fears for "the lives & property of the good citizens, [who] will be at the mercy of the indians and the bad." After plainly stating that "to sum [up] in a few words nothing will be done but *gold digging* [Temple's emphasis]," he informed his family that while his cattle and horse ranching kept him more than busy and he had no intention to go to the mines, "Pliny I think will go next spring and try his hand at gold digging," something F.P.F. did not mention in his letter of just two days before![1] It is possible that F.P.F. did indeed head for the north in the spring of 1849, as he indicated in his 1877 dictation for Bancroft, that he worked for his brother until that year. If he did go to the diggings, he likely found, as did the other cattle ranchers of the south, such as his brother and father-in-law, that the path to wealth was not paved by back-breaking manual labor but by the slow, steady trod of the hooves of his cattle.

In his letter, Jonathan Temple mentioned, "My daughter [Francisca] was married on the 1st of this month [September 1848] to a gentleman belonging to Spain by the name of Gregorio de Ajuria."[2] This marriage was to bring about some fascinating consequences and financial rewards to Temple. In regards to the rising tide of the Gold Rush, the Temples and Workmans joined their cattle-raising compatriots in the Los Angeles region by sending their animals north to supply fresh beef to the hordes of miners and other residents of the gold-country. Although little is known of the specifics of this trade regarding the families, there are some hints as to the range of their enterprises. Jonathan

---

1   F.P.F. Temple to Abraham Temple, 20 September 1848, F.P.F. Temple's copy courtesy of Josette Temple; Jonathan Temple to Abraham Temple, 22 September 1848, from a copy of the original in the Homestead Museum Archives.

2   Gregorio de Ajuria and Francisca Temple, in 1850, were in Los Angeles living with Jonathan and Rafaela Temple and without children. Ten years later, they were in New York, with several children, born in France, Mexico, and New York. Soon after, the family relocated to Paris, where Gregorio de Ajuria died by 1865. Francisca raised her children in France and died there in the 1890s. Years later, a daughter-in-law, Oria, and her daughter relocated to New York and then Los Angeles and, in the 1920s and 1930s, corresponded with the Walter P. Temple family of La Puente.

Temple, for example, was half-owner of the Rancho El Tejon from 1857 until 1865. It seems plausible that the ranch was used as a stopping point for herds being shipped to the gold fields from southern California, although the heyday of the Gold Rush came before this period. Unfortunately, as Temple experienced with his Los Cerritos rancho, the devastating drought of 1863 and 1864 forced he and his partner at Tejon, Antonio Del Valle, to sell the enormous property to Edward F. Beale, under whom the Tejon became widely known.[3] Temple was also the owner of the Rancho El Consuelo in Tulare County. The surviving 1858 tax receipt for the property shows that the value was almost $95,000 at a time when this was considered a handsome sum for a person's entire estate. On the El Consuelo were nearly 750 head of horses, over 3,500 head of cattle, and even a few American-bred bulls. Adding this to Tejon and Cerritos, it can be surmised that Temple had a very lucrative gold country cattle trade.[4]

The same success can also be attributed to Temple's brother. It is known that F.P.F. Temple had quite an investment in Gold Rush towns in Tuolumne County dating from the early 1850s. According to a researcher, Temple "owned at least a dozen butcher shops, seven or more slaughter houses, a small residence in Springfield and a bakery lot which backed up to the residence lot, and several houses in Sonora. These properties were located in Springfield; Columbia; Shaw's Flat, near Springfield; Sonora; and Saw Mill Flat, south east of Columbia."[5] It is likely from this statement that Temple used these holdings, which he maintained well into the 1870s, to process and sell the cattle he imported from southern California. Temple also leased a portion of the Rancho El Tejon after his brother had sold his interest to Edward Beale and was, from 1864, part-owner of the nearby Rancho San Emigdio with David W.

3   Earle Crowe, *Men of El Tejon* (Los Angeles: The Ward Ritchie Press, 1957), pp. 46–47.
4   *Receipt and List of Property of John Temple, Rancho El Consuelo, Tulare County*, 27 September 1858. Original in the possession of Charles and Margaret Coker. Copy in the Homestead Museum Research Archives. Temple's agent in the payment of taxes, totaling $1609.56, on the El Consuelo was his long-time partner and friend, David W. Alexander.
5   Barbara Eastman to Thomas W. Temple II, 24 April 1968, Thomas W. Temple II Collection; copies of research cards on F.P.F. Temple's holdings from Columbia State Historic Park Archives, Homestead Museum Research Archives. Eastman noted that the Columbia *Courier* of 28 July 1866 recorded, "Mr. Temple has opened a New Butcher Shop in the brick building on Main Street next to Charley Brown's News Depot." This holding, known thereafter as the Temple Block, was sold in September 1874. Temple also owned a frame building in the town in June 1857, which he sold about 1865. He was also assessed in 1866 for the People's Market building in Columbia, which was still in his name as late as 1871, when it was a restaraunt. According to Eastman, the latest date of Temple's interests in the area was when he sold his Springfield properties in early 1875. Two of Temple's structures are extant at Columbia.

Alexander. Alexander, who came to California with John Rowland in 1842 was a business partner of Jonathan Temple and a two-time Los Angeles County Sheriff. Alexander became close with William Workman's son, Joseph, when both were supervising the ranchos at Tejon and San Emigdio, and he named one son Joseph Workman Alexander and another Samuel Temple Alexander.[6] As in the case with his brother, Temple's investment in these properties was undoubtedly for their use as resting points for the transfer of cattle before crossing the San Joaquin Valley toward the mines.

The effects of the Gold Rush on southern California's cattle industry are well documented. Inflated by the "unequalled quantity of gold" Jonathan Temple referred to, rancheros earned profits far greater than those earned in the days of the hide and tallow trade. Amidst the general affluence in California during the halcyon days of the Gold Rush, a good deal of money found its way down to previously cash-poor Los Angeles.[7] Again, specific evidence is generally lacking regarding the extent of the material wealth of the Temple and Workman families in the Gold Rush years, but the extensive expansion of their ranching enterprises and land holdings, as well as some indicators like tax assessments, suggest they made fortunes in this period. Beyond material concerns, the salad days of the rush enabled William Workman to make his only return trip to England in early 1851, when he commissioned an ornate headstone at the family plot in the graveyard of St. Cuthbert's Church, where the remains of his parents and those siblings who stayed in England were buried.[8]

---

6   William Harland Boyd, *A California Middle Border* (Richardson, TX: The Havilah Press, 1972), pp. 38–39; Los Angeles *Star*, 30 April 1870. Boyd noted that Temple ran cattle on the ranch after the departure of David W. Alexander, sometime in the 1860s. Temple pastured his stock, under the management of Adam Malezewski, "until [he] disposed of his stock and entered the banking business in Los Angeles." Actually, Temple did not sell his interest in San Emigdio until after he became a banker, disposing of the ranch in 1871, when he built an addition to his Temple Block, in which he opened the Temple and Workman bank. The Los Angeles Public Library has a photograph of Temple's ranch house at Tejon. It is possible that both interests were obtained by 1864. "Certificate of Tax Sale" for one-half of Rancho San Emigdio to David W. Alexander and F.P.F. Temple, 20 January 1864 and Deed from William C. Owen, Sheriff of Tulare County to David W. Alexander and F.P.F. Temple for one-half of Rancho San Emigdio, 4 November 1864, courtesy of Josette Temple.

7   In the abovementioned letter of 28 June 1847, F.P.F. noted that, while ten years previously "the country was in a flourishing condition" (though he was not there at the time), in 1847 Los Angeles, "The missions are nearly broken down, a very few cattle in comparison with those items, money scarce, and a greater number of people to do the [mercantile] business."

8   Workman was in Veracruz in February; stopped in New York with close friend David W. Alexander, where the earliest known photograph of Workman, with Alexander, was taken by Mathew Brady of later Civil War fame; and was in Clifton in late March just in time to be recorded in the British national census of the end of that month. The gravestone in Clifton Workman erected for his family on this trip survives. Another tangential anecdote to Workman's English homecoming was his purchase of a clock as a wedding present for John Rowland and his second wife, Charlotte

Jonathan Temple's fortune was probably already significant before 1848, but in the 1850s, he reached levels of wealth and influence unequalled by any citizen in southern California, save Abel Stearns. He is believed to have pastured as many as 15,000 cattle at Los Cerritos, which undoubtedly brought him a good income in the hide and tallow trade and a great deal more money in the marketing for beef later. His activities in the former regard were boosted by his ownership of the store and warehouse in San Pedro, at least until 1852 at the latter when he sold out of the partnership there. Meanwhile, Ygnacio Garcia managed his store in Los Angeles from 1849 until 1856, when Temple closed the enterprise.[9] He reputedly had interests in trading ships plying the coast between Acapulco and San Francisco and ownership of large areas of coastline land between Acapulco and Mazatlan.[10] Temple's wealth may also be measured by the fact that his county property assessment in 1851 was valued at $79,000, and the following year he paid the highest tax in the county.[11]

Harris Newmark recalled that these many enterprises developed in the late forties and early fifties and made Temple "a very rich, if miserly, man."[12] Newmark also noted that Temple, "who had a ranch or two in the North (from which he sent cattle to his agent in San Francisco), generally had a large reserve of cash to his credit with butchers or bankers in the Northern city, and he was thus able to issue drafts against his balances there..."[13] This shows that some

---

Gray, married at El Monte in the spring of 1852. Rowland's first wife, Encarnacion Martinez, died the previous year. Evidently, Workman planned a second trip to England very soon after returning to La Puente and intended to take his son, Joseph, with him, but plans were changed when David Workman was invited to come to California and brought Joseph with him in 1854, Mary Workman to Joseph Workman, 2 November 1852, Krebs Collection, copy in the Homestead Museum Research Library.

9 Harris Newmark, *Sixty Years in Southern California*, ed. by W.W. Robinson (4th ed., Los Angeles: Zeitlin and Ver Brugge, 1970), p. 66; Los Angeles *Star*, 17 May 1856, for the auction of Temple's entire stock of merchandise.

10 Biographical sketch from the California Biography File, Los Angeles Central Public Library.

11 Robert G. Cleland, *Cattle on a Thousand Hills* (5th ed., San Marino: The Huntington Library, 1975), p. 314, note 2.

12 Newmark, *Sixty Years in Southern California*, p. 66. Temple was not above making loans to his friends, though, as one such advance was made to his former partner David W. Alexander and Phineas Banning when the latter two terminated their business at San Pedro in 1856. An interesting outgrowth of this is that William W. Jenkins, a family friend of the Temples (see the section on Chapter Two regarding Alcatraz Island) and estate administrator of F.P.F. Temple wrote Banning's sons almost half a century later to inform them that he still held Alexander & Banning's promissory note to Jonathan Temple and that while he had "never made any formal demand for money...and am not doing so now" wished to "hear from you in the matter." It was probably from his administration of F.P.F. Temple's estate that the note passed into Jenkins' hand. The note is in the possession of Margaret Coker, the widow of Jenkins' grandson, Charles Coker.

13 Ibid., p. 129.

enterprising southern Californians utilized San Francisco's enormous resources as well as those from the comparatively underdeveloped Los Angeles.

As an indication of the changing conditions in Los Angeles, Temple used his considerable financial resources to erect business buildings in the town. In 1850, he built a two-story adobe at the intersection of Spring and Main Streets known as the Temple Block, the town's first substantial business building.[14] Seven years later, he erected a business building on Main Street that was "fitted up in style of magnificence far surpassing anything of the kind in this section of the State."[15] Among the merchants in this building were the Hellman Brothers, whose later prominence in the city was matched by few families. Temple's longest-standing landmark and a memorable one for many a nineteenth-century Angeleno was his 1859 Market House fashioned loosely after Faneuil Hall, one of the notable landmarks of Boston. The structure's first floor was occupied by market stalls (although this soon changed to more conventional store fronts), and its second level became a meeting hall and theater. Another notable feature of the building was the tower clock, a landmark timepiece for the city's residents that was utilized on two subsequent county courthouses, long after the original was razed. Given that Los Angeles was a small, isolated frontier town of fewer than 5,000 persons and that its architect, W. H. Dearien, was probably more accurately a contractor and builder rather than a trained architect, the building seemed a giant step in its architecture. Harold Kirker, however, in a study of California's nineteenth-century architecture, called the structure "a primitive, badly proportioned copy of Faneuil Hall" and agreed with the 1870s comment of German noble Ludwig Louis Salvator that the building was an architectural aberration with a noisy clock in

---

14 The lot had been owned by William Wolfskill, another of Los Angeles' early American residents. It was sold to Richard Loughlin, who was a member with William Workman of the 1827 trapping expedition referred to in Chapter One. Loughlin built a one-story adobe home there. Jonathan Temple bought the lot in June 1848 from a Juan Bouet. Layne refers to the adobe, which he said was built "in either the latter part of 1851 or early part of 1852" as the fourth two-story structure in the city. Layne, however, confused this site with that of the one-story adobe house and store Temple had used since his arrival to Los Angeles and which was also removed in 1871 by Temple's brother F.P.F. and replaced with a three-story brick building that became the final addition to the new Temple Block. The building referred to here was torn down in 1871 and replaced by a brick structure erected by John G. Downey. J. Gregg Layne, "Annals of Los Angeles," *Historical Society of Southern California Quarterly*, XIII (December 1934): 325. See also, Newmark, *Sixty Years in Southern California*, p. 66, and Henry D. Barrows, "John Temple," Los Angeles *Times*, 5 March 1887, p. 1 and "Recollections of the Old Court House and Its Builder", pp. 41–42, *Historical Society of Southern California Annual for 1894* (Los Angeles: Historical Society of Southern California, 1894.)

15 Los Angeles *Star*, 14 November 1857.

92

MARKET HOUSE, CIRCA 1870
SECURITY PACIFIC COLLECTION/LOS ANGELES PUBLIC LIBRARY

its tower.[16] Temple first made his proposal to build the structure to the town's common council in late January.[17] In October shortly after its completion, the city council passed an ordinance in relation to the function of the new structure: "The brick building lately erected by John Temple between Main and Spring Streets for the use of the City of Los Angeles shall be, and the same is hereby declared to be the City market and the City Hall of said city for the purpose of a public market and shall be known as the City Market and City Hall of said city."[18]

Regarding the theater, it was referred to as "the first theater [in Los Angeles] equipped to house American professional companies." It was finished in February 1860 and had a stage measuring 45 by 25 feet, with painted scenery, private boxes on the side, a two-tiered gallery with raised benches and a parquette furnished with armchairs. That fall, the first American dramatic

---

16 Barrows, "Recollections of the Old Court House and its Builder," p. 40; Harold Kirker, *California's Architectural Frontier: Style and Tradition in the Nineteenth Century* (New York: Russell & Russell, 1970), 72. A portion of one of the courthouse clock faces now has a prominent place in the California history exhibit at the Natural History Museum of Los Angeles County.
17 "Proposition of John Temple", 25 January 1859, Common Council Records, Book 6: 341, Los Angeles City Archives.
18 Marco R. Newmark, "The Life of Jonathan (John) Temple," *Historical Society of Southern California Quarterly*, 36 (March 1954): 47. See also Temple's offer to sell the building to the city for $30,000 in installments with interest: John Temple to Mayor and Common Council of Los Angeles, 8 July 1861, Common Council Records, Book 6: 486, Los Angeles City Archives.

company to perform in Los Angeles played the Temple Theater. Occasionally, troupes from Mexico performed Spanish plays, as well. Henry Barrows, in an 1887 article on Temple, recalled one American and several "Spanish" companies—these latter Barrows remembered "used to have crowded houses" and "gave admirable representations of standard drama." Barrows also described the commemorative service after the assassination of Abraham Lincoln.[19] In 1861, a failure as a financial building due to a depressed economy, the Market House was leased to the city and county for use as administrative offices and the courthouse, which was initially on the first floor, but the theater seems to have lasted until at least 1866, when the Temple estate sold the building to John S. Griffin. In 1871, the county purchased the building from Griffin, and the theater was removed so more courtrooms could be added.[20] Although all of Jonathan Temple's buildings were gone by 1925, one downtown element remained to perpetuate his name: Temple Street, which he opened in the 1850s heading west from the intersection of Spring and Main streets to Fort Street (now Broadway). As insignificant as the street's beginnings were, it was extended in the 1870s as part of the development of Bunker Hill. Although Harris Newmark and others who make mention of the opening of the street attribute its naming as a complimentary gesture by city officals, city attorney Frank H. Howard in an 1871 report on F.P.F. Temple's proposal to make an addition to the Temple Block wrote, "Temple Street was donated to the City by John Temple."[21] Regardless of its origins, the street is today an important thoroughfare at the heart of the civic center of the city.

An early signpost to the conscious development of Los Angeles' emergence from a pueblo to a city was the drawing of the first survey of the town- the Ord survey. This was also one of Temple's lasting contributions to Los Angeles because of his role as negotiator on behalf of the city. In June of 1849, the town *ayuntamiento*, the equivalent of the city council, met to discuss an order from the governor for a survey "to serve as a basis for granting vacant lots out of the unappropriated lands belonging to the Municipality." A month later, Temple,

---

19 Henry D. Barrows, "John Temple: Interesting Sketch of a Los Angeles Pioneer," Los Angeles *Times*, 5 March 1887 and "Recollections of the Old Court House and Its Builder," *Historical Society of Southern California Annual, 1894* (Reprint ed., Los Angeles: Dawson's Book Shop, 1966), 42.

20 Moshe Yaari, "The Merced Theater," *Historical Society of Southern California Quarterly*, 37 (September 1955): 196; Los Angeles *Semi-Weekly Southern News*, 22 February and 31 October 1860.

21 Newmark, *Sixty Years in Southern California*, pp. 61, 66; F.H. Howard to the Mayor and Common Council of the City of Los Angeles, *Report on Proposed Temple Block Addition*, 12 April 1871, Common Council Records, Book 7: 263, Los Angeles City Archives

the only American or European on the council, "moved that a Com[mittee] be appointed to confer with the surveyor [Edward O. C. Ord] who is to make a Map of this City as to the means & bills relating to the accomplishment of the undertaking." After he and Manuel Requena accepted appointment to be the commission, Temple reported, in mid-July that Ord, "demands a compensation of fifteen hundred dollars in coin, ten lots selected from among those demarked in the map, and vacant land to the extent of one thousand *varas*...or, in case the proposition is refused, then he wants to be paid the sum of three thousand dollars in cash."

Temple recommended paying Ord the $3,000, because, he argued, the value of the land the surveyor would have received would have been worth substantially more. He did note, however, "The City funds cannot now defray this expense, but...a loan of that amount may be negotiated." The council then followed Temple's recommendations, although the question of who would provide the funds for the loan was not evidently answered immediately. On 22 July a contract was made with Ord, defining the area which he was to survey and indicating the amount of money he was to receive. Temple and ayuntamiento President Jose del Carmen Lugo were the pueblo's signatories. By mid-September Ord completed his task and Temple convened a meeting of the ayuntamiento to formally present the survey. The minutes of the meeting recorded that "the Syndic [Treasurer, being Temple himself] thereupon submitted the finished City map as well as the receipt showing that he himself had paid the surveyor the sum of three thousand dollars, this amount being a loan made by the Syndic to the City to enable it to pay for said map." To repay Temple for his loan the city conducted an auction of city lots in November. It appeared to be a success, because at a meeting the following month he reported the "auction of lots produced $2490 & there still remains $510 due Temple." Temple was evidently fully reimbursed his loan through future auctions. Temple's role in the survey extended beyond securing Ord's contract and making the advance payment. According to an August 1849 letter from Ord's assistant, William Rich Hutton, "he would talk to me sometimes about the work. One day he said to me, pointing to a stone at one corner of a square, 'Well, you must come here again; here is only one stone; there must be four.' I did not say anything, but pointed to the three others, which were plain enough to be seen, only he was looking the wrong way for them. He did such things several times &, after he found that he was always wrong, he kept on his side of the street." Hutton also wrote that Temple accused Ord of cheating the city in their negotiations and threatened to contract with John C. Fremont, of all people, but that "after a good deal of haggling with Johnny Temple, [Ord] contracted to do the survey..." Moreover, Hutton claimed that Temple was the town's treasurer because the Californios "were afraid to trust their own people." Another notable reference to Temple in Hutton's letters is that "Temple has a lien on the San Pedro ranch (Domingues') &, if he can get the part he wants, intends to lay out a town immediately; but he will not be able to do anything for several months yet." Evidently, this plan for a townsite did not pan out. If anything, Hutton's impressions of Temple's seem closely aligned to Harris Newmark's description of the merchant as "miserly".[22]

As the only American or European on the ayuntamiento, Temple was seemingly the logical choice to represent the town in negotiations and the implementation of the survey. As one of Los Angeles' wealthiest citizens, it was not surprising that he expended the funds to pay Ord and then suggested an auction of lots to obtain repayment. Temple's role in the process also reveals the change in the political millieu of Los Angeles that led to the decline of Californio power and the ascendancy of American control of the public scene in southern California. Further evidence of change lies in Ord's decision to list the streets in the survey area in English as well as in the Spanish by which they were known to the residents of Los Angeles. Streets like *Loma, Forte, Principal, Flores,* and *Primavera* became familiarly called Hill, Fort, Main, Flower and Spring as Americanization gained ascendancy.

Perhaps Temple's most fascinating, if little-known, project in this period came outside of California with his arrangement with the Mexican government to lease its national mint. Temple's son-in-law, Gregorio de Ajuria, had come to California in 1845 as a speculator and became the son-in-law and a confidant of Temple. In 1854, Ignacio Comonfort, a Mexican attorney, army general and self-proclaimed revolutionary, met Ajuria while in the United States and sought funds for a planned revolt against the Mexican government. De Ajuria loaned Comonfort $60,000 on agreement that he would be repaid $250,000 if the revolution succeeded. The next year, Comonfort succeeded in overthrowing the government and became Mexico's President. Hoping to

---

22 W. W. Robinson, "The Story of Ord's Survey," *Historical Society of Southern California Quarterly,* 19 (September-December 1937): 121-127; William Rich Hutton, *Glances at California, 1847-1853* (San Marino: The Huntington Library, 1942), 14-32.

capitalize on his dealings with the new leader, de Ajuria moved with his wife, Francisca Temple, and children to Mexico City. The lease of the national mint, contracted to the firm of Roche and Company, expired that year and Alejandro Bellange, a former employee of the facility, sought to take up the new lease. However, he lacked the financial means to do so and apparently came into contact with de Ajuria through Comonfort. De Ajuria then enlisted the support of his father-in-law. Temple made advance rental payments aggregating some $500,000, an enormous sum in the 1850s, making Temple and Bellange partners in the operation of the mint. The lease was signed in July 1856 and approved a few days later by the Mexican Congress. The new owners took possession of the facility the following spring.

Given the continually troubled Mexican economy, the Comonfort administration drew heavily upon Temple's advance payments. The regime, however, collapsed very quickly and, by 1858, Comonfort and de Ajuria had fled Mexico City, the latter taking his family to New York and then Paris, where he lived until his death three years later. What was surprising was that the lease Temple and Bellange had arranged was not revoked, even in the tumultuous years of the invasion of France, the short-lived empire of Maximilian, and the resulting renewal of native Mexican rule. Of course, Temple himself probably only made an occasional visit to Mexico City, while Bellange saw to the day-to-day affairs of the mint. When Temple died in 1866, the lease was retained by his widow and their daughter, then residing in Paris, and their interests overseen by a representative in Mexico. The Temples retained the lease of the mint until 1893 when the government nationalized the operation of the facility.[23]

Land Claims and Politics in the Early American Period

While Jonathan Temple was engaged in construction and development in the city and financial investments in Mexico City, he, his brother, and William Workman were entangled, at great length, in the complex process of land claims involving the ranchos La Merced, La Puente, Los Cerritos and other properties.[24]

---

23 The information for the lease of the mint was drawn from Sol Alexander, "Juan Temple and the Mint of Mexico," *Plus Ultra*, 116 (May 1973): 3–5.
24 W.W. Robinson's *Land in California* (2nd ed., Berkeley: University of California Press, 1979), pp. 91–109, was the basis for the following background material on the land claims process.

TEMPLE ADOBE, RANCHO LAMERCED, CIRCA 1870

COURTESY OF PHILIP NATHANSON

Regarding La Merced, Workman had obtained the 2,363-acre property by mortgage foreclosure from original grantee Casilda Soto de Lobo in 1850. He then deeded the rancho to his *mayordomo*, or ranch foreman, Juan Matías Sanchez and F.P.F. Temple. When the Sanchez family moved into the Soto adobe, now a historic site in Montebello, F.P.F. and Margarita Temple built their own adobe house in 1851.[25] Born in New Mexico about 1808, Sanchez may well have known Workman in Taos and is believed to have come to California about 1846, when he registered a cattle brand in Los Angeles, driving, evidently, his cattle on Workman's share of La Puente. He appeared on the 1850 census as Workman's foreman. Sanchez and his family shared lasting friendships with the Temple and Workman families, an example of the amity that often existed between Americans, Europeans and Latinos in an era when racial and ethnic tensions between the two were prevalent. Aside from

25 Maria Casilda Soto to William Workman, Mortgage of Rancho La Merced, 18 December 1850, Book 1, Page 99; Maria Casilda Soto to William Workman, Deed to Rancho La Merced, 30 April 1851, Book 1, Page 39; William and Nicolasa Workman to F.P.F. Temple and Juan Matias Sanchez, Deed to Rancho La Merced, 15 September 1852 and 29 November 1875 [recorded], Book 41, Page 60, Los Angeles County Archives; John Q. A. Warren, California Ranchos and Farms (Madison: State Historical Society of Wisconsin, 1967), pp. 98-100, 110.

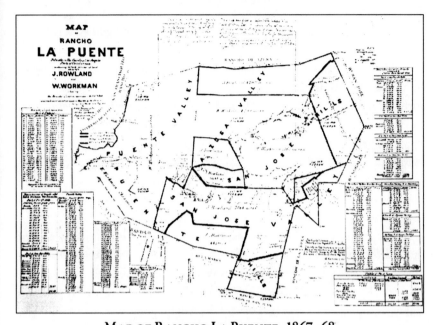

MAP OF RANCHO LA PUENTE, 1867–68

COURTESY OF THE HOMESTEAD MUSEUM, CITY OF INDUSTRY, CALIFORNIA

serving as sponsors at baptisms and naming their children after their friends and other expressions, another example of the abiding friendship between the three families was when Sanchez obtained the Rancho Potrero Grande (located in present-day South El Monte and Monterey Park) in 1852 and, five years later, sold equal shares to Workman and Temple.[26]   Twenty-five years later, the strong bond was taken to an extreme in a time of exceptionally strained circumstances.

Just as Workman was transferring La Merced to Sanchez and Temple, the federal government in Washington, D.C. was deciding the thorny question of land ownership in California. The Mexican system of grants was considered by many Americans to be hopelessly inferior and chaotic in comparison with their own, but though private property protections were guaranteed in article eight of the Treaty of Guadalupe Hidalgo, which ended the Mexican-

---

26 Thomas W. Temple II, *Don Juan Matias Sanchez and Rancho La Merced*, unpublished manuscript, 1959, pp. 2–4 and appendix, pp. 8–10. Copy in the Homestead Museum Research Archives. An interesting artifact of the relationship between Workman and Sanchez is a cancelled note for over $3,000 borrowed by the former from the latter in 1850 and paid off four years later, a transaction witnessed by F.P.F. Temple. Courtesy of Josette Temple.

American War, article nine, dealing specifically with land grants, was stricken by President James Polk and the U. S. Senate, with the American position being that land grants were a matter to be debated and decided by Congress. Matters were complicated in that, before any grace period could elapse to deal with the transfer of systems, the Gold Rush brought teeming hordes of gold seekers to the territory. As the rush peaked then sputtered by the mid-1850s, squatters became numerous and many new land-hungry immigrants believed that, because California was American territory, the Mexican land system was void. Many of the new arrivals cast envious eyes on the staggering land holdings possessed not only by Californios but by early American and European transplants like William Workman and F.P.F. Temple. [27]

In response to the crisis that was developing over land, Congress passed the California Land Claims Act of 1851, which created a three-person commission, based in San Francisco, to hold confirmation hearings about any land granted to persons before the American takeover. A report by William Carey Jones, who was sent in 1849 by the federal government to investigate the land situation in California, stated that most of the titles granted under the Mexican system were valid. Jones had the support of his influential father-in-law, Senator Thomas Hart Benton of Missouri, and his colorful brother-in-law, John C. Frémont, one of California's United States Senators during the land claims dispute and husband of another of Benton's daughters. Frémont, consequently, proposed a bill for land settlement based upon Jones' report. California's other senator, William Gwin, accepting a report by California Secretary of State and Civil War-era Union General Henry W. Halleck that many grants were fraudulent, believed that the state should be opened up to new settlers and that the huge Mexican land grants should be determined either false or outside of American law and policy, despite the provisions of the Treaty of Guadalupe Hidalgo. Gwin's populist position, despite an amendment pushed through by Benton to provide some safeguards for owners, was much more appealing to Congress. His bill passed both houses and became law on 3 March 1851.

The Act created a three-member commission, appointed to meet for three years (although this was later extended to five). A secretary, clerk and an agent were appointed and interpretation was provided for Spanish speakers to pro-

---

27 See page 109-110 for examples of how Workman and Temple occasionally dealt with squatters.

vide, at least from an official standpoint, fairness to all claimants. All persons who had claims on land granted before 7 July 1846, when the Americans took possession of Monterey, were to argue their cases before the board in San Francisco and present documentary evidence and witnesses to substantiate their claims. The commission was then required to make a decision within thirty days which would be forwarded to the U.S. District Attorney. The Act was amended in August 1852 to make every decision eligible for appeal by either the claimant or the government as far as the United States Supreme Court. If the claimant received a confirmation and a certificate and had the property properly surveyed, then a patent was to be issued by the government. Fortunately, for southern California landowners, such as the Workman and Temple families, a session of the commission was held briefly in Los Angeles during the autumn of 1852.

With government bureaucracy and prolonged judicial review, as well as distractions like the Civil War, the average claim took seventeen years to complete. This was a trial, even for successful claimants, since many owners, particularly Californios, were unable to afford lawyers and extensive surveys and live long enough or retain enough financially to wait for their patent. In all, the commission heard over 800 claims and, though two-thirds of these were confirmed, many were sold, mortgaged and foreclosed upon, and subdivided. The process was so prolonged that an act of Congress in June 1860, authorized the District Courts to handle survey examinations and decisions, bypassing the General Land Office and seeking to handle land claims more expeditiously.

In the cases of the family ranchos of Los Cerritos, La Puente, and La Merced, Jonathan Temple, F.P.F. Temple and William Workman all received preliminary confirmation. Upon automatic federal appeal, all three won the second round of hearings and subsequent challenges as well. The claims for La Merced and Los Cerritos were settled by the late 1850s, although the patents were not issued until 1872 for the former, and 1867 for the latter.[28] By the time the Los Cerritos patent was issued, Jonathan Temple had sold the rancho to Flint, Bixby, and Company at a pittance as a result of the dark years of the great drought of 1862–64, and had moved to San Francisco, where he died in late May of 1866. William Workman had claims to other properties besides La Puente, including the Mission San Gabriel. With a new co-claimant, Aaron

---

28 Jacob N. Bowman, *Index to Spanish-Mexican Land Grant Records and Cases of California* (Berkeley: Bancroft Library, 1941), pp. 66, 176.

Pollard, succeeding Hugo Reid after Reid's death in 1852, Workman won confirmations by the Commission and federal District Court, before the United States Supreme Court overruled the confirmation in April 1864. The court's ruling was that California Governor Pío Pico had no authority to make the grant. In regard to the mission buildings, President Lincoln had, by then, issued an order returning all such property to the Catholic Church.[29]

Another claim was for the Rancho Cajon de los Negros, a three-square league parcel near Cajon Pass in San Bernardino County granted by Pío Pico to Ygnacio Coronel in May 1846. Five months later, Workman obtained the rancho from Coronel. Having filed his claim in October 1852, Workman's case was heard by the Land Commission in 1854, but was rejected on the grounds that it was believed Pico had made his grant after the July 7th seizure of Monterey and antedated the grant to Coronel. Workman's appeal to the U. S. District Court in 1856 also was unsuccessful. Despite these defeats, Workman still considered himself owner of the property, as is judged by his sale of half of the rancho in 1870 to California's Secretary of State Drury Malone.[30]

It was the challenge to La Puente that proved more substantial and makes for an interesting case study in the history of the land claims process. The original grant by Alvarado in 1842 was for four square leagues or about 18,000 acres. Three years later, although Pío Pico's grant indicated a larger acreage, though not in specific numerical terms, the provincial Assembly confirmed the new grant for the same four square leagues. Board of Land Commissioners member Robert Thompson heard the case and decided that Pico had intended to grant the entire amount of land between the boundaries that were specified, despite the Assembly's decision otherwise. Thompson thereby confirmed the grant; although, like Pico, he made no mention of leagues or acres, extending then the dispute over acreage to further levels in the process.[31]

29 There are also some surviving correspondence concerning the San Gabriel land claim, including Aaron Pollard to William Workman, 27 September 1852 and 15 July 1854, in which, in the former, Pollard introduces himself as the assignee of the claim of Hugo Reid, Workman's co-grantee, who had just died. Also, attorney Volney E. Howard, then in San Francisco, but soon to move to San Gabriel in the wake of his voluntary exile during the Second Vigilance Committee, wrote letters to Workman on 15 July 1854 and 16 February 1856. These letters provided courtesy of Josette Temple; *United States v. Workman et. al.*, 68 U. S. Reports (December term 1863), pp. 745–769.
30 Ibid., p. 41; James F. Shunk, *Photographic Exhibits in California Land Cases from the Mexican Archives* (San Francisco: n.p., 1861), pp. 38–47; Los Angeles *Star*, 23 October 1852 and 12 November 1870;
31 Robert Thompson, *Opinion in the Claim of the Rancho La Puente*, Board of Land Commissioners Docket No. 127, pp. 57–60 California Private Land Claims.

The United States government, in its appeal, took the position that the Assembly's decision for four leagues was the legitimate official act, regardless of Pico's assumed intentions and Thompson's opinion. When the case was heard before the federal District Court in the spring of 1856, Judge I.S.K. Ogier agreed and issued a decree specifying four square leagues.[32]

Rowland and Workman, represented by William G. Dryden, their associate in the Texas-Santa Fe Expedition affair of 1840–41 and a lawyer in Los Angeles, filed for appeal to the U.S. Supreme Court, although it was decided instead that a rehearing before Judge Ogier in the winter term of 1856–57 was in order.[33] Ogier reversed himself, vacated the prior decree, and ruled that the confirmation for Rowland and Workman was for eleven square leagues.[34] It is likely that precedence established in other land commission decisions asserting the primacy of boundary specifications, rather than size delineations, convinced Ogier to issue the new ruling.

Though it appeared that Rowland and Workman had only to survey their land and submit the plat to the General Land Office in order to receive their patent, further obstacles arose. Because the General Land Office handled adjudication of the plats so slowly, an 1860 amendment to the Land Claims Act brought survey hearings back to the District Court. The federal government made its motion for exceptions, and in October 1862, ten years after the process began, federal District Judge Fletcher M. Haight heard new arguments regarding the survey.[35] As in many appeals by the government, any pretext that appeared to be remotely justifiable seemed to have applied here. Questions directed toward surveyor Henry Hancock referred to discrepancies over the boundaries of La Puente with the adjoining ranchos La Habra and Nogales, although an agreement with the owners of the former and a court ruling on the latter were cited by the surveyor as proof that these issues were

---

32 Judge Isaac S.K. Ogier, *Decree in the Land Claim of Rancho La Puente*, Case No. 385, 1 March 1856, Board of Land Commissioners Docket No.127, p. 133, California Private Land Claims.
33 William G. Dryden to John Rowland, 2 December 1855 and William G. Dryden to John Rowland and William Workman, 17 March 1856. Originals with the La Puente Valley Historical Society.
34 Judge Isaac S.K. Ogier, *Decree in the Land Claim of Rancho La Puente*, Case No. 385, 13 February 1857, General Land Office Docket No. 160, pp. 13–14, California Private Land Claims.
35 J.W. Mandeville to J.A. Hendricks, 4 November 1859, General Land Office Docket No. 160, p. 71, California Private Land Claims.

moot.[36] Haight agreed and decreed that the federal objections were overruled and the plat valid.[37]

At this point, the government had six months to appeal the matter to the Supreme Court and why it didn't, after taking the matter so far, is a mys-

JOHN ROWLAND,
CHARLOTTE GRAY
ROWLAND AND
UNIDENTIFIED CHILD,
CIRCA 1860
*COURTESY OF
LA PUENTE VALLEY
HISTORICAL SOCIETY*

tery. The statute of limitations had expired when in, 1864, the issue of the size discrepancy was raised again in correspondence between the General Land Office commissioner and the Secretary of the Interior. Rather than act at all, the General Land Office chose to do nothing and the patent remained unissued.[38]

Undoubtedly exasperated, Rowland contacted Henry W. Halleck, who had filed the less approbationary of the two reports on California land grants

---

36 Henry Hancock, *Deposition in the Land Claim Survey Hearing of Rancho La Puente*, Board of Land Commissioners Docket No. 127, pp. 179–185, California Private Land Claims.
37 Judge Fletcher M. Haight, *Decree in the Land Claim Survey Hearing of Rancho La Puente*, General Land Office Docket No. 160, pp. 17–20, ibid.
38 J.M. Edmunds to Edward Bates, 22 February 1864, General Land Office Docket No. 160, pp. 23–26, ibid.

before the passage of the Land Claims Act. Halleck, responding in June 1865, was blunt in his assessment, "There seems but one way to expedite business in that office, hire an agent & give him plenty of money."[39] Rowland either took Halleck's advice or came to that conclusion on his own, because he and son-in-law John Reed hired a lawyer in San Francisco to press the government for their patent. The attorney contacted Washington lawyer Henry Beard, who examined the claim's history and presented a forceful argument to the Secretary of the Interior in early 1867 that led, finally, to the deliverance of the patent in April.[40] After fifteen years, Rowland and Workman had official confirmation of the ownership of La Puente, enduring trials that were at once common and unique to the land claims process.

From the beginnings of the American period, the Workman and Temple families participated in the affairs of the southern California political arena. Jonathan Temple's role in politics was especially noteworthy between 1846 and 1850. As seen above, he served as alcalde of the pueblo in 1846 after the first American seizure of the city and he served on the ayuntamiento during 1849. When the newly incorporated city conducted its first elections on 4 April 1850, Temple was elected to the inaugural common [city] council, which featured a mixed membership of Americans, Europeans, and *Californios*. Temple's term on the council lasted only from July through early December and was his last turn in political office.[41] He thereafter contented himself with managing his various economic interests, although he made one last stab at political office, conducting a losing campaign for county supervisor in 1860.[42]

F.P.F Temple also entered into early American-era politics in Los Angeles, serving as the city treasurer from 1850–52 and winning election to the first Los Angeles County Board of Supervisors in 1852. He ran for political office four additional times; for county supervisor in 1863 and 1871, and county treasurer in 1873 and 1875, mostly as an independent, though he was also a Republican Party loyalist, in an era of near complete Democratic Party dominance in Los Angeles politics, and only his last attempt was successful. Even

---

39 Henry W. Halleck to John Rowland, 2 June 1865, MS, [James] Perry Worden Collection, Henry E. Huntington Library, San Marino, CA.

40 Henry Beard to John Rowland, 8 April 1867. Original with the La Puente Valley Historical Society; Henry Beard, *In the Matter of the Application of John Rowland and William Workman for the Patent to the Rancho La Puente* (Washington D.C.: Gibson Brothers, 1866.), pp. 1–19; General Land Office Docket No. 160, pp. 86–104, California Private Land Claims.

41 California Biography File, Los Angeles Public Library; Maymie R. Krythe, "Daily Life in Early Los Angeles", *Historical Society of Southern California Quarterly*, 36 (December 1954): 322.

42 Los Angeles *Southern News*, 14 November 1860.

William Workman made a bid for political office in 1859 when he ran for supervisor as part of a People's Party, made up primarily of disaffected Democrats. Workman's one and only attempt at politics failed.[43]

"Good Taste and Liberality"—
The Halcyon Days of the Ranchero

Economically, William Workman, Jonathan Temple and F.P.F. Temple remained primarily involved with their ranching enterprises in the years during the Gold Rush and up until the drought years of the early 1860s. Jonathan Temple, as was noted above, diversified in ways that the other two did not and probably lessened his dependence on cattle and agriculture. By 1856, the year the mint arrangement was made, he closed his store with an auction of the establishment's inventory. Shortly before his death in May 1866, and after a devastating period of flood, followed by drought, he sold his Rancho Los Cerritos for well under a dollar an acre and moved to San Francisco, nearly divesting himself from southern California entirely, with the conspicuous exception of his prime real estate holdings in the center of Los Angeles.[44] For Workman and F.P.F. Temple, even with the nullification of land grants, such as Alcatraz and San Clemente islands, the mission San Gabriel, and a rancho in San Bernardino County, their acquisition of southern California real estate intensified during the first years of the Gold Rush and continued until the mid-1870s. Aside from their home ranchos of La Puente and La Merced, the two men obtained the whole of the 2,042-acre Rancho Potrero de Felipe Lugo, flanking the west bank of the San Gabriel River adjacent to La Puente and La Merced, and one-quarter interests each in the adjoining Rancho Potrero Grande, which covered 4,431 acres.[45] Temple and Workman also owned a portion of the tiny 83-acre Rancho Potrero Chico, also known as the Misíon

43 Los Angeles Star, 9 July 1859 and 27 August 1859

44 A later instance of Temple's investment enterprise was in 1860 when Temple was a "stockholder to the amount of a number of thousand dollars" in a proposed telegraph line from the eastern states to the Pacific coast via a southern route. Los Angeles *Semi-Weekly Southern News*, 10 October 1860.

45 For transactions concerning the Workman and Temple interests in Potrero de Felipe Lugo, commonly called the Dolores or Morillo rancho, see Maria Verdugo and Rafael Lunaga to William Workman and F.P.F. Temple, 7 January 1857, Book 3: 536, George Morillo and Madelena Vejar to William Workman and F.P.F. Temple, 27 February 1857, Book 3: 566 and Maria Romero and Jose Espinosa to F.P.F. Temple, 25 April 1857, Book 3: 617, Los Angeles County Archives. The interests in Potrero Grande came from their compadre Juan Matias Sanchez, Sanchez to Workman and Temple, 7 March 1857, Book 3: 580. Ibid.

MISSION SAN GABRIEL, CIRCA 1878
COURTESY OF THE HOMESTEAD MUSEUM,
CITY OF INDUSTRY, CALIFORNIA

Vieja, because the original site of the Mission San Gabriel was located nearby.[46] Outside of the San Gabriel Valley, Temple owned property in the Plaza area of Los Angeles as early as 1847 and had land along the east bank of the Los Angeles River from 1852.[47] Workman, meanwhile, in 1864, took over 4,400 acres of the Rancho Rodeo de Las Aguas, now encompassing the Beverly Hills area, by foreclosure on Henry Hancock, as well as Hancock's vineyard in Los Angeles near the Los Angeles River.[48] A year earlier, he had become the owner of Scott's Ranch, a parcel owned by prominent Los Angeles attorney

---

46 Francisco Vejar, et. ux. to Juan Matias Sanchez and F.P.F. Temple, *Deed to the Rancho Mission Vieja de San Gabriel [Potrero Chico]*, 1 September 1851, Book 1: 52. Ibid. Juan C. Vejar to William Workman, F.P.F. Temple, and Juan Matias Sanchez, Deed to Rancho Potrero Chico, 9 May 1863, Book 6, Page 184, Ibid; Salome Valenzuela et. al. to William Workman, F.P.F. Temple, and Juan Matias Sanchez, Deed to Rancho Potrero Chico, 4 March 1863, Book 6, Page 205, Ibid.

47 See the copy of an 1847 deed to Temple from pueblo officials in the Homestead Museum Research Archives; also, Los Angeles Common Council Records, Book 5: 67, Book 6: 443 and 447 and Book 8: 85 and Los Angeles County Archives Deed Books 3: 389, 5: 231; 5: 233, 5: 235, and 13: 73 for transactions regarding acreage along the east side of the river between the roads to San Gabriel and to El Monte.

48 *Tax Assessments for 1864*, Los Angeles County, Seaver Center for Western Research. Workman's copy of an undated memorandum of agreement between Hancock and Gabriel Allen, concerning 1,500 acres of the northern end of the ranch, is in the possession of Josette Temple.

and judge Jonathan R. Scott, located on the southern half of the Rancho San Rafael and flanked on the west by the Los Angeles River.[49]

In this period of unprecedented financial success and land acquisition, there were concomitant difficulties to occasionally deal with, including problems with thieves, counterfeiters, and squatters. One such situation is seen in an advertisement taken out in the Los Angeles *Star* in early 1854, in which William Workman and John Rowland warned others "from settling, cutting timber, or in any way infringing upon our Rancho de la Puente" on threat of prosecution.[50] There were also several recorded instances of difficulties regarding horse and cattle thievery, as well as the counterfeiting of brands, which were all-too-common occurrences. In 1855, Workman, to stave off counterfeit use of his brand, issued this proclamation,

> To Whom It May Concern—the undersigned having found several of his horses, with a false counter-brand, he has now registered a new counter-brand, which shall be the only evidence of his having legally sold any horse or horses; therefore all persons purchasing any animal with my brand, will be particular to see that it is properly counter-branded, otherwise it will be reclaimed by its proper owner.[51]

A year later, Workman, John Rowland and his son-in-law, John Reed, F.P.F. Temple and Jonathan Temple teamed with other rancheros to issue this statement:

> Rancheros and all other owners of stock are hereby cautioned that they cannot be too watchful of the same. A lot of 26 heads belonging as follows, viz.—8 to John Rowland, 2 to John Reed, 3 to F.P.F. Temple, 5 to W. Workman, 2 to John Temple...were taken from a drove that left Mission San Gabriel, about ten days since. It is to be regretted that some few Rancheros in this County employ thieves as vaqueros,

49 Jonathon R. Scott to William Workman, *Deed to Land in the Rancho San Rafael*, 28 July 1863, Book 6: 241, Los Angeles County Archives. This parcel was sold by Workman to Alexander Bell in 1866, William Workman to Alexander Bell, *Deed to Land in the Rancho San Rafael*, 17 September 1866, Book 8: 174, Ibid.
50 Los Angeles *Star*, 11 February 1854.
51 *The Southern Californian*, 16 May 1855.

whose stealings are sometimes winked at by their employers. By keeping a good look out, those fellows may be detected and finally all driven from the county.[52]

Sometimes, cattle and horse thieves were captured, as evidence in a surviving "invoice" from 1861, in which Henry D. Barrows, a well-known Los Angeles teacher, wrote William Workman calling for the latter's payment of $100 for a subscription to pay for a posse which successfully caught the thieves of horses belonging to several area ranches, including Workman. A receipt on the same document, signed by Joseph Pleasants, foreman of Workman's long-time friend, William Wolfskill, who owned a ranch in present northern Orange County, confirmed Workman's payment.[53]

It seems that Workman also was vigilant about tracking down his stolen animals, if a repentant and apologetic letter from 1856 is any indication. Sent by San Gabriel farmer Thomas van Deusen, the letter seeks forgiveness from Workman for a mistake in which van Deusen wrote, "I have only to say that a Cow, bearing your Brand, was found tied to my Rope. But in what manner it came there, were my life to pay the penalty for failing, I should be unable to save it, for I am as yet totally ignorant of when how or by whose agency it came there." After explaining (or trying to) why the cow's appearance on his farm was not his doing, van Deusen vowed, "I shall use my utmost endeavors to discover the author of the deed, and have him brought to justice" and concluded, humbly, "Therefore if you see fit to prosecute I have only to say I shall suffer innocently." Clearly, Workman was a man respected (perhaps feared?) by his neighbors![54]

Regarding the problem of squatters, which may have been a consequence of the Workman and Temple ranches' proximity to El Monte, where many new arrivals ended their migration to southern California from the east, there are a few documented cases of conflict. In 1862, Workman, F.P.F. Temple and Juan Matías Sanchez received a court ruling to eject twenty-seven squatters from their Rancho Potrero Grande.[55] Another ruling, twelve years later, for Temple and Sanchez on the same property led to a violent clash between one squatter and Sheriff William R. Rowland, son of John Rowland. The per-

52 Los Angeles *Star*, 19 April 1856.
53 Henry D. Barrows to William Workman, 11 October 1861, Courtesy of Josette Temple.
54 Thomas van Deusen to William Workman, 5 October 1856, Courtesy of Josette Temple.
55 Los Angeles *Star.*, 12 April 1862.

petrator surrendered, but another claimed he would fight to the death over his home.[56] A reprinted article in the *Star* in late 1876 made allusion to "the Temple & Workman grab of old settlers homes and very valuable homesteads at El Monte" in support of those listed in the two above examples.[57] There were some contemporary accounts though, such as that of El Monte farmer William B. Lee in an 1873 newspaper article, that gave unstinting praise to Workman and Temple for their assistance to new arrivals.[58] It appears that, while the families were willing to help immigrants, they also could be firm in dealing with those who squatted, rather than solicited.

In reviewing available data about the extent of their ranching enterprises, one can see why thieves would target the Workman and Temple families: they possessed considerable property, but also had wide-spread development of their animal and agricultural resources. Though one source notes that F.P.F. Temple in 1860 had about 1,200 cattle and that Workman pastured 1,500, another account which also gives figures for that year but does not list the size of F.P.F. Temple's herds, showed Jonathan Temple possessing some 4,000 head and William Workman 5,000, the county's third-highest total, after Abel Stearns and Juan Avila.[59]

John Quincy Adams Warren, a traveler who stayed at the Workman ranch, gave this description, published in 1860, of Workman's stock raising activities:

> The ranch...is devoted, with the exception of a few acres, entirely to stock raising. Wm. Workman has some 3,000 head of cattle and about 600 head of horses, nearly all California stock, with the exception of a few half-breeds. The stock in the dry season roam over the range of hills in pursuit of forage, and are nearly lost to sight; but in the spring when the new grass makes its appearance, the plains are covered, presenting an attractive appearance.

56 Los Angeles *Express*, 13 and 14 January 1874.
57 Los Angeles *Star*, 23 November 1876.
58 Ibid., 21 August 1873.
59 Warren, *California Ranchos and Farms*, notes, pp. 109–110; Layne, "Annals of Los Angeles", p. 349.

Warren continued, "There is not that much attention paid to improvement of stock which perhaps a few years hence may witness." With the onset of the great droughts just a few years later, Warren's predictions were not borne out and poor market conditions served as a precursor to the decline of cattle raising and the ascendancy of agriculture.[60]

An interesting artifact from these last days of the so-called "cow culture" comes from a newspaper account of a *recogida*, or roundup, of horses on Workman's rodeo grounds northwest of his home in 1859. Here some idea of that pastoral culture that had predominated for generations in the region is discerned:

> The scene was most exciting. The plain was literally covered with horses; they were driven into the corrals, in bands of from twenty to fifty, and there examined and parted. The proceedings were conducted under the superintendence of Don Felipe Lugo, a Judge of the Plains, but there were several others present—Messrs. Workman, Temple, Rubottom, &c.—There was a very general attendance of the neighboring rancheros, besides farmers from the Monte and vicinity, to all of whom, Mr. Workman dispensed his hospitalities in the most liberal and profuse manner. The feats of horsemanship performed by the Californians were astonishing; but the facility and percision [sic] with which the "lasso" was thrown could scarcely be credited by those who have not witnessed such experts. The animal aimed at was secured, whether in the band or running at full speed over the plain; and that, too, by the neck or limb at the fancy of his pursuer. The proceedings occupied two days.[61]

At the same time, both F.P.F. Temple and Workman supplemented their cattle income with agricultural pursuits. Early signs of this activity by the family, aside from the mention of Workman's crop of corn and beans during his first year at La Puente, are mention of grape raising at La Puente in the 1850

---

60 Warren, *California Ranchos and Farms*, pp. 110–111.
61 Los Angeles *Star*, 26 February 1859.

federal census, and this advertisement in the summer of 1854 in *The Southern Californian* newspaper:

> Grapes! Grapes!! The subscriber offers his crop of Grapes at three cents per lb. delivered at the heap in his vineyard, in the Rancho of the Puente. Hauling can be procured on reasonable terms in the Monte. For further particulars, apply to David W. Alexander, Los Angeles, or William Workman, at La Puente.[62]

Henry Miller, an artist known for his drawings of the California missions and who visited La Puente in October 1856, noted that Workman had "a fine and large vineyard and orchard in which grow 12,000 grape vines and an abundance of fruit of all kind..."[63] The 1860 census agriculture schedule reported that the production of wine by Workman was 6,000 gallons.[64] It seems that, before this period, Workman confined himself to raising the grapes and selling them to vintners. By 1860, though, he joined the ranks of such contemporaries as Kohler and Froehling, Mathew Keller and Benjamin D. Wilson as a manufacturer.

J.Q.A. Warren's 1860 visits to the ranchos La Merced and La Puente also detailed their burgeoning agricultural enterprises, and the point can be extended to say that, compared to the years prior to and during the Gold Rush, there was a dramatic rise in the practice of agriculture. At La Merced, which at 2,363 acres was a moderately sized ranch, the Temples had some "100 acres of which are inclosed to garden, vineyard, and agricultural purposes...Fifty acres are devoted to orchard and vineyard, the latter containing about 20,000 vines." In the orchard, Warren reported there was "a large variety of fruit trees, pear, peach, plum, apricot, olive, figs, and English walnuts." Of the latter, there were some 200 successfully bearing trees. Field crops under cultivation included such staples as corn, wheat, barley and rye. At La Puente, where Workman had much more room on which to expand his enterprises, Warren saw ten acres of vineyards and orchards; a small beginning, but upon which

62 *The Southern Californian*, 31 August 1854.
63 Henry Miller, *California Missions* (Santa Barbara: Bellerophon Books, 1983), p. 63.
64 Los Angeles *Star*, 15 October 1859. Iris Higbie Wilson, in her biography of William Wolfskill, alluded to the fact that Henry D. Barrows had written in the *Star* on 24 October 1859 that prominent winemaker John Frohling had made wine at the vineyard of both Workman and John Rowland the prior week. The author could not, however, locate this article in searching the *Star*.

were "about 10,000 vines, which have the past season produced an extra crop. There are some 50,000 new vines set out and doing well." This latter number meant an additional fifty acres devoted to viticulture. Warren listed peach, pear, apple, fig and pomegranate trees in the Workman orchard. This description shows that even before the collapse of the cattle economy, some ranchers were experimenting, and often quite successfully, with a large variety of crops on southern California's fertile soil.[65] An original source that documents how some of this experimentation was conducted is found in an 1856 letter from F.P.F. Temple's brother-in-law. In it, John H. Bancroft makes reference to a request the previous year from Temple's nephew and foreman, Thornton Sanborn, for "a box about one foot square, with the best Peach, Plum, and Cherry stones you can find in the market, all kinds of garden seeds, the best, all kinds of flour seeds also Hovey & Co. Catalogue of trees," which items were sent in the fall of 1855.[66]

Even the means of production were enhanced by the establishment of mills. By 1860, F.P.F Temple had a thriving mill on La Merced that was converting corn and wheat into corn meal and flour valued at $21,000.[67] William Workman would not construct his own until after 1864, but had access to the facility of his friend John Rowland, who, in 1847, built one of the earliest mills in southern California.

With the rapidly growing agricultural production of the families, it is worth recalling that, with the semi-arid climate, despite the importance of dry-farming, especially in wheat, irrigation was indispensable. Along the San Jose Creek, William Workman had a mile-long ditch that brought water to the farmlands immediately south of his home. Three and a half miles west, a ditch was dug for the Workman mill, which was established sometime in the latter 1860s. Then, along the east bank of the San Gabriel River, a third Workman irrigation ditch drew the waters off of the "new" channel, created after an 1867 flood, though it is not known if this ditch or another existed to the "old" Rio Hondo course previous to the flood. F.P.F Temple had a four-mile long ditch dug in 1854 on the west bank of the San Gabriel extending

65 Warren, *California Ranchos and Farms*, pp. 110–111.
66 John H. Bancroft to F.P.F. Temple, 2 August 1856, courtesy of Josette Temple.
67 *Schedule of Products of Industry, El Monte Township, 1860 Census*, National Archives and Records Administration, Laguna Niguel, CA. This schedule also noted the mill of John Rowland producing 2,000 barrels of flour and 3,000 barrels of corn meal, valued at $46,000. We can assume that some portion of this produce came from the fields of William Workman, whose mill was built later in the sixties, unless he used F.P.F. Temple's mill.

southwest through between 300 and 400 acres of the Ranchos Potrero de Felipe Lugo and La Merced. Although these ditches watered fairly small and highly localized farm patches, it is evident that they had a high value since they were in use for many years before the great water projects of the early twentieth century.[68]

During these prosperous times, even with the ongoing land claims proceedings and the uncertainty of their results, the Workman and Temple families made many striking improvements to the homes and outbuildings on their properties, particularly at La Puente and La Merced. At the latter, J.Q.A. Warren visited the Temple home, built in 1851, and noted, "The mansion is adobe, built in substantial and comfortable style, and like the usual Spanish houses forms a half-square 110 feet by 70."[69] Although the home continued for years to maintain the appearance of a ranch-style adobe, it was later remodeled with the addition of a wooden second floor. By about 1870, a French Second Empire-style brick residence was constructed adjacent to the adobe, which clearly showed the contrasts of the former Californio period with the nascent Americanization then underway. Perhaps another example of this latter process or a reflection of overall modernization, as well as an indicator of the wealth F.P.F. Temple possessed in this period, is the expenditure of $40,000, an immense sum, for lumber purchased from Phineas Banning to fence the Temple portion of the La Merced rancho.[70]

There were also substantial expenditures on improvements across the San Gabriel River at La Puente. Sometime before 1856, Workman enlarged his adobe from three rooms to thirteen. There are several known accounts of this configuration of the house, though none, unfortunately, of its earlier appearance. Henry Miller's 1856 account includes the earliest description found of the building: "Mr. Workman's house is a one story building of adobe and forms a square with a yard in the middle. The house is well-finished, and painted with oil colors on the inside and outside, imitating marble, and afterwards varnished."[71] Two years later, the visiting members of the Committee of the California State Agricultural Society noted: "His buildings are of adobe, colored and penciled to represent stone. They form an oblong square court, 75 by

---

68 William H. Hall, *Irrigation in [Southern] California* (Sacramento: State Office Printing, 1888), pp. 485–486; 575–577.

69 Warren, *California Ranchos and Farms*, p. 110.

70 Maymie R. Krythe, *Port Admiral: Phineas Banning, 1830–1885* (San Francisco: California Historical Society, 1957), p. 97.

71 Miller, *California Missions*, p. 63.

150 ft., in which many of the tropical fruits are sufficiently protected to flourish the entire year."[72] Warren, in his 1860 sojourn had this to say about the structure: "The main building or residence is in the form of an oblong square; in the center is a large open court yard, containing tropical fruits and an arbor of trellis work, covered with grape vines running the entire distance."[73]

The most detailed description of the house comes from Workman's grandson John H. Temple, who had his early education at the private school located at the house in the 1860s and early 1870s, and who owned the house between 1888 and the turn of the century. Temple's account is of added interest because of his identification of the service and storage spaces located in the wings, which extended to the south of the house and were razed in a late-1860s remodeling. These rooms included a smoking or rest room with a fireplace; a sitting room; the well room (the well survives today, though after Workman's death it was replaced by a pump house and water tower that also remain on the grounds, just south of the home); a commissary for the ranch employees; a butcher shop; a smithy; and storage rooms for saddles, saddle trees and the vaquero's accouterments and grain; and the school room. Among the teachers employed by Workman to educate the Temple grandchildren were Thomas Scully, who married one of the Yorba family from today's Orange County and for whom Scully Hill in present-day Yorba Linda is named, and, from 1860, English native Frederick Lambourn, who became Workman's ranch foreman and was later a State Assemblyman and successful Los Angeles merchant with Workman's miller, William F. Turner. At the end of the wings, remembered John H. Temple, was a gate "some fifteen or twenty feet wide, with a massive lock" surmounted by "an elaborate pigeon house, from which the family derived their squabs and pigeons." Echoing earlier descriptions, Temple recalled the patio, grape arbor, and orange trees.[74]

The Workman House before 1865 with its homogeneous melding of living spaces and work areas, reflected the era of self-suffiency that marked the Mexican period and the generation after the American conquest. This would be dramatically altered, though, in a remodeling of the house by 1870, so that the home today does not give that sense derived from the accounts above. By

---

72 Quoted in Leonore Rowland, *The Romance of La Puente Rancho* (Covina: Neilson Press, 1958), p. 26.
73 Warren, *California Ranchos and Farms*, p. 110.
74 From a biographical sketch of Workman in John Steven McGroarty, *Los Angeles: From the Mountains to the Sea*, (Chicago: American Historical Society, 1921), pp. 922–923.

SAINT NICHOLAS CHAPEL, CIRCA 1870s
COURTESY OF HOMESTEAD MUSEUM, CITY OF INDUSTRY, CALIFORNIA

contrast, Jonathan Temple's Los Cerritos adobe still retains its basic form and well illustrates this home/workplace quality.

Certainly, the quadrupling in size of Workman's house was a direct result of increased income in the Gold Rush-era beef trade. Earlier, Workman's home had reflected a somewhat spartan and functional appearance, though in the 1850s he could choose to show some of his wealth and success and incorporate changes to his residence that were more aesthetic and luxurious, such as the varnished walls described in the aforementioned contemporary accounts. This was also extended to his outbuildings and other sites of the ranch, most particularly in the establishment of the *El Campo Santo* Cemetery some three hundred yards east of the house. Used as early as 1850, perhaps at the same time as the enlargement of the Workman House, the cemetery eventually featured a brick enclosure wall, of which the west or entrance side is extant; a cast-iron fenced family plot, which survives intact; and a Gothic-revival chapel that was named St. Nicholas in honor of Workman's wife, Nicolasa.

When Henry Miller visited in the fall of 1856, he was asked by Workman to prepare some plans for several proposed structures and wrote, "Amongst the drawings which I made for Mr. Workman was a plan for a chapel which

116

he is going to build here for the benefit of his Indians who live near his house in their shantees and who work for him, earning 50 cents a day."[75] On 30 May 1857, Bishop Thaddeus Amat blessed the cornerstone for the new edifice, which appears to have taken two to three years to complete. The California State Agricultural Committee in 1858 noted that Workman was "about to erect a church edifice at his own expense, in which he designs to maintain the form of worship adopted by the Roman Church, for the benefit of his workmen and neighbors."[76] J.Q.A. Warren's 1860 description, the most detailed of the chapel extant, stated that Workman "has just erected upon his place a large and commodious brick church for the benefit of those who may wish to avail themselves of the opportunity of worship." In noting the dimensions and wall thickness of the structure, Warren was sure to add that "the mechanics are the best that can be procured" and that "no regard has been had to cost, that being a secondary consideration." Although there were other private chapels being built at the same period—the Vejar family, neighbors to the east on the Rancho San José, and the Yorbas, on the Rancho Cajon de Santa Ana in present-day north Orange County, were contemporaries who were constructing houses of worship—Warren commented on St. Nicholas' that "when completed [it] will be an ornament to the neighborhood, as well as a novelty, in point of location, reflecting credit upon the founder." In fact, Warren's high praise of Workman included the pronouncement that "everything about the place evinces good taste and liberality," and the conclusion that, "I have dwelt somewhat at length upon La Puente ranch, it being one of the most prominent on my route in point of location, picturesque beauty and position."[77]

With such an impressive home and ranch, as well as a significant income to maintain it all, Workman's successes in California may have been an inspiration to his brother, David, a reversal of the events of thirty years before when William followed David to the United States. Although David kept his home in central Missouri, he was a frequent traveler throughout the southwest, joining trading caravans as far south as Chihuahua City, Mexico. It was the Gold Rush, however, that turned his attentions to California. David's son, William Henry, later described his father's growing interest in the west:

---

75 Miller, *California Missions*, p. 63. The mention of the chapel being built for Workman's native American laborers is one of the few known instances where the Gabrieliño/Tongva Indians on the ranch are mentioned.
76 Quoted in Rowland, *The Romance of La Puente Rancho*, p. 26.
77 Warren, *California Ranchos and Farms*, pp. 110–111.

[I]n 1849, attracted by the gold discoveries, he came to California for the first time. Seeing the opportunities that lay in selling supplies to the miners, Father returned to Missouri in 1850. He purchased a train load of supplies and equipment and came back across the plains to California. He then opened a merchandise store in Sacramento, but on November 2, 1852, the store and its entire stock were destroyed by a great fire that wiped out seven-eighths of the city.

Deeply discouraged by his loss, David paid a visit to his brother and received consolation and encouragement. William Henry's narrative continued: "It was at the Puente that William persuaded David Workman to bring his wife and three sons to Southern California to live. Father came home in the summer of 1853, bringing news that the following spring we would all head for California." Joining them was William Workman's son, José, known commonly as Joseph, who had, as early as 1847 ("in his infancy" according to a biographical account), lived with his aunt, Agnes Workman Vickers, her husband John, and son James, in Baltimore. In 1852, there were indications that Joseph might join his father on a trip to England, but this may have changed with the Sacramento disaster and the subsequent decision to bring the David Workman family to La Puente.[78]

David Workman prepared three wagons with a carriage for Mrs. Workman, and in April 1854, the family set off from Boonville, following the Oregon and California Trail opened in the great migrations of 1843. William Henry vividly recalled the trip in his later years from the vantage point of a teenager on a great adventure. The party met occasionally with Indians, including an encounter with Sioux and Cheyenne that resulted in the party's entire provisions being surrendered. In Utah, Brigham Young came to the encampment and sought to persuade the emigrants to stay in the land of the Saints. The Workman group later passed Lake Tahoe, through Sacramento, and then Stockton, where they disbanded and sold their outfit and took a boat to San Francisco. A steamship brought them to San Pedro where, in October 1854,

---

78 Mary Workman to Joseph Workman, 1 November 1852, transcription by David A. Workman, copy in the Homestead Museum Research Library; *An Illustrated History of Los Angeles County, California*, (Chicago: Lewis Publishing Co., 1889), p. 683.

six months to the day after they left Boonville, they were met by William Workman and taken to La Puente.[79]

As William Henry wrote, "Their joy [at reuniting], however, was to be short-lived."[80] David was employed as his brother's agent to drive cattle and sheep to the mines of northern California. On one such trip in the summer of 1855, in a Stanislaus County encampment, David went on a mule to fetch a missing heifer and did not return. The next morning, a search party found

**DAVID WORKMAN,
CIRCA 1854**
*COURTESY OF THE
WORKMAN FAMILY
COLLECTION*

his body at the bottom of a 200-foot precipice. David Workman's remains followed the same route of the family's journey from Stockton the year before and were brought back to La Puente for the funeral.[81] The Los Angeles *Star* reported "The Obsequies of David Workman, Esq." at the Workman House. Because the reporter, as well as the Workman brothers, was a Mason, he reported in great detail on the event, which was the first family burial in the cemetery. First, the funeral cortege, numbering some fifty Masons, was preceded by the Los Angeles Brass Band in its solemn march to the home. After the ceremony, details of which were not elucidated in keeping with Masonic practices, the group marched in procession to the cemetery for graveside ser-

---

79 The above description of the David Workman's family trip is based upon William H. Workman, "Reminiscence of My Coming to California", pp. 3–9, *Annual Report of the Pioneers of Los Angeles County, 1908–1909* (Los Angeles: Pioneers of Los Angeles County, 1909.)
80 Workman, "Reminiscence of My Coming to California", p. 9.
81 Los Angeles *Star*, 25 August 1855.

vices, which would "long be remembered as one of more than ordinary grandeur in Southern California."[82]

David Workman's widow, Nancy, and their three sons remained at La Puente for a short time before moving into Los Angeles. The eldest, Thomas, went to work for Phineas Banning and his steamship company at Wilmington, and, as with his brothers later, was inclined to the pursuit of political office, serving as Justice of the Peace at San Pedro and running for County Clerk in 1861.[83] Thomas, though, died at thirty in 1863 in the explosion of the steamship *Ada Hancock*, one of the more notable tragedies of the period in the Los Angeles area.[84] Elijah, the middle son, also worked for Banning, then for the federal government at Fort Tejon, and as a salesman before he took up the occupation of his father and uncle and went to work as a saddler in his own business by 1857. William Henry, the youngest, who had learned the newspaper trade in Missouri, took employment with the Los Angeles *Star* and *The Southern Californian* newspapers. After 1860, he was associated in Elijah's saddlery. In the ascendancy of Americanization that marked later decades, Elijah and, especially, William Henry would play important roles in local politics, adding a new and wider scope to the involvement of the Workman and Temple families in southern California's public sphere.

As for Joseph Workman, it does not appear that he remained long at La Puente, either. From 1856, shortly after his arrival, Joseph was sent to Kern County where he supervised cattle on the ranches El Tejon and San Emigdio, which were part-owned by his brother-in-law, F.P.F. Temple. He remained at Tejon for some fifteen years, not returning to La Puente until after his marriage to Josephine Belt, a Stockton native, in January of 1870.[85]

Noah's Flood and The Great Drought

The successes of the families during the prosperous years of the 1850s was subject to the changing conditions of cattle raising in southern California. First, the Gold Rush slowed and production in the gold fields dropped appreciably by mid-decade. Miners turned to other occupations, such as cattle ranching, and raised the competitive stakes among the state's established ranchers.

---

82 Ibid, 17 November 1855.
83 Ibid, 7 June 1856; Los Angeles *Semi-Weekly Southern News*, 7 August and 6 September 1861.
84 Los Angeles *News*, 1 May 1863; Los Angeles *Star*, 2 May 1863.
85 *An Illustrated History of Los Angeles County, California*, p. 683.

Additionally, the cattle ranches of the middle states, particularly Texas, were producing a better breed of animal and the demand for beef from the midwest raised a stiff challenge to this region's rancheros. Finally, there were threats from the wildly divergent weather patterns in southern California.

While known for its recurring pattern of drought, the region has also been vulnerable to flooding. One of the worst downpours in southern California history, sometimes called Noah's Flood, began on Christmas Eve 1861, when a hard, steady rain pelted the southern California region. For a month, the rain fell almost continually. For modern Angelenos who live amidst one of the most complex and finely engineered flood control systems in the world, the idea of massive flooding is only a remote threat. But at a time when the region was mainly undeveloped and without any drainage system of significance, the southern Californians of January 1862 found themselves inundated by water. Because many homes, such as those of the Workmans and Temples, were built near water courses to take advantage of whatever water was available under normal semi-arid conditions, coverage in the Los Angeles *Star* was typified by the effects of the flood at F.P.F and Margarita Temple's home on the east bank of the San Gabriel River (now the Rio Hondo after an 1867 deluge changed the river's course.) The home had been flooded completely and the Temples "effected their escape from the house on a raft."[86] The results of the flood were disastrous to agriculture and stock raising throughout the region. Historian Robert G. Cleland estimated that the disaster caused a loss of 200,000 cattle—and this was before the droughts that followed and eclipsed the damage caused by the flood of 1861–62.[87]

Still, the advent of the flood and the wake of its destructive force did not seem to herald any portentous change for the cattle industry in the immediate aftermath. Jonathan Temple, for example, purchased, at the end of January 1862, a soap factory at San Pedro with the intention of adding candle manufacturing, indicating that he planned to continue dealing extensively with cattle.[88] A few months later, the *Star* reported , "Within the last twelve months, considerable attention has been given to the improvement of stock of this country...There are several rancheros who have enriched their stalls with these imported animals—among whom are pre-eminent, Messrs F.P.[F.] Temple and

86   Los Angeles *Star*, 25 January 1862.
87   Cleland, *The Cattle on a Thousand Hills*, p. 130.
88   Los Angeles *Star*, 1 February 1862.

F.W. Gibson". The article noted that the two were investing more in mules and horses than all of the other ranchers in southern California combined.[89] Fielding W. Gibson, a native of Kentucky, lived just north of El Monte and later in the decade collaborated with Temple in an early suburban subdivision that became Compton. Undoubtedly, his connections to his home state led to the purchase of pureblooded horses from Kentucky. Temple also bred horses on property he owned in Alameda County and, with partner Samuel A. Jackson, bought, in 1863, a horse named Black Warrior for the princely sum of $7,000.[90] Though on a smaller scale, Temple seemed to be a precursor to such contemporaries as Leonard J. Rose, who bred fine race horses on the famous Sunnyslope ranch in today's Pasadena, and Elias J. Baldwin, whose Rancho Santa Anita birthed a great tradition of horse racing that continues today with its landmark racetrack in present-day Arcadia.

This increased investment in animal husbandry came on the eve of another natural disaster which has become an epoch-delineating signpost for southern California history: the great drought of 1862–64. The drought was so severe that a quarter to a third of normal rainfall was estimated. The result, not surprisingly, was the devastation of the cattle industry. Ranchers desperately sought to move their animals hundreds of miles in some cases to seek any appreciable pasture land. Many finally resorted to slaughtering their animals wholesale, even though they already faced depressed market conditions, which had in Jonathan Temple's case, led him to slaughter some 2,000 cattle in 1861 for an extraordinarily low return.[91] The impact of the drought was such that, just before his death in 1866, he sold Los Cerritos to Flint, Bixby, and Company for only $15,000. At 27,000 acres, that amounts to just a little more than 50 cents an acre.[92]

At La Puente, William Workman, according to an account given by his grandson, John H. Temple, to John Steven McGroarty,

---

89 Ibid, 10 May 1862.
90 See the advertisement for Black Warrior in the Los Angeles *Star*, 21 February 1863, giving the horse's pedigree and announcing its standing for mares for the upcoming season. Jackson was listed as a horse trainer in the 1870 census two households from Temple.
91 Ibid, 27 April 1861.
92 At this time, F.P.F. Temple offered notes bearing heavy interest for sale at fifty cents on the dollar "and found few takers." William A. Spalding, comp., *History and Reminiscences: Los Angeles City and County California* (3 vols., Los Angeles: J.R. Finnell and Sons Publishing Company, n.d. [1931]), I: p. 166.

was compelled to kill some two thousand head to save their hides. The cattle were driven into a large corral from day to day and were shot. John H. Temple recalls seeing cattle go up to a cactus patch so weak that they could scarcely walk and in attempting to get something to eat would literally cover their heads and mouth with cacti. It was one of his greatest ambitions to follow his grandfather through the corral and see him bring his bullock down. He [Workman] was considered one of the best shots in the West, and proved it many a day, though he was sixty-three years of age.[93]

Although John H. Temple was but seven or eight years old while watching his grandfather perform as, archetypically, "one of the best shots in the West," his recollection reveals the desperate measures taken during those gloomy years of the drought.

Despite this remembrance, it appears that Workman and John Rowland did not suffer the type of attrition that many of their peers did. According to an account written by Joseph Pleasants, foreman of William Wolfskill's Rancho Lomas de Santiago in present Orange County, Wolfskill invited Workman and Rowland in January 1864 to join him in removing their cattle to the Mojave River area north of the San Bernardino Mountains. With Pleasants guiding the Wolfskill herds and Rowland's son, William, in charge of the La Puente animals, a total of 5,000 cattle and 1,000 horses left for the long journey to the fringes of the high desert. By March the drive had reached the desired pasturage, despite traveling in cold mountain weather through the Cajon Pass. Although rain finally fell in the Los Angeles area in November, Pleasants and Rowland did not return to their respective ranchos until May 1865, after over a year away. According to Pleasants' account, Wolfskill, Workman and Rowland only lost a quarter of their stock, considerably less than other ranchers.[94]

Like most historians writing of the period, McGroarty wrote that the drought "practically put an end to cattle raising in southern California."[95] While cattle raising was no longer the primary economic activity in south-

---

93 McGroarty, *Los Angeles: From the Mountains to the Sea*, p. 923.
94 Joseph E. Pleasants, "Ranging on the Mojave River in 1864," *Touring Topics*, 22 (March 1930): 42, quoted in Iris Higbie Wilson, *William Wolfskill, 1798–1866: Frontier Trapper to California Ranchero* (Glendale: The Arthur H. Clark Company, 1965), pp. 203–204.
95 McGroarty, *Los Angeles: From the Mountains to the Sea*, p. 923.

ern California, some ranchers recovered and replaced their decimated herds, a fact not typically noted by the region's chroniclers. According to accounts in the *Star* in 1868 and 1870, William Workman, for example, kept his herds at numbers that were as high as those before the drought.[96]

WORKMAN HOUSE, CIRCA 1870
POSSIBLY **WILLIAM WORKMAN** STANDING ON FRONT STEPS
COURTESY OF THE HOMESTEAD MUSEUM, CITY OF INDUSTRY, CALIFORNIA

Nonetheless, by 1866, southern California was in the throes of a tumultuous economic transition. Many rancheros who subsisted on cattle for their livelihood found themselves bankrupted or, like Jonathan Temple, got out of the business. With the replacement of cattle ranching by agriculture as the backbone of southern California's economy, the prominence of local Californio traditions, so largely supported by the culture of the cattle ranch, also began to disappear. The rise of agriculture, post-Civil War immigration, bringing many farmers from the eastern states, increasing communications with the Eastern states and other factors, led to Los Angeles' first boom period, beginning in the late 1860s. Within a few years of the drought, the American

---

96 See accounts for 1868 and 1870 in Chapter Four.

and European population, for the first time, surpassed that of Californios and Mexicans. Some long-time ranchers, like F.P.F. Temple and William Workman, who had diversified themselves by engaging in agriculture and had built up substantial savings, survived the drought and continued to keep their enormous landholdings, still engaging in the long-standing traditions of the pastoral ranching culture. In the post-drought period, however, the two men also took to new paths in terms of economic pursuits. Younger and more in tune with developments in Los Angeles, Temple gravitated to the development of business in the city, becoming one of its biggest boosters. Although Workman remained one of the last of the old-style rancheros, keeping most of his immense share of La Puente until the mid-1870s and largely confining himself physically to his ranch as he reached his seventies, he allied himself with his son-in-law financially and legally—F.P.F. Temple was given his father-in-law's power of attorney by legal agreement in 1868 and had his trust.[97] Where F.P.F. Temple went, and he aimed high, so went his aging father-in-law, an anomaly in southern California's latest transformation.

---

97 Power of Attorney, William Workman to F.P.F. Temple, 29 May 1868, courtesy of Josette Temple. This was revoked in February 1876 and the aftermath of the failure of the bank of Temple and Workman when Workman assigned power of attorney to F. P. F.'s son, Francis. See footnote 22, p. 188.

CHAPTER FOUR

Southern California Transforms

∾ 1864–1876 ∾

The Preeminence of Agriculture

The end of the great drought of 1862–64 was followed by a period of in-creased immigration, partially spurred on by the end of the Civil War and composed significantly of migrants from the ravaged South. There was also an increasing awareness in the East of the value of California's salubrious cli-mate for health-seekers. Finally, there was a significant immigration from northern California as the decline in gold production led many residents of the North to seek their fortunes in the Los Angeles region. When these new arrivals reached southern California, land was available because the end of the Gold Rush, drought, and attendant economic stagnation, as well as the demands of pursuing claims under the California Land Claims Act, had led to the foreclosure, sale, and subdivision of many of the long-held ranchos. To meet the needs of the residents of a burgeoning Los Angeles, an increasingly sophisticated system of schools, transportation projects, fraternal clubs and community organizations and a growing business community, among other components, developed. With new growth, the economic keystone of the fu-ture was going to lie increasingly with the business of the city rather than in the traditional country pursuits of ranching and agriculture, but the latter con-stituted the major industry in the region for decades. From 1868 until 1876, Los Angeles and outlying areas experienced the first sustained development boom in its history. While miniscule compared to its antecedents, the town began to look increasingly like a city and the Temple and Workman families played a significant part as business leaders, while continuing pastoral and agricultural pursuits, in this first of many booms that have characterized the history of American-era Los Angeles.

While the boom continued, however, the social, as well as the economic, world in southern California shifted. The enumeration in the 1870 census revealed that, for the first time, those with Spanish-language surnames were outnumbered by Americans and Europeans.[1] Economic domination by the latter, through agriculture and the new, emerging sphere of urban business activity, was nearly complete. Moreover, the diminished herds of cattle on fewer and fewer ranchos led to a concomitant loss of much of the culture of the Californio, which was largely centered around the cattle economy and rancho society. The economic and political deprivation of Californios and Mexicans were essentially mutual and, by the 1870s, only a handful of them had any positions of power and high standing in the community, such as Antonio F. Coronel, who was state treasurer in the early 1870s, and respected jurist Ygnacio Sepulveda.

Another recent development concerned the newly arrived Chinese, many of whom were imported to build the region's new railroads. Just as poorer Californios and Mexicans tended to live in the increasingly declining Plaza area, the Chinese, who were more subject to segregation, settled in the same section. These changes in the physical landscape were not merely confined to the Plaza. Throughout the city, old adobes, seen as anachronisms and blights on the community, were razed to make way for new buildings, most of them built by Americans and Europeans, with some conspicuous exceptions by the few prominent Californios remaining. The last years of the sixties and first half of the seventies did indeed bring an unprecedented transformation to southern California in ways both beneficial and destructive.

An interesting rhetorical question, therefore, revolves around how the Workmans and Temples balanced the cultural perspective in their own mixed-heritage families. Of Nicolasa Urioste de Workman, for example, next to nothing is known-there are, it seems, no photographs extant of her, few descriptive comments have been passed down, and almost no family record so far known mentions her.[2] Concerning her daughter, Margarita Temple, there is more information available, but it is spotty at best, although this sad circumstance is the norm when it comes to the story of women, particularly *Latinas* in nineteenth century southern California. We do know that the children of Margarita and F.P.F. Temple, while given English-language names and

---

1 In 1870, 50.4% of Los Angeles residents were American or European, while 42.8% were Spanish-surnamed. Paul R. Spitzzeri, "What a Difference a Decade Makes," *The Branding Iron* (No.248), Winter 2007.

2 See Walter P. Temple to Francis W. Temple, 15 February 1888, Homestead Museum Research Archives, which refers to the 86-year old widow, saying, "Grandmother is as usual, still gets her weekly wine sometimes."

solidly American and British educations at such institutions as Santa Clara College, M. I. T., Harvard University, and the Inns of Court in London, did maintain strong ties to their Californio and Mexican culture that extended well into the twentieth century. Their father, however, was a Yankee, whose prominence in the emergent community was predicated on his connections with the now-dominant American and European economic and social class and his advancement of those interests.

There were members of the Workman family who did not share dual cultures and who, like F.P.F. Temple, operated firmly within the sphere of the new majority. William H. Workman and his brother, Elijah, were coming into prominence in these years, operating as partners a successful saddlery in Los Angeles for some fifteen years, each serving on the Board of Education and serving multiple terms on the city council throughout the 1870s. William H., who married Maria Elizabeth Boyle, daughter of prominent viticultrist Andrew Boyle, inherited, through his wife, his father-in-law's valuable bluff-top holdings across the Los Angeles River from the town after Boyle's death in early 1871. Although his earliest pursuits there were agricultural, he began, in 1875, what would be one of the most successful subdivisions in southern California, Boyle Heights.[3]

Meanwhile, Jonathan Temple and William Workman were aging patriarchs who represented the last of the old guard who had come to Mexican territory in the 1820s. Temple, in his final years, had moved from southern California. His daughter and son-in-law had fled to Paris after the overthrow of the French empire in Mexico and Gregorio de Ajuria fell ill, perhaps insane, dying there in 1861. His widow and children remained in Paris, and John and Rafaela Temple had an extended stay with them. When the two returned to California, they made their home in San Francisco. Having disposed of Rancho Los Cerritos and having his other enterprises in Los Angeles managed by an agent, Temple remained at his Bush Street residence until his death in May 1866. Afterwards, Rafaela Temple sold her husband's holdings in Los Angeles and moved to Paris, where she lived the rest of her life with her daughter. Among these transactions was the sale, in April 1867, of the Temple Block to F.P.F. Temple.[4]

---

3   Los Angeles *Herald*, 24 May 1875.
4   Rafaela Cota de Temple to F.P.F. Temple, Deed to Land in Los Angeles, 4 June 1867, Los Angeles County Archives, Book 8: 567–68. This document refers to an earlier agreement on 8 April for the sale of the Temple Block parcel between Court Street on the south, Spring Street on the west,

William Workman, in his late sixties, remained on his Rancho La Puente property and was increasingly isolated from the change that swirled around him. In 1868, shortly after receiving the federal patent to Rancho La Puente, Workman and John Rowland executed a formal partition of the ranch, each taking exactly 24, 395 acres with even amounts of valley (more valuable) and hill (less so) lands. He and Rowland were among the last of the few old large landholders and, with Rowland's death in the fall of 1873, Workman was truly an anomaly. Yet, he also showed an ability to stay in tune with trends and a willingness to modernize and innovate, making many more improvements to his ranch in the mid to late 1860s.[5] These showed that he was sprightly enough to continue supervising large-scale farming and stock raising operations at La Puente.[6] Except for the investments he had in Los Angeles through F.P.F. Temple, he was still living the pastoral life of the Californios. Indeed, though the drought of 1862–64 had decimated the cattle industry, Workman was one of the few ranch owners to still own large herds of cattle afterwards. In 1868 and 1870, the *Los Angeles Star* reported that Workman possessed several thousand animals.[7] Rare examples of documents detailing stock raising in the post-drought years include a letter from agent William Ramshay, written from Owens Lake in Inyo County in June 1870, to F.P.F. Temple, which details a trip to Salt Lake City to sell animals belonging to Temple and Workman, and a letter from Temple to his son, Francis, in the fall of 1873 that notes:

> Mr. Ramshay is still in Inyo County with our stock, he has had more trouble with them this season than usual on account of the very large number of sheep drove from the vallies [sic] on to his mountain range. I think it will be advisable

---

Main Street on the east, and the "Square" or open space on the north where Spring, Main, and Temple then intersected.

5   Workman did begin selling off portions of his rancho in the late 1860s. One such sale was made in December 1868 for 5,316 acres, William Workman to Peregrine Fitzhugh, *Deed to a Portion of the Rancho La Puente*, Los Angeles County Archives, Book 13: 497–498. It appears, though, that this sale was defaulted, as Fitzhugh wrote to Workman in August 1870 asking for a settlement on the purchase, Peregrine Fitzhugh to William Workman, 16 August 1870, courtesy of Josette Temple. Subsequently, in 1871, F.P.F. Temple took out an advertisement to sell the same 5,316 acres, Los Angeles *Star*, 20 December 1871. At Workman's death in May 1876, he held just over 17,500 of the original 24,395 acres, *Inventory and Appraisement of the Estate of William Workman*, 26 October 1876, Probate No. 781, Superior Court, Los Angeles County Archives.

6   Occasional problems with trespassers (see Chapter 3) continued to pester Workman and John Rowland, who took out an advertisement warning others from pasturing their animals on La Puente, Los Angeles *Star*, 20 March 1869.

7   Los Angeles Star, 6 June 1868 and Los Angeles Star, 29 January 1870

to drive them off or dispose of them in the spring, as I think Ramshay is getting tired out taking charge of them for such a length of time."[8]

In the meantime, there was a burgeoning sheep industry in the region and F.P.F. Temple used some of the land around the Workman Mill, recently deeded by William Workman to his daughter, to raise sheep and Cashmere goats.[9]

Even though Workman kept most of his holdings intact until 1876, the boom of the late 1860s and early 1870s led Benjamin C. Truman, editor of the Los Angeles Star and author of the booster narrative, Semi-Tropical California, published in 1874, to conclude that the rancho, "in time must become the seat of thriving communities," and that La Puente and its neighbors would become "human hives." Truman's prophecies concluded rather grandly with the prediction , "Farm houses and villas will dot the plains, and crown the beautiful rolling hills which surround them, and school houses and churches will take the places of huts of the herders and vaqueros."[10]

Regarding the improvements to the Workman ranch, the most significant was the extensive remodeling of the house. The U-shaped adobe, dating to at least 1856, with its intertwining of domestic and work spaces in one building, was transformed. The southward-extending 150-feet long adobe wings were razed, but the 1842 three-room core was retained, as were two later adobe rooms at the northeast and southeast corners. At each corner, brick rooms were added and a second floor, also of brick, was constructed. A significant change was the extent of the addition of exterior ornamentation. Stucco with Gothic quoins (or blocks carved to look like stone) on the corners of the new brick wings; large arched windows with Greek columns and capitals on the additions; posts, balusters and stair rails at the porches on both sides of the dwelling; Italianate brackets at the eaves of the roof; these, and more, brought a distinctive blending of architectural styles to the house that can only be described as "picturesque". In the interior, at least two marble fireplaces, designed to burn coal, were added, as was a substantial wood staircase,

---

8   William Ramshay to F.P.F. Temple, 22 June 1870 and F.P.F. Temple to Francis W. Temple, 25 November 1873, courtesy of Josette Temple.

9   Temple and Andrew Kittilson, a Norwegian native, signed a memorandum of agreement in February 1869 for the raising of goats. In the 1870 census, Kittilson is the householder enumerated after William Workman and his profession was given as "sheepherder." It is unknown how long the Temple/Kittilson arrangement lasted or how long Temple raised sheep and goats near the Workman Mill.

and presumably there were other significant changes, though later uses have left the interior dramatically altered.[10] The second floor remained unfinished until three bedrooms and a bathroom were added in the early 1940s, leading to speculation that the addition of the upstairs area might have been to make the house appear larger and more imposing. Although not documented, the remodeling has been traditionally assigned as the work of Ezra F. Kysor, the first trained architect to practice in Los Angeles. Kysor, listed only as a "laborer" in the 1870 census, designed the Pico House hotel (1870) as well as St. Vibiana's Cathedral (1876). In 1882, he designed the Boyle Heights home of Joseph Workman. Also uncertain is the completion date of the remodeling, though an October 1870 map of the southwestern portion of Workman's La Puente holdings contains an image of the reconfigured dwelling, suggesting it was completed by then. Moreover, correspondence from the spring of 1870 concerning picket fencing, which surrounded the house, may be indicative of a completion date, because it was unlikely that an enclosure would be added before the construction work was finished.[11] In any case, the "picturesque" Workman House, with the earlier Gothic Revival St. Nicholas Chapel in the family cemetery, must have presented quite a picture in the sparsely-populated, rural setting of Rancho La Puente in the early 1870s!

Other examples of improvements to the ranch were the Workman Mill, mentioned previously as constructed about 1865, and the construction of three large brick wineries, built at about the same time.[12] Workman had been engaged in viticulture since at least 1850, although he sold the grapes off the vine for several years, rather than engaging in the manufacture of wine. A history of the San Gabriel Valley, for example, notes that Workman's wine production in 1859 stood at 8,000 gallons, likely done by outside pressers.[13] In an October 1859 article, the *Star* mentioned that southern California's winemakers were engaging in pressing their product, including those "of the Puenta."[14] In 1860, Workman was listed in an industry addition to the federal census as

---

10 Surviving wood paneling in window and door openings and wainscoting may date from this remodeling, though some profiles indicate possibly earlier dates.

11 Blochman and Co. for Levi E. Smith to William Workman, 29 March 1870; Benjamin Dreyfus to William Workman, 7 April 1870, courtesy of Josette Temple.

12 Workman's grandson John H. Temple attributed the construction of the mill to 1865, "Some Side Lights on the History Puente Valley and Rancho La Puente," *La Puente Valley Daily Journal*, 5 July 1918. Courtesy of Josette Temple. At about the same time, tax assessment records show the production of wine, indicating the wineries were erected by 1865.

13 King, *The San Gabriel Valley: Chronicles of an Abundant Land*, p. 19.

14 Ernest P. Penniou and Sidney S. Greenleaf, *A Directory of California Wine Growers and Wine Makers in 1860* (Berkeley: Tamalpais Press, 1967), p. 29.

having fifty acres of improved vineyards and carrying 5,000 gallons of wine on-hand.[15] Two years later, the *Semi-Weekly Southern News* reported that Workman had made 6,000 gallons in 1861.[16] To illustrate the growing production of the Workman vineyards, another newspaper article, from 1868, of major wine producers in the southern California region listed Workman's output at 11,000 gallons per year.[17] Seven years later, it was noted that Workman's distillery was one of thirty in Los Angeles County and that the output of his vineyards combined, for some reason, with those of San Fernando, was 75,000 gallons during the previous year.[18]

The wineries were probably built about 1866 because tax assessment records before that date make no mention of wine-making supplies in Workman's list of property. Additionally, the previous year's California Agricultural Society noted "At Mr. Workman's...we found a very thrifty vineyard of about 10,000 vines, from which we obtained some remarkably fine bunches of the sweetest grapes we have anywhere tested in this, or indeed, in any other country." It is interesting to note that this high praise was followed with the notation that "these vines, however, were not so well pruned, nor so free from weeds as they should be."[19] Yet, no mention was made of whether Workman produced wine directly or what apparatus he possessed to do so. By contrast, in 1867, Workman was assessed for six fermenting tubs, forty-five wine pipes (or barrels), a still, 1,755 gallons of wine, and 694 gallons of brandy.[20] The wineries stood directly south of the house and two of them existed until the early 1970s.[21] Workman's grandson, John H. Temple, noted that he "built three large wine cellars, one used for a crushing and fermenting cellar, the other for white wine, and the third for red wine. These wines were sold all through the state, but the principal market was Boston, Massachusetts."[22] The Temples

---

15 Ibid..

16 Los Angeles *Semi-Weekly Southern News*, 12 February 1862.

17 Los Angeles *Star*, 14 November 1868.

18 Los Angeles *Herald*, 7 January 1875.

19 Report of the Visiting Committee, California State Agricultural Society, 1865, from a transcription by Thomas W. Temple II in the Homestead Museum Research Archives. The last documented statement regarding Workman's viticultural enterrpise was an inventory of his estate in January 1876 which showed he owned six pipes, or 6,700 gallons, of white wine, 102 empty wine pipes, and fourteen wine vats. Los Angeles *Herald*, 5 February 1876.

20 *Tax Assessments for 1867*, Seaver Center for Western History Research. Workman's 28 September 1866 license to manufacture wine for the 1866–67 tax year also survives in the possession of his great-great granddaughter, Josette Temple.

21 See Chapter Six for Workman's grandson Walter P. Temple's use of the wineries as an auditorium and dining hall.

22 McGroarty, *Los Angeles: From the Mountains to the Sea*, p. 923. There is no other known documentation regarding the market for Workman's wines.

were from Reading, not far from Boston, so those connections were possibly utilized for the trade. Another grandson, Francis W. Temple, was responsible for the management of the Workman vineyards and wine-making operation and continued the business when he assumed ownership of the homestead after Workman's death.

Aside from the vagaries of the weather, there were occasionally perceived threats from other sources. When the state government announced in 1869 "an onerous tax of dollars per diem" from wine growers and brandy distillers, an ad-hoc committee of Los Angeles-area viticulturists, with Workman as a vice-president, sent a petition of protest, claiming that federal law limited taxation according to the Internal Revenue Bill of 1868. The signers of the petition, including prominent southern California wine growers such as Phineas Banning, Benjamin D. Wilson, Leonard J. Rose, Matthew Keller, Henry Kohler, Jean Louis Sansevain, Edward Vache, J.J. Warner, and Workman's neighbor, Henry Dalton, claimed that the tax burden "would be so great an extent as to operate as a national calamity."[23]

In the aftermath of the drought of 1862–64, Workman expanded his other agricultural holdings so that according to John H. Temple, Workman had some 5,000 acres, known as the Wheatfield Ranch, under cultivation of that crop and a wheat ranch house constructed a few miles northeast of the homestead.[24] The 1865 California State Agricultural Society report, coming just at the end of the horrendous drought of 1862–64, gave the following description of Workman's small agricultural domain, "Mr. Workman has about 10 acres of Corn; 100 Peach; 40 Fig, 14 years old; 15 Pear; 3 Apricot; 30 Apple, grafted, and 40 Pomegranate trees." In describing the Workman House, the enthusiastic visitors noted that it was "a well-built adobe, cemented...", by cemented referring no doubt to the painted wall observed by the 1858 committee, and measuring 90 by 200 feet with an enclosed courtyard. This is the last known description of the original adobe, for within five years the house was to be dramatically remodeled. The committee concluded by calling the homes of William Workman and F.P.F. Temple, "the best built adobes we have seen in the State." Extolling the "beautiful flower garden, well protected by a good brick wall," various outbuildings, and the home itself, the committee

---

23 Los Angeles *News*, 30 March 1869; Los Angeles *Star*, 3 April 1869.
24 McGroarty, *Los Angeles: From the Mountains to the Sea*, p. 923. The ranch house appears on an 1868 map of the Rancho La Puente.

used the interesting metaphor of the Southern plantation in paying praise to Workman's domain.[25]

Speaking of the South, while the aforementioned agricultural products were generally common on the ranches and farms of southern California, Workman was among the few to experiment with cotton, likely because of the destruction of Southern cotton fields and the need of the Union for access to the crop. Harris Newmark offered this explanation for the experiment in his autobiography:

> In February [1863], the editor of the *News* advised the experiment of growing cotton...Whether this suggestion led William Workman into cotton culture, I do not know; at any rate, late in November of the same year F.P.F. Temple was exhibiting about town some well-matured balls of cotton raised on Workman's ranch...[26]

The *News* reported on the exhibition of the Workman cotton, adding that the trial, "proved so successful as to induce him to try the experiment on a larger scale the coming season."[27] Other cotton fields were started in El Monte and on other southern California farms. The industry was highly promoted by the *News* in 1864, which reported, at the end of the year, that French Consul Jean Morenhaut had "sent to France five samples of cotton cultivated in this county," including some grown by Workman and F.P.F. Temple.[28] Still, the crop did not find an adequate market and did not become much more than a novelty.

Contemporary reports indicate, though, that Workman had more than enough success with established crops. In the spring of 1868, after a season of heavy rain, the Los Angeles *Star* reported that Workman, John Rowland, and Rowland's son-in-law, John Reed, had sown a record amount of grain crops on La Puente.[29] A week later Workman exhibited a staggering 125 stalks of barley grown from a single seed, attesting, in addition to copious water supply,

25 *Report of the Visiting Committee*, California State Agricultural Society, 1865. Typescript copy in Homestead Museum Archives.
26 Newmark, *Sixty Years in Southern California*, p. 317.
27 Los Angeles *Semi-Weekly Southern News*, 20 November 1863.
28 Ibid., 17 December 1864. See also 17 February and 20 April 1864.
29 Los Angeles *Star*, 16 May 1868.

to the great fertility of the soil on the rancho.[30] The prosperity continued the next year as it was reported, "Mr. Workman's mill is running on his last year's crop, turning out plenty of good flour. He has four or five thousand quintals [a quintal being one hundred kilograms] yet to make up."[31] Despite a rather severe drought in 1870, it was reported, "Mr. Workman's mill at the Puente is the only one in the vicinity making flour, and it is kept constantly running to the height of its capacity."[32] Finally, as late as March 1875, the remarkable state of volunteer crops in La Puente's fertile fields was reported in the *Express,* including the note that "Mr. Workman, of the Puente Ranch, informed us that a barley field of three hundred acres sowed by him has yielded four crops, three of them volunteer, and that the last crop was the heaviest of the four."[33]

With yields such as these, Workman was able to expand his agricultural enterprise beyond the sale of raw products. By 1868, he constructed a mill three miles west of his home, close to the conjunction of the San Jose Creek and the San Gabriel River at the base of the Puente Hills. Until then, he undoubtedly had used the mill of his partner, John Rowland, built considerably earlier, or after about 1860, that of his son-in-law, F.P.F. Temple.[34] Although Workman deeded the land around the mill to his daughter in 1868, he maintained the building and kept the proceeds.[35]

One of the superintendents of the mill, perhaps the only one, was William Turner, whose wife, Rebecca, wrote her memoirs in 1929, which were published some thirty years later. Turner had experience in the business, as his father, John, was the operator of the Eagle Flouring Mill in Los Angeles for many years. Although it is not known when Turner began runnng the mill, it would seem to be about 1868. His wife, Rebecca, recalled that the two were engaged about two years after he assumed the position and they were married in May 1871. Workman, meanwhile, gave the couple the use of a house at the site. Mrs. Turner also described the arrangements Workman and her husband had made, noting that "Mr. Workman told my husband he would pay

---

30 Ibid., 23 May 1868.
31 Ibid., 23 June 1869.
32 Ibid., 29 January 1870.
33 Los Angeles *Express*, 18 March 1875.
34 The Los Angeles *Star*, 21 October 1871, notes that the Rowland mill was the oldest in Los Angeles County, built in 1847, although this, undoubtedly meant the oldest private mill, since the El Molino Viejo of the Mission San Gabriel dates much earlier. Mention is made in the article of Workman's mill and that the San Jose Creek furnished the water power for the two.
35 William Workman to Antonia Margarita Workman de Temple, *Deed to the La Puente Mill Property,* 5 March 1868, Book 9: 323–324, Los Angeles County Archives. The deed refers to "the Mill of William Workman lately built."

him thirty dollars a month to run the mill, and he could have in addition, all the money taken in from those who paid cash to have their corn ground." As an artifact describing from a female perspective, rural ranching life far from the growing city of Los Angeles, Mrs. Turner's memoirs are a rare window into that world:

> If I had not been so completely happy [with her marriage] I might have felt the lack of neighbors, for we were alone—absolutely alone. True, the Workman ranch was only three miles away, but it was hidden by a fold of the hills. As far as one could see, in every direction, not a house, not a barn, no vineyards nor orchards; the road, little traveled, running east and west was the only sign, the only indication, that people ever passed that way.

In the summer of 1871, Workman's dam on San Jose Creek burst, and for "several months" the mill was shut down because it operated from a ditch filled by the dam's runoff. Although the dam was repaired and the mill re-opened, the end of the year brought Workman's refusal to pay Turner for the period that the mill was shuttered, and he noted that the mill did not make a profit, although he did offer the Turners the house and any cash that came in from the mill. The next day, Frederick Lambourn, the tutor of the private school in the Workman home and then manager of Workman's ranch, visited the Turners. Lambourn, who left Workman's employ in 1875 to serve in the State Assembly, made a proposal to the Turners about opening a general store at the mill with him. An old supply house was refurbished and the store opened, probably in early 1872. The store, which catered largely to a Californio and Mexican clientele, operated profitably, but in June 1874 a robber nearly killed the Turners, slashing William with a knife and shooting the pregnant Rebecca in the upper back, leading to her miscarriage. The case was a notorious one because the alleged attacker, Jesus Romo, was lynched by Lambourn, El Monte merchant Jacob Schlessinger, and Walter Drown, son of the late Ezra Drown, former Los Angeles District Attorney, who after being orphaned by his father's death had William Workman as his legal guardian and F.P.F.

Temple as his mentor.[36] The Los Angeles newspapers devoted considerable space to the aftermath of the hanging and the tensions between Pío Pico and other Californios, Mexicans and Americans and Europeans who defended the execution of Romo, if not the principle of lynching.[37] The Turners did not stay in La Puente much longer. In June 1875, William Turner and William Workman dissolved their partnership with the former moving to El Monte where he ran a store with a partner. In later years, Turner and Lambourn operated a highly successful wholesale grocery business in Los Angeles.[38]

Workman's interest in improving the ranch extended to the public roads that passed through his immense domains, as evidenced from a surviving letter from Los Angeles County Supervisor M. F. Quinn, from 1870. In the missive, Quinn detailed how the rerouting of the old "Colorado" road, then known as the "La Puente and San Jose Road," now Valley Boulevard, reflected, as Quinn wrote, "the conditions you consented to have the road to pass through your Land." Moreover, it appears that Workman proposed "planting trees on both sides of the road and also of the building of a fence on both sides of the road." With these improvements, Quinn enthused, "this Avenue would be an ornament to this County. Yes! Even to this state." One of the conditions was the closing of what was then called "the Mud Spring road," Mud Spring being a stage stop in what is now San Dimas. Notably, Quinn reported that, although the other supervisors were initially opposed to closing this thoroughfare, which seems to have crossed the "La Puente and San Jose Road" and run northeastward toward Mud Spring, a little explanation as to the "conditions" imposed by Workman led the board to reconsider and "they all agreed that you might close the Mud Spring road."[39]

Workman's burgeoning agricultural enterprise also led him to search for ways to facilitate the shipment of his products from the ranch to ocean-

---

36   A statement of property in the guardianship of William Workman for Joseph Walter Drown, 4 November 1865, is in the possession of Josette Temple. Drown resided on the Workman Homestead, owned by Workman's grandson, Francis W. Temple, in the 1880 census. By 1885, he was a foreman for Workman's nephew, future Los Angeles mayor and treasurer, William Henry Workman, in Boyle Heights. In 1890, he was a boiler foreman for the Los Angeles Cable Railway Company in Boyle Heights. Drown died in 1899 at age 47.

37   Rebecca Turner, *My Story* (Los Angeles: Typecraft, Inc., 1960) pp. 119–67; Los Angeles *Star* and Los Angeles *Herald*, 4–12 June 1874. For more on the Romo lynching, see Paul R. Spitzzeri, "The Last Lynching in Los Angeles County: The Incident at Workman Mill", *Brand Book* 22 (Los Angeles: Los Angeles Corral of The Westerners, 2003,) 61–84; and Paul R. Spitzzeri, "Judge Lynch in Session: Popular Justice in Los Angeles, 1850–1875," *Southern California Quarterly*, Volume 87, Number 2 (Summer 2005) , 111–113

38   Los Angeles *Herald*, 2 June 1875.

39   M. F. Quinn to William Workman, 8 June 1870. Courtesy of Josette Temple.

bound vessels for transport. In the late 1860s, some enterprising residents of Anaheim developed a small wharf near the opening of the New San Gabriel River, which, due to flooding in 1867–68, diverted course from the old route (now the Rio Hondo) which emptied into the Los Angeles River, to a new one that overtook the course of Coyote Creek in Orange County and emptied into the Pacific Ocean. This new facility, called Anaheim Landing (now Seal Beach), sought to compete with the near monopoly exercised by Phineas Banning at his Wilmington location to the west and attracted the attention of Workman, who invested in the enterprise. As an economic downturn hit by the end of the decade, however, Workman seems to have toyed with backing out of his support for the nascent wharf. An extant letter from August Langenberger, one the proprietors, to Workman opened with the admonition that "I must state that for the present I could not buy your shares as times are so very hard." Calling for patience, Langenberger assured Workman that "I honestly think that in one year from now, we are out of debt, if we have no Banning & Co. to freeze us out." He begged that "a few hundred dollars is a small object to you and I hope that you will not help our enemy to put a wedge in our body for the sake of this small sum." Seeking to appeal to Workman's pride, Langenberger noted "If it had not been for you and Don Juan Forster our Lighter Co. would not exist anymore, of which we all live in happy remembrance, and therefore hope you will not sell to Banning & Co."[40]

Meanwhile, on another portion of La Puente was William Workman's son Joseph, who returned from the San Joaquin Valley where he had lived since 1856 as superintendent of the Tejon rancho holdings of his father and brother-in-law.[41] In San Francisco in January 1870, Joseph, at thirty-nine, married nineteen-year-old Josephine Belt of Stockton. The newlyweds received some 800 acres of land on the western edge of La Puente to live on, property that was later in the year willed to Joseph and his future children by William Workman.[42] Building a house a few miles northwest of his father's, the younger Workman raised sheep, farmed and raised a family with his wife, and he ap-

---

40 August Langenberger to William Workman, 8 March 1870. Courtesy of Josette Temple. Established in 1864, the landing continued to operate into the 1880s, but it is not known if Workman divested himself from his investment in 1870 or later.
41 *An Illustrated History of Los Angeles County*, p. 683.
42 The elder Workman, however, did not release the deed to his son until late March 1873, evidently, according to court testimony in 1922, because Joseph lived somewhat of a dissolute life as a young man and was not trusted by his father. Upon receiving the deed, Joseph raced into Los Angeles to have it recorded before his father changed his mind, claiming to have set a speed record from La Puente in the process!

peared to have little involvement outside the sphere of his ranch, aside from agricultural organizations, such as heading the sheep and wool contingent of the Farmers' Club of the San Gabriel Valley in the mid-1870s.[43]

Although on a far smaller scale than that of his father-in-law, F.P.F Temple's ranching activities at La Merced also remained thriving and productive, as seen from this quite complimentary description of the property by the California Agricultural Society in 1865:

> His ranch contains 2300 acres mostly grazing hill land. 250 acres are capable of cultivation, but 80 acres only are at present well cultivated. The houses, fences, out-buildings and general arrangements of the place indicate more thrift and energy than is common, as yet, even among the more wealthy inhabitants of the lower country.

> He has in orchard 200 Peach, 50 Olive, 50 Fig, 20 Pear, 15 Apple, and 50 Apricot trees, all two years old. Has also 5 acres of Melons, Pumpkins, &c...His 20 Acres of Corn is also very fine.

Similar to Workman's cotton experimentation, Temple's farm included some novelties for the area including, "about 1/8 of an acre of Tobacco, which was planted much too close, but which nevertheless appeared very well" and "a better article of sugar-cane than we have elsewhere seen. It covers about 3/4 of an acre, is of a thrifty growth, and praises well. It is said to be a superior article, granulating well, and making an excellent quality of white sugar." It is worth noting that on this visit of September 1, 1865, Temple was recorded as having 1000 head of cattle, "[t]hese latter had been driven out of the valley to feed [recall the drive to the Mojave River area for grass mentioned in Chapter Three], Los Angeles county being this year so affected by the drought as to force the sale or removal of almost all the cattle."[44] His farming and ranching activities, although overshadowed by his business activities, continued to be diverse and

---

43 Joseph and Josephine Workman had six surviving children: Mary (b. 1870); Agnes (b. 1872); Lucille (b. 1874); William (b. 1876), George (b. 1879), and Josephine (b. 1882). An infant, Nellie, died in 1888. All but the youngest two were born in La Puente. Josephine and Nellie were born in Boyle Heights. See Los Angeles *Star*, 28 March 1873 for the Farmers Club notice.
44 *Report of the Visiting Committee*, California State Agricultural Society, 1865.

successful. As late as the summer of 1875, his twelve-acre hop field was cited for its productivity and was used as an encouragement for others to plant the crop.[45] Temple continued his interest in purebred horses and kept a half-dozen mares in Alameda County to breed animals for his ranch at La Merced.[46] He also was quite active in agriculturally related organizations, including service as a trustee of the Los Angeles Wine Growers Association (1868), a commissioner of the Southern District Agricultural Association (1870), and treasurer of the Farmers' Club of the San Gabriel Valley (1873).[47]

During this period of successful crop cultivation and ranching, the Temples made more improvements to their ranch including, by the early 1870s, the addition of a two-story brick house next to the adobe they had been living in for some twenty years. While ranching certainly provided the family a prosperity that few others in southern California could match, F.P.F. Temple turned his attentions increasingly to the city.

F.P.F. Temple: City-Maker

F.P.F Temple was best known for the development of his Los Angeles business interests, and he was one of southern California's wealthiest citizens in the post-Civil War period. In 1869, he was second to Abel Stearns in the amount of taxes paid in Los Angeles County, based on assessments of property.[48] Three years later, after the death of Stearns, Temple had the county's highest tax assessment, at over $150,000.[49] In 1875, a chart listing the "Solid Men" of Los Angeles County showed that Temple was worth $1.5 million, a half-million more than his nearest peers, John Downey and William Workman.[50]

Regarding Temple's involvement in the emerging business arena in Los Angeles, historian Remi Nadeau's term, "City Maker," used in his work on the boom of the late 1860s and early 1870s, applies well. Unfortunately, Temple's place as an early booster of so many new business activities, such as oil, rail-

---

45 Los Angeles *Herald*, 14 and 17 August and 17 October 1875.
46 Los Angeles *Express*, 13 March 1875.
47 John A. Wilson, ed., *Thompson and West's History of Los Angeles County, 1880* (Reprint ed., Berkeley: Howell-North, 1959), p. 66; Los Angeles *Star*, 12 October 1870, 5 November 1870, 28 March 1873.
48 Los Angeles *News*, 15 December 1869.
49 Los Angeles *Star*, 9 August 1872. In 1877, the year after the collapse of his financial fortune, Temple's tax assessment, at over $204,000, was still the highest in Los Angeles County, ibid., 15 April 1877. In both 1872 and 1877, William Workman ranked eighth in assessments.
50 Los Angeles *Express*, 27 March 1875.

F.P.F. TEMPLE, CIRCA 1875
COURTESY OF THE HOMESTEAD MUSEUM,
CITY OF INDUSTRY, CALIFORNIA

roads, and especially, banking has been overshadowed by the spectacular collapse of his Temple and Workman bank in early 1876. Banking, of course,
was a necessary prerequisite for any serious entertainment of business expansion in southern California. The Temple and Workman bank, created in 1871
from a rift between Temple and Isaias Hellman in their Hellman, Temple, and
Company banking house opened in 1868, was the base from which Temple
and his managing cashier, Henry S. Ledyard embarked on a remarkable run
of business projects (William Workman was a silent partner, investing his
money in the business but having no involvement in its management). The
headlong embrace of the mania for development that characterizes any boom
period, and Los Angeles has essentially been one extended sequence of booms

after another, can both propel the successful speculator to dizzying heights of wealth and influence or send an overextended capitalist into irreparable ruin. As a rancher-cum-nouveau capitalist, Temple overreached in his developmental schemes and his failure remains one of the most significant events in southern California in the quarter-century after American occupation and statehood. In Los Angeles' emergent transformation from a Mexican pueblo, to a remote town, to a nascent city, F.P.F. Temple and William Workman by association, symbolize the passing of the old order, though they tried to keep pace with new developments. Still, the efforts were varied and intense with a signal impetus for Temple's foray into capitalism traced to the 1867 purchase of his recently deceased brother's valuable Temple Block from his sister-in-law.[51] From this central vantage point in the new center of Los Angeles, Temple's activities radiated throughout southern California. His spectacular financial crash prevented him from joining John Downey, Isaias W. Hellman, Elias J. "Lucky" Baldwin, and Harris Newmark among the business elite in the region.

Another early development was in April 1867, a month after the Temple Block transaction, when Temple and Fielding W. Gibson of El Monte, who purchased 4,000 acres of the Rancho San Pedro two years before from the Dominguez family, decided to create a subdivision as Jonathan Temple had contemplated doing in 1849.[52] Like so many Californio cattle rancheros in the post-drought period, the Dominguez' were pinched financially and forced to sell this parcel for a mere seventy-five cents an acre. Situated along the Los Angeles River and the important road between Los Angeles and the harbor at San Pedro, the property was subdivided by the two as Gibsonville and placed for sale in the summer. Along with a few predecessors, including El Monte, Anaheim and San Bernardino, the new subdivision was a precursor to later tracts that sprung up throughout the region. Three years after its creation, a large portion of the subdivision was purchased by newcomer George D. Compton, and a town bearing his name was developed by him and others,

---

51 Rafaela Cota de Temple to F.P.F. Temple, *Deed to the Property of Jonathan Temple*, 4 June 1867, Book 8: 567–568, Los Angeles County Archives. This deed was an outgrowth of an agreement between the two, dated 8 April 1867. F.P.F. Temple's copy, dated 9 April 1867, is in the possession of Josette Temple. Actually, Jonathan Temple had taken out an advertisement in March 1866, two months before his death, offering what seemed to be all of his downtown property—presumably there weren't any buyers for those portions F.P.F. Temple obtained. See Los Angeles *Semi-Weekly News*, 23 March 1866.
52 Los Angeles *Semi-Weekly News*, 26 April and 11 June 1867.

replacing Gibsonville. Compton was one of the first successful subdivisions outside of Los Angeles and Pacific Railroad in the post-Civil War period.

It was another seven years before Temple again delved into a major real estate subdivision project, but by 1874–75, Los Angeles was deep in the throes of the boom. In the midst of other new communities, such as Artesia and Pomona, which arose at this time, Temple joined forces with other prominent southern Californians in two projects. The first, Centinela, was created from two ranchos in the area, now known as Inglewood, Westchester, and Baldwin Hills. The Centinela Land and Water Company, incorporated in late November 1874 with Temple as President, included as officers Daniel Freeman and Jonathan S. Slauson, whose names continue to be a presence in the area. The subdivision, modeled after a successful project in Lompoc in Santa Barbara County, proved to be especially ambitious. Temple and his associates planned to construct the Los Angeles and Pacific railroad from the city to the salt works located where Ballona Creek emptied into the ocean and where the syndicate intended to build a wharf for commercial shipping. Land sales were held in the spring of 1875 and were heavily promoted and covered in the Los Angeles press. Shortly afterward, in May 1875, Temple formed a partnership with Benjamin D. Wilson and Wilson's son-in-law, John DeBarth Shorb to form the Lake Vineyard Land and Water Company, with Temple as treasurer. Their subdivision, Lake Vineyard, was on a very desirable portion of Wilson's property that now encompasses today's Alhambra and San Marino.[53] The company's first project was a water transport system from the San Gabriel Mountains down the Arroyo Seco to the site. Sales for the subdivision were first held in December 1875. In addition to these two enterprises, there was some mention in 1875 that Temple was ready to subdivide his holdings at La Merced and the surrounding ranchos and add to the rapidly growing numbers

53 Los Angeles *Star*, 8 May 1874, 2 December 1874, 17 December 1875; Los Angeles *Herald*, 2, 5, 8, and 10 December 1874, 1 January 1875; Los Angeles *Express*, 2, 8, and 14 December 1874. The Centinela Land Company was incorporated on 21 November 1874 and Temple was elected president of the organization. See Thomas A. Sanchez, *et. al.* to F.P.F. Temple *et. al.*, *Deed to the Rancho Centinela o Paso de la Tijera*, 3 March 1875, Book 36: 161, Los Angeles County Archives and *Certificate of Incorporation of the Centinela Land Company of Los Angeles*, No. 105, 21 November 1874, Seaver Center for Western History Research. Temple was the treasurer of the Lake Vineyard Land and Water Association, formed in May 1875, Los Angeles *Star*, 8 and 27 May 1875; Los Angeles *Herald*, 15 May 1875; F.P.F. Temple to Lake Vineyard Land and Water Association, *Deed to Interest in Lake Vineyard*, 11 December 1875, Book 41: 216, Los Angeles County Archives; *Articles of Incorporation of the Lake Vineyard Land and Water Association*, No. 120, 7 May 1875, Seaver Center for Western History Research.

TEMPLE BLOCK, CIRCA 1877

COURTESY OF THE HOMESTEAD MUSEUM, CITY OF INDUSTRY, CALIFORNIA

of townsites emerging in southern California.[54] The fate of these projects, as with many others that Temple was party to, hinged upon the fortunes of the Temple and Workman bank, which will be discussed later in this chapter.

In the downtown section of Los Angeles, with his brother's holdings as a base, Temple expanded his ownership of property and erected many buildings noteworthy for the time. The first addition to the Temple Block, started by his brother, Jonathan, in 1857, was a two-story structure on Main Street in 1868 that housed Harris Newmark and Company's warehouse and the headquarters of Masonic Lodge No. 33, of which Temple was an officer.[55] Two years later,

---

54 Los Angeles *Herald*, 1 January 1875.
55 Temple and William Workman were active masons, holding membership in three different lodges: No. 42, a Free and Associated lodge, which was the first in southern California; No. 33, a Royal Arch lodge in Los Angeles, and No. 104, a Free and Associated lodge in Lexington, now part of El Monte. Temple frequently served as an officer in these lodges, holding the title of Master at the Lexington lodge in 1869–70. He was involved in several other fraternal and social clubs, including the Coeur de Lion Commandery of the Knights Templar, of which he was a founder in 1869; the Knights of Pythias, which he helped initiate in 1874; and the Cosmopolian Club, changed later to Union Club, which began in the spring of 1875 in a building constructed by Temple and of which he was a founder and treasurer. Los Angeles *Star*, 25 July 1868, 7 November 1868, 8 April 1875 and 6 May 1875; Wilson, *Thompson and West's History of Los Angeles County, California, 1880,*

he built a three-story addition that contained the city post office.[56] The final installment, and the centerpiece of Temple's downtown projects, was another three-story edifice, erected in 1871, that housed the Temple and Workman bank. The building was one of the city's landmarks until razed in 1925 for Los Angeles' current city hall.[57] James J. Ayres, former owner and editor of the Los Angeles *Express* newspaper provided a fine, detailed account of what he called "the great beehive of commercial and professional activity in the middle seventies," describing the many businesses housed in the four buildings of the Temple Block.[58] In the surrounding area on Spring and Main streets, Temple erected other structures, including, in 1872, a business building on the west side of Spring Street, and by early 1875, another large two-story building on that street that became the new post office and meeting rooms for the Union Club, a newly-formed social club of which Temple was treasurer.[59] There were other major building proposals in the works for 1875, including an elaborately designed theatre with a seating capacity for 1,800 persons and a large building for printing offices.[60] Events of the following months, discussed later, precluded the realization of these projects.

A likely link between Temple's real estate holdings and his burgeoning development of downtown Los Angeles property with business buildings is represented in his significant investment in San Joaquin Valley ranch land throughout the 1860s. Starting in 1860 and continuing throughout the decade, Temple acquired, from individuals and through public land purchases from the state, over 8,000 acres of land in present northwestern Fresno County and southwestern Madera County, lying along the San Joaquin River. By decade's end, however, Temple sold off these holdings, mainly to the state's preeminent cattle barons, Miller and Lux. It may well be that these sales were used to finance his projects in downtown, which began in earnest in 1869.[61]

The scope of F.P.F Temple's corporate activities, especially in the boom years of the first half of the 1870s, is rather staggering, considering that Los

---

pp. 121, 124; *Historical Review of the Los Angeles Lodge No. 42, F & A.M.* (Los Angeles: Los Angeles Lodge 42, F & A.M., 1929), pp. 55, 81–83; *Centennial History of Lexington Lodge No. 104, F & A.M.* (El Monte: Lexington Lodge 104, F & A.M., 1955), pp. 67–68.

56 Los Angeles *Star*, 12 March and 7 May 1870.

57 Los Angeles *Star*, 24 March and 24 September 1871.

58 Spalding, *History and Reminiscences*, pp. 198–202

59 Los Angeles *Star*, 11 January 1872, 6 August and 13 October 1874; 3 May 1875.

60 Los Angeles *Herald*, 26 February and 22 July 1875.

61 Listings of these transactions are found on the website of the federal General Land Office and in the appendices of a California Water Resources Board document.

Angeles was still a small, emerging city. We are able to trace his capitalistic activities, however, as early as 1858, when he purchased an interest in the Los Angeles Water Works.[62] However, it was after 1867, the year that he obtained his brother's downtown property and established the townsite that became Compton, that his presence in the early corporate development of Los Angeles was made most manifest. In that year he was a partner with James Allen in a castor oil mill. Then, in 1868 he became part-owner of the Los Angeles Woolen Mills and President of the Los Angeles Homestead and Building Association, the latter a partnership including architect Edward J. Weston, who designed some of Temple's subsequent buildings.[63] In 1870, Temple was a founding trustee of the Los Angeles City Gas Works.[64]

In the heat of the rush to speculate and profit during the peak boom years of 1872 through 1875, Temple's membership in a wide array of companies formed a fascinating and varied portfolio. They included several corporations that dealt in insurance, a new concept in southern California. He was a director of the State Investment Insurance Company, Vice-President of the Los Angeles branch of the Life Association of America, housed in the Temple and Workman bank, and a trustee, with his bank serving as treasurer, of the local branch of the Home Mutual Insurance Company.[65] The Temple and Workman bank was also the depository for the local branch of the Trust Fund Insurance Association of the Pacific Mutual Life Insurance Company.[66] Among the more interesting of the organizations Temple belonged to was the Forest Grove Association, of which he was treasurer. This corporation, founded in 1874, planted and sold eucalyptus trees on the Rancho San Antonio, southeast of Los Angeles.[67] In recognition of the need for improved health conditions in the Southland, the Southern California Sanitary Hotel and Industrial College Association was founded in 1873 with Temple as its treasruer.[68] As

62 Los Angeles *Star*, 25 December 1858.
63 Ibid., 26 November 1867, 27 March 1868, and 5 May 1868; *Los Angeles News*, 6 March and 27 March 1868; Wilson, *Thompson and West's History of Los Angeles County, 1880*, p. 70; F.P.F. Temple to John Rowland, 31 July 1868, MS, Huntington Library; *Certificate of Incorporation of the Los Angeles Woolen Mill Company*, No. 108, 10 December 1874, Seaver Center for Western History Research.
64 Los Angeles *Star*, 23 July 1870.
65 Los Angeles *Herald*, 10 May 1874; Los Angeles *Star*, 8 May 1872, 22 December 1874.
66 Los Angeles *Herald*, 15 July 1875.
67 *Articles of Incorporation of the Forest Grove Company*, No. 102, 16 November 1874, Seaver Center for Western History Research; Los Angeles *Herald*, 22 November 1874; Los Angeles *Express*, 28 November 1874.
68 Los Angeles *Star*, 13 May 1873.

part of an effort to improve the port at San Pedro, Temple, along with such local luminaries as Phineas Banning, Benjamin D. Wilson and Leonard J. Rose, was a founding director of the Southern California Cooperative Warehouse and Shipping Association, which constructed a wharf and supply warehouses there.[69] He was the president of the Board of Stock Brokers, organized to buy and sell real estate and conduct a general brokerage and commission business.[70] The Los Angeles Cooperative and Fruit Nursery Company, whose leading officials Thomas Garey, Luther Holt, Milton Thomas, and Robert Town, were the founders of the townsites of Artesia and Pomona, enlisted Temple as its treasurer.[71] Temple also owned and operated a saw mill and lumber hauling operation at San Jacinto, near present-day Idyllwild, and owned and operated a mill in San Antonio Canyon, above today's Claremont and Upland.[72] Finally, he joined future mayor Prudent Beaudry, Thomas Garey, Jotham Bixby and others in forming the Los Angeles City and County Printing and Publishing Company, which took over the management of the Los Angeles *Herald* newspaper in early 1874.[73] It was the *Herald*, ironically, which was an avid booster for the kind of speculative projects listed above and, yet, was the most vigilant of the city's papers on reporting on the collapse of the Temple and Workman bank, a failure brought about by that very speculation. By then, Temple had divested himself of his ownership in the paper and, according to the *Herald*, had become a major financier of its rival, the *Express*.[74] During Temple's campaign for county treasurer in 1875, the Independent Party, for whom he was a candidate, ran a small sheet aptly titled the *Independent*. It is possible that Temple was the major financial backer for this topical paper.[75]

---

69 *Articles of Incorporation of The Southern California Cooperative Warehouse and Shipping Association*, No. 82, 12 January 1874, Seaver Center for Western History Research; Los Angeles *Express*, 6 January 1874; Los Angeles *Herald*, 7 January 1874 and 1 January 1875.
70 Los Angeles *Star*, 4 and 11 June 1875.
71 Ibid., 19 June 1875.
72 Ibid., 11 September 1875; Los Angeles *Herald*, 18 May 1876. The *Star* noted that the mill, which was steam powered, processed sugar pine, fir, and oak and that the lumber was hauled eleven miles to San Gorgonio Pass and to the new Southern Pacific terminus at Colton, where it was brought to Los Angeles; John W. Robinson, "San Antonio Canyon Before 1880", pp. 178–180, *Pomona Valley Historian*, IX (Fall 1973) cites an article from the 23 July 1881 issue of the Los Angeles *Herald*, in which one "J.A.G." noted that a wagon road in the canyon was "built by the late F.P.F. Temple, who constructed a sawmill 10 or 12 miles from the canyon mouth."
73 *Articles of Incorporation of the Los Angeles City and County Printing and Publishing Company*, No. 86, 16 February 1874, Seaver Center for Western History Research; Los Angeles *Herald*, 1 and 7 March 1874; Los Angeles *Express*, 6 March 1874.
74 Los Angeles *Herald*, 24 August 1875.
75 Ibid., 26 and 27 August 1875.

Aside from all of the above interests, it was in oil, railroads, and banking that Temple was most active. With the subsequent history of oil in the region well-known and documented, little has been mentioned about Temple's role as a pioneer in southern California's fledgling oil industry. In July 1873, he was an incorporator of the Los Angeles Petroleum Refining Company.[76] This organization was formed to develop oil on property owned by Temple in the Newhall area and, in June 1874, the equipment was delivered there to begin work on the well.[77] A month later, Temple was elected treasurer of another concern, the Lesina Oil Company.[78] In August 1874, oil was struck eighty feet down at the Temple claim with an output of a rather paltry three to four barrels a day.[79] In January 1875, however, the Los Angeles *Star* reported that the Temple well was producing forty to one hundred barrels of oil per day, an indication that matters were improving greatly, although little was subsequently mentioned in the press about the claim.[80] Also in 1874, Temple was a founder of the Citizens Gas, Light and Oil Refinery, a concern formed to bring locally produced and refined crude to the local market, reducing the costly dependence on imported products.[81] Finally, in the summer of 1875, he was an officer of two companies that, like so many of that period, were largely financed by San Francisco capitalists. One was the Los Angeles Boring Company, of which Temple was treasurer and which had a well at San Fernando that reached nearly 200 feet in the summer of 1875, but like others, yielded nothing.[82]

The other company was the Los Angeles Gas Company, which had been in operation for several years and had been owned by Perry, Woodworth, and Company. Both of these companies were controlled by Charles Simpkins, who had experience operating gas works in northern California towns.[83] Temple's involvement in gas and oil enterprises ceased in the economic crisis that overwhelmed his bank in late 1875, and a simple epitaph to his oil interests was recorded in the 21 December 1875 issue of the *Herald* which noted, "We hear

76 *Articles of Incorporation of the Los Angeles Petroleum Refining Company*, No. 76, 24 July 1873, Seaver Center for Western History Research; Los Angeles *Star*, 16 July 1873 and 3 June 1874; Los Angeles *Herald*, 7 October 1873; Los Angeles *Express*, 29 January 1874.
77 Los Angeles *Star*, 2 June 1874.
78 *Articles of Incorporation of the Lesina Oil Company*, No. 94, 2 July 1874, Seaver Center for Western History Research; Los Angeles *Express*, 25 July 1874.
79 Los Angeles *Express*, 3 August 1874.
80 Los Angeles *Star*, 7 January 1875.
81 Ibid., 29 January 1874.
82 Los Angeles *Herald*, 2 July and 12 August 1875.
83 Ibid., 3 July 1875.

that the machinery is being moved from the Temple oil well."[84] Although the petroleum craze yielded some useful product for Los Angeles' homes and businesses, it was not until the Star Oil Company's successful well at Pico Canyon in 1876 and, still later, the activity of the 1880s and 1890s that the oil industry began to be a serious presence among southern California's capitalistic enterprises. Forty years after F.P.F. Temple's forays in the oil business, his son, Walter, revived the family's fortunes in oil development through his repurchase of land on the La Merced property once owned by his father and the subsequent discovery of the Montebello oil field there.

It is, of course, water that has always been southern California's most precious natural resource, and Temple was among the first to launch a full-scale water development project that had its source in Los Angeles. In the summer of 1873, he and some associates, most prominently his bank's managing cashier Henry S. Ledyard, formed the Cerro Gordo Water and Mining Company, an Inyo County venture financed by depositors of the Temple and Workman bank.[85] The plan was to build a water pipeline from Miller Springs to the silver mines of Cerro Gordo, an area initially developed by Remi Nadeau, owner of a mule-team transport system from the silver mines at Cerro Gordo and Panamint to Los Angeles.[86] These mines were a major source of profit to Los Angeles and transporting water eleven miles from the springs to the mines was an ambitious project. In May 1874, the first shipments of water from Miller Springs poured into the mines at Cerro Gordo, seemingly a spectacular success for Temple, his associates and the bank.[87] Unfortunately, in the spring of 1875, the springs unexpectedly dried up and the demise of the enterprise proved to be costly, especially in light of subsequent events in that pivotal year.

There were other mining interests pursued by F.P.F. Temple, including such areas as the Piru mining district near today's Santa Clarita, Catalina Island and an antimony mine near his Rancho San Emigdio at the southern extremity of the San Joaquin Valley. The Catalina and San Emigdio interests were with Stephen Boushey, and the latter also included architect Edward J. Weston, who designed some of Temple's early Los Angeles structures. After

---

84 Ibid., 21 December 1875.
85 Seven stock certificates for the Cerro Gordo Water and Mining Company belonging to William Workman, along with four Temple and Workman bank checks to pay for the stock subscription, are in Workman's papers, owned by Josette Temple.
86 Los Angeles *Star*, 22 and 25 June 1873.
87 Ibid., 14 May 1874.

Temple left the San Emigdio project, Boushey and Weston with new associates successfully shipped some ore to San Francisco.[88]

Transportation was especially crucial to development in Los Angeles, a city isolated, hemmed in by mountains and deserts, without a navigable river, lacking immediate access to a true harbor, and without a railroad until 1869. Temple's role in improving the transportation resources of southern California, though largely forgotten, is yet notable. An early transportation project was a cooperative venture in 1867 with William Rubottom, who had just settled on land on the Rancho San Jose purchased from rancher Louis Phillips, and opened a hotel and tavern in the new community he named Spadra, now in present-day Pomona. Rubottom and Temple teamed up to open a cut-off road from Los Angeles to San Bernardino. This route passed from the Los Angeles River to Temple's place at La Merced, across the San Gabriel River into La Puente at William Workman's mill and through Workman's portion of the rancho until it passed Rubottom's inn at Spadra and reconnected not far east of that with the main road to San Bernardino.[89] With regard to what we now call "urban transit," Temple, as treasurer, joined in 1874 with Robert M. Widney and others in the formation of the Spring and Sixth Street Railway Company. Although consisting of modest cars pulled on a single-gauge track by a lone horse, the railway was functional and proved the viability of street railways, which proliferated in the city in the 1880s.[90]

It was to railroads that southern California looked as the key to unlocking the barriers that prevented the city from significant growth. Prefiguring later developments, Temple was one of several Los Angeles businessmen who met in late 1864 to discuss the possibility of constructing a railroad line from the city to San Pedro.[91] In the summer of 1868, Temple, William Workman

88 See Boyd, *A California Middle Border*, p. 39; Los Angeles Star, 7 November 1872; Los Angeles Times, 21 April 1886; General Land Office records, Patent Lands, F.P.F. Temple, Stephen Boushey, and E. J. Weston, for thirty-eight acres in Kern County antimony mines, Documents 583-586, 27 June 1873 from www.glorecords.blm.gov.; Stephen Boushey to William Workman and F.P.F. Temple, Five-Twelfths of Little Hill Mining Claim, Santa Catalina Island, 17 June 1868; Albert B. Hayward to F.P.F. Temple, Half-interest in fifty feet of Little Hill Mining Claim, Santa Catalina Island, 5 February 1869, courtesy of Josette Temple

89 Los Angeles *Semi-Weekly News*, 26 September 1867.

90 *Articles of Incorporation of the Spring and Sixth Street Railroad Company*, No. 83, 6 February 1874, Seaver Center for Western History; Los Angeles *Star*, 7 and 19 February 1874; Los Angeles *Express*, 10 February 1874 and 13 January 1875; Los Angeles *Herald*, 10 February and 10 June 1874. The Spring and Sixth reincorporated in the summer of 1875 to extend the line north from the Arroyo Seco to the Plaza and then either to Figueroa Street or the depot of the Los Angeles and Independence Railroad on San Pedro Street. Los Angeles *Herald*, 15 July 1875.

91 Los Angeles *Tri-Weekly News*, 3 December 1864.

and others commissioned an engineer to examine the possibility of building a railroad terminus at Dead Man's Island. This was likely in anticipation of the construction of the Los Angeles and San Pedro line, the area's first railroad, led by such local notables as Phineas Banning, John Downey, and Benjamin D. Wilson.[92]

Still, the larger goal in the minds of Los Angeles' leading citizens was a line to link the city with San Francisco and the eastern states. In 1870 Temple, participating in an informal meeting at Downey's Los Angeles office, began making an important contribution in helping to secure the Southern Pacific Railroad line from San Francisco through the city, after that company announced their intention to build a track to San Diego.[93] In November 1871, three days before the Workman and Temple bank opened, a convention was held in Anaheim to organize southern Californians for the task of wooing Southern Pacific. Temple was one of only a handful of members to receive three votes in the electoral process attesting to his position of respect among his contemporaries. He was elected to serve on the Committee of Resolutions, which drafted a statement of what was decided in the session.[94]

The next major meeting was held the following May at which William Workman was a participant. The discussion by then expanded to whether the city should negotiate with the Southern Pacific or the fledgling 35th Parallel Railroad, soon called the Texas and Pacific Railroad. Temple was appointed to serve on a Committee of Thirty people that mapped out objectives towards these negotiations.[95] A week later, still another committee, this time of nine persons, including Temple, was created to begin direct contact with both of the companies under consideration.[96] In late July the Committee of Thirty appointed Temple, lawyer Henry O'Melveny, and Harris Newmark to draft a resolution for presentation to the Los Angeles County Board of Supervisors asking the board to put a bond issue on the ballot for the November general election.[97] Working for two days, the three men prepared a resolution that was submitted to the committee. The resolution made some extraordinary concessions to the Southern Pacific, which publicly contemplated bypassing Los Angeles by running the line through San Bernardino, a ploy intended to

---

92 Los Angeles *Star*, 4 July 1868.
93 Los Angeles *News*, 21 January 1870.
94 Los Angeles *Star*, 20 November 1871.
95 Ibid., 20 May 1872.
96 Ibid. 27 May 1872.
97 Ibid., 23 July 1872.

maximize the railroad giant's negotiating power with a city eager for access to an outside rail line.

Among these concessions was an offer to give the Southern Pacific $150,000 worth of stock and, essentially, the controlling interest in the Los Angeles and San Pedro Railroad, as well as $300,000 in cash. Additionally, the county was to pay for the fifty miles of track heading north from Los Angeles through the Grapevine to the border with Kern County. In return, the Southern Pacific would build the line coming from San Francisco to the Kern County line, construct a line east to the Colorado River through Temple and Workman's San Gabriel Valley ranchos, and another from Florence, south of Los Angeles, to Anaheim from the Los Angeles and San Pedro's track.[98] It was an agreement that railroad supporters argued was the only way to get the railroad line to Los Angeles, end the city's isolation, and propel it further in its development, even if it meant acquiescing to the demands of the Southern Pacific.

In early August the Board of Supervisors approved the motion to put the bond issue to a vote at the November election, but added a twist to the process by allowing another new competitor, the San Diego and Los Angeles Railroad, to compete for the bonds with the Southern Pacific.[99] Astounded, the stoutest supporters of the Southern Pacific agreement, with Temple among them, protested vehemently and rushed to make an arrangement with the Southern Pacific in selecting a depot site in Los Angeles, which was finalized in late October at First and Alameda streets. Temple was once more centrally involved in these developments.[100]

The election in early November resulted in the passage of the bond issue giving the "subsidy" to the Southern Pacific. After nearly a year of hard work, Temple and his colleagues succeeded in their efforts to secure the line. Over the course of the next year, the SP finalized the purchase of right of ways throughout southern California, including in late 1873 and early 1874, those areas through Temple's Rancho La Merced and Workman's Rancho La Puente. Construction of the eastern line through La Puente, where a depot was built not far from the Workman and Rowland homesteads, was completed in April, 1874 before terminating first at Spadra and then, in 1875, at Redlands. A rare

---

98 Ibid., 25 July 1872.
99 Ibid., 7 August and 3 October 1872.
100 Ibid., 15 and 30 October 1872.

example of a contemporary reference to the building of the railroad line comes in a November 1873 letter from F.P.F. to his son Francis:

> The rail road is progressing rapidly the San Fernando and Nietos branches are nearly completed, and most of the forces are now on the eastern branch leading from town through the Mission San Gabriel, Monte, Puente, and San José, twenty nine miles will be built in this direction, the road will pass near your grandfather's fence, the station will probably be nearly opposite the old adobe walls, which will be very convenient for the Puente people, there is two steam pile drivers at work in the San Gabriel river bed, they will probably have the bridge completed in two or three weeks, so that trains can pass to San Jose about the first of Jany.[101]

The all-important line from San Francisco was completed in September of 1876, but by then, Workman was dead and Temple was not able to savor the moment he had been so instrumental in arranging.

Having played such an important part in the movement to bring the Southern Pacific to southern California, Temple then became a competitor to the Big Four by serving as a major promoter in three locally based railroad projects. The largest was the Los Angeles and Independence Railroad, founded in early 1874 with Temple as president, after a bill was passed in the Assembly and signed by the governor granting Los Angeles the right to the Cajon Pass for a rail line to the prosperous silver mines of Cerro Gordo in Inyo County, where Temple's water project was busily at work.[102] The second effort, never realized, was the aforementioned Los Angeles and Pacific Railroad, incorporated later in the year, with Temple again as president, as part of the Centinela land subdivision.[103] The third was a road known as the

---

101 F.P.F. Temple to Francis W. Temple, 25 November 1873, courtesy of Josette Temple. The reference to the "old adobe walls" may be about the Mission San Gabriel granary ruins which were just north of the Workman House.

102 Ibid., 19 April 1874. The three Los Angeles newspapers, the *Star*, the *Herald*, and the *Express* gave extensive coverage to the Los Angeles and Independence, which was seen as the means to giving Los Angeles the freedom to control its own trade, independent of the powerful Southern Pacific. See also Paul R. Spitzzeri, "The Road to Independence: The Los Angeles and Independence Railroad and the Conception of a City," *Southern California Quarterly*, 83:1 (Spring 2001): 23–58.

103 *Certificate of Incorporation of the Los Angeles and Pacific Railroad Company*, No. 107, 9 December 1874, Seaver Center for Western History Research; Los Angeles *Herald*, 9 December 1874.

Los Angeles and Truxton, the latter a proposed townsite on the coast west of Los Angeles.[104] This latter company, however, was sublimated into the Los Angeles and Independence, which struggled to raise the ardor and financial support of southern Californians until the obtainment of support and capital of Senator John P. Jones of Nevada, who was developing a seaside resort called Santa Monica, where Truxton had initially been.[105] Jones entered the project in return for a line, to be built first, from his fledgling town to Los Angeles. Temple, who stepped down from the presidency in favor of Jones, became treasurer, oversaw the fundraising, and went with Jones in early 1875 to solicit support from San Francisco capitalists who promised to put forward $300,000 if southern Californians would match the offer.[106] After months of traveling through the region, Temple and others obtained the amount needed and construction began in earnest. This project was not without its controversy. The railroad intended to run its line through the ranches of Temple and Workman on its way to Cajon Pass and build a depot outside Los Angeles city boundaries.[107] Both the route and the depot location did not sit well with many in the community, including Temple's friend, Mayor Prudent Beaudry, who vetoed a common council ordinance establishing the San Pedro Street site.[108] Then, after the suspension of the Temple and Workman bank in late August 1875, Senator Jones, who suffered losses in the San Francisco panic that affected the bank, was said to have wanted to sell out his interest. Though he did not, he did turn over the management of the railroad to another San Franciscan, J.P. Jackson.[109] In mid-October a nineteen-minute test run of the line was made from the Cienega station in today's west Los Angeles to the wharf at Santa Monica.[110] Work on the line to the San Pedro Street station was completed on 27 November and the trains began to run two days later.[111] By the end of the year, meetings were held to try and convince Angelenos to support a

104 Los Angeles *Herald*, 21 May 1874.
105 *Articles of Incorporation of the Los Angeles and Independence Railroad Company*, No. 109, 2 January 1875, Seaver Center for Western History Research; Los Angeles *Star*, 7 January 1875.
106 Los Angeles *Star*, 6 January 1875. Both F.P.F. and Thomas W. Temple owned lots in Santa Monica, no doubt through their association with Jones, see Los Angeles *Star*, 17 February 1879 for their names on a list of delinquent taxpayers showing their holdings in the resort town.
107 Los Angeles *Herald*, 24 July 7, 12, 23, and 25 September 10 October 30 November 1875. The depot was originally planned for a Figueroa Street location and was eventually built on San Pedro Street, south of the city's center.
108 Ibid., 25 September 1875.
109 Ibid., 7 and 12 September 1875.
110 Ibid., 19 October 1875.
111 Ibid., 27 and 30 November and 1 December 1875.

subsidy for the continuance of the line to Utah for the connection with the Union Pacific. This, however, evoked reminders of the controversial Southern Pacific subsidy of 1872 and was hotly disputed.[112] But, further talk of a direct transcontinental link were made moot by other events involving the demise of the Temple and Workman bank and the related financial downturn that lasted until the 1880s, when revived talk of the link to the east led to its fruition later in the decade. In the meantime, the Southern Pacific acquired the Los Angeles and Independence line in 1878 and continued much of the plans of the latter concern, especially in completing the Cajon Pass line.

In something of a complement to his avid pursuit of business interests, Temple continued seeking political office, running for County Supervisor in 1871 and County Treasurer in 1873 and 1875. He lost the first two campaigns, with the 1873 Treasurer's race pitting Temple, as an Independent, against incumbent Democrat Thomas Rowan of Farmers and Merchants Bank.[113] One of the main issues in this campaign, which contained the usual invectives in the newspapers, was Temple's status as owner of a bank and how this might conflict with holding the treasurer's office, notwithstanding Rowan's association with banking, albeit as but a cashier in Farmers and Merchants Bank. Occasional discussions of this issue appeared, including a communication from an unnamed reader who expressed, "You cannot vote for Mr. Temple as Treasurer without at the same time giving him the power to use the public moneys in his business" and that, "these funds are a means of strength to his bank, of multiplication to his resources, and are necessarily used in his business."[114] Responding to such opinions, Temple, in a "Card To The People Of Los Angeles County," published in the Los Angeles *Star*, answered, "My object and intent in seeking the office, is not to secure the use of the public moneys for the banking institution with which I am connected." Appealing to his sense of standing in the community, he continued, "And, if the public, with their knowledge of me, extending through over thirty years of what I hope and have considered has been an honorable connection with the business interests of the county, now have confidence in the integrity of my word, I hereby pledge myself to obey, in every particular, the law of the land." He then quoted from the state political code against the use of public moneys

---

112 Ibid., 17, 22, and 29 December 1875.
113 F.P.F.'s son, Thomas, had announced his intention to run for the seat, but yielded to his father. Los Angeles *Star*, 11 March and 14 June 1873.
114 Ibid., 13 August 1873.

for private interests. Temple concluded by stating that the public "may elect to prevent that the banking institution—with which I have so long had the honor of sharing the public patronage—shall not monopolize this evidence of the public trust."[115]

The *Star*, for one, was highly supportive of Temple, so much so that its endorsements rang with rather ostentatious terms of praise. For example, Temple was said to have "never offended a human being" and to have "done much to succor and encourage the poor farmer and struggling mechanic." Further, it was claimed, "No living man can say aught of him socially, morally or politically," and "there has never been in Los Angeles county a man placed before its people so overwhelmingly in popular favor."[116] By contrast, Rowan, although recognized as a good man, was "merely the figurehead of a gigantic political organization [said to be headed by Rowan's employer at the Farmers and Merchants Bank, Isaias Hellman, Temple's rival banker] that is sucking from the body politic its very heart's blood."[117] Perhaps the most interesting endorsement of Temple came from El Monte farmer William B. Lee, who stated, "The noble deeds of charity of which he has been the doer will live long after the buildings (he erected) have crumbled to dust. Our children's children will reverence the name of Temple." After relating that Temple and William Workman assisted many emigrants to the El Monte area without recompense, Lee called Temple "the poor man's friend," and as if to make the most persuasive point of all, noted that "last, but not least, he was never known to hire a Chinaman." This is an interesting statement, especially in light of Temple's railroad activities in 1875, when large numbers of Chinese were hired to lay track for the Los Angeles and Independence.[118] Despite this, the result of the elections was a narrow victory for Rowan who had 1,859 votes to Temple's 1,726.[119]

The 1875 election featured a rematch between Temple, again running as an Indepedent, and Rowan. While the campaign repeated many of the same aspects of the earlier campaign, the repositioning of the press is notable. By 1875, the *Star* had a new owner and editor and, consequently, was nearly mute

---

115 Ibid., 26 June 1873.
116 Ibid., 31 July and 13 August 1873.
117 Ibid., 2 September 1873.
118 Ibid., 21 August 1873. Lee's enthusiasm may have largely stemmed from the assistance William Workman gave in helping to sell Lee's property to raise funds for his defense in an 1854 murder charge. Lee was found guilty and sentenced to hang, but his conviction was overturned by the State Supreme Court. Workman's papers relating to the property sale are in the collection of Josette Temple.
119 Ibid., 5 September 1873.

in its coverage of Temple's candidacy. This was more than made up for by the fact that the *Express* took on a highly vocal advocacy of Temple's candidacy, sounding much like the *Star* of two years before. Early in its coverage, the paper called Temple "modest, public-spirited, generous, and alive to the rights of the humblest—a millionaire who has no more thought of arrogance than the man who carries his hod."[120] Subsequent issues continued along the same lines in promoting Temple's campaign, which was also benefitted by a short-run sheet called the *Daily Independent*, formed to push the Independent Party's candidates. The opposition's viewpoint, as expressed by the *Herald*, is interesting to contemplate and was also underscored by the economic panic that gripped Los Angeles, due to the suspension of the Bank of California, just a few days before the election. The fact that the *Herald* was a vociferous opponent of Temple is ironic, given his part-ownership of the paper in 1874 and its previously enthusiastic support of Temple's Los Angeles and Independence Railroad project. Here again, a change of ownership and Temple's probable financial investment in the rival *Express* were the reasons. The *Herald* curtly dismissed the views of its rival by claiming that its competitor "is published at the expense of F.P.F. Temple and John P. Jones," and stating that it "covers Mr. Temple with the most fulsome and nauseating adulation."[121] Meanwhile, the *Independent* was described as a "one mule power concern," followed by a downgrading to "one donkey power" and as "Mr. Temple's special organ."[122] The *Herald* also offered the interesting opinion that the Independent party was "willing to sacrifice the entire ticket" for Temple and another candidate because Temple "is rich and they can therefore assess him heavily for money to carry on the Republican Presidential campaign of next year."[123] Echoes of 1873 were also heard in such statements as, "We heard an Independent remark yesterday that Mr. Temple wanted the treasurer's office for the money he could make out of the county funds. We presume this is true..."[124]

Even as the banking houses of Temple and Workman and Farmers and Merchants banks suspended business on the eve of the election, Temple narrowly defeated Rowan, who still cashiered at Farmers and Merchants, by a tally of 2,648 to 2,365.[125] In the resulting demise of his bank, however, Temple

120 Los Angeles *Express*, 5 August 1875.
121 Los Angeles *Herald*, 24 August 1875.
122 Ibid., 27 August 1875; Los Angeles *Daily Independent*, 17 August 1875.
123 Ibid., 24 August 1875.
124 Ibid., 29 August 1875.
125 Los Angeles *Express*, 7 September 1875.

refused calls and successively fought lawsuits that sought his resignation and served his office, albeit through a deputy, from 1876 to 1878. Certainly, his administration was unique in southern California's political history: a bankrupted financier sitting as county treasurer!

Temple and Workman: Bankers

Ultimately, the demise of the Temple and Workman bank is F.P.F. Temple's legacy in southern California history. As a long-time rancher trying to be a capitalist in the heightened atmosphere of a boom, Temple exemplified the transition underway in southern California during the period. Unlike I.W. Hellman, his former partner, and E.J. "Lucky" Baldwin, who took over most of Temple's princely holdings, the "modest, public-spirited, generous" banker lacked the experience and prudence of the former and the ruthlessness and savvy of the latter. Investing his full confidence, financial backing, and power of attorney with his son-in-law, William Workman followed F.P.F. Temple to failure.

Initally, though, Temple and Workman made the right choice in linking their fortunes (literally and figuratively) with Isaias W. Hellman as Los Angeles was introduced to the concept of banking. The genesis of the industry dates to February 1868, when John Downey, unable to induce southern California investors to join him, formed a partnership with twenty-two-year-old San Franciscan James A. Hayward and opened southern California's first banking house, Hayward and Company.[126] The institution was short-lived, lasting until the summer of 1870, and was soon followed by a second institution, formed by the collaboration of Temple, Workman and Hellman. The Los Angeles *Star* ran this announcement in early June 1868:

> We understand that Messrs. Wm. Workman, F.P.F. Temple and Isaiah [sic] W. Hellman have associated for the purpose for carrying on a banking business in this city. They are having a building erected adjoining the Bella Union Hotel for their accomodation. Mr. Hellman, we suppose, will be the business manager, under whom the affairs of the establish-

---

126 Hayward was the son of a wealthy mine operator from northern California and namesake of the northern California city of Hayward.

ment will no doubt be most ably conducted. It is expected to be in operation about the first of next month. The firm name will be Hellman, Temple, & Co.[127]

Hellman, a native of Bavaria, emigrated to Los Angeles in 1859 and, after working in his cousin's store, purchased a mercantile business at Main and Commercial Streets in 1865. His success may be measured by the fact that within three years he had doubled the size of the business and established himself as an avid buyer of real estate. In time, he also set up an informal banking establishment in his store with a safe kept in the building.[128] How Hellman and Temple decided to work together is probably based on the former's banking services."

The partners were an interesting combination. Temple and Workman represented the long-standing, stable, propertied and moneyed class of the community, whose ample cash resources were to supply most of the start-up money, $50,000 each, for the new institution. Hellman, who put $25,000 of his money in the institution, exemplified the new type of American-era businessman in Los Angeles. He was an American-era arrival and an exemplar of the new business class in the city. Hellman's establishment was far more sophisticated, for example, than Jonathan Temple's store had been a generation before, although he sold his store to devote himself to making the bank a success. With Hellman's expertise and community respect as a hard-working and adept man of business, and with Workman and Temple's positions among the established elite in southern California, the partnership seemed to be an ideal one for creating a powerful banking institution in the emerging city. Hellman was managing cashier, assisted by James Toberman, a future mayor of Los Angeles, and Thomas Rowan, who in addition to being county treasurer, as noted above, was city treasurer from 1868 to 1870, and was mayor in the 1890s.[129]

---

127 Los Angeles *Star*, 6 June 1868.
128 Robert G. Cleland and Frank Putnam, *Isaias W. Hellman and the Farmers and Merchants Bank* (San Marino: The Huntington Library, 1965), pp. 9–13. Among the surviving William Workman papers is a letter and receipt from Hellman, dated 25 December 1866, concerning a note from Pío Pico to Workman and money drawn on Hellman and a 23 June 1866 cancelled note, in which Workman borrowed $2,000 from the merchant. These examples of Hellman's informal banking are courtesy of Josette Temple.
129 Ibid., pp. 15–16.

The bankers intended to make quite an impression with their facility. The partners signed a lease to house their institution in a smart, new brick building erected by Temple and Workman's friend, Pío Pico, and designed by early Los Angeles architect Edward J. Weston. The edifice stood on the east side of Main Street adjacent to the landmark Bella Union Hotel. Its location near the triple intersection of Main, Spring, and Temple Streets was part of the movement of the center of town away from the Plaza and, ironically, Pico's hotel, completed two years later.[130]

The bank did not open at the beginning of July as originally envisioned, and despite its first advertisement that it would open at the beginning of September it was not until the 8th that, "[T]he banking house of Messrs. Hellman, Temple, & Co., was thrown open for public accomodation. On the occasion, the managing partner, I.W. Hellman, Esq., issued invitations to a large number of citizens, who met in the bank parlor and quaffed generous wine, to the prosperity of the new banking institution."

In a sign that the city was ready to push for more development and an indication of the yearning some citizens had to make Los Angeles a "real city" like San Francisco, the *Star* exclaimed, "The building erected for the accomodation of the bank marks a new era in our architectural designs—or rather, it is the first building erected here with any regard to elegance...and is highly creditable to the architect and proprietors."[131]

The first day's accounts showed some $38,000 in deposits made, nearly a third of that by Temple alone. Well-known denizens of Los Angeles like Pico, Diego Sepulveda, Manuel Coronel, Henry D. Barrows, William Workman's nephew, William Henry, and Workman's tutor and foreman, Frederick Lambourn, were listed as inaugural depositors as well.

From the figures for deposits and loans during the bank's history, it would appear that the bank was doing well. At year's end in 1868, the bank had $94,000 in deposits and had loaned $149,000. Deposits increased from $117,000 in 1869 to $141,000 in 1870, while loans rose from $209,000 to $258,000 in the same period. In all, some 1,400 loans amounting to over one million dollars were made during the two and a half years the bank existed. Yet, it was the issue of loaning policy that was one of the main causes of the bank's disintegration within two and a half years. A work on Hellman's bank-

---

130 This is now the site of the Hollywood Freeway.
131 Los Angeles *Star*, 12 September 1868.

ing career simply noted that Hellman and Temple had basic philosophical differences on how to run a bank and make loans, noting, "Workman [who may be excluded from any real involvement in the institution] and Temple held the naive heresy that the bank should lend to anyone in need." Hellman, not surprisingly, "believed that loans should be made only to those who gave satisfactory evidence of an ability and willingness to repay."[132]

Whether it was only this question that caused the rift or whether there were other more sensitive issues at hand, it was the matter of loan policy given above that led to Hellman's offer, at the end of January 1871, to buy out Temple and Workman for $58,000 in cash and promissory notes totaling $84,000. Temple and Workman, in exchange for the compensation provided, yielded all interest in the bank's affairs to Hellman.[133] Perhaps Temple's ideas were too liberal, and certainly the later careers of the two principals proved Hellman to be correct. This telling statement, attributed to Hellman, and possibly apocryphal, has been related in several histories of southern California: "Mr. Temple's only qualification in a borrower was that he must be poor. I saw that doing a banking business on that basis would soon leave me poor also, so I dissolved the partnership."[134] Still, it appears that the breakup of the concern was not conducted too acrimoniously, as is suggested in a letter Hellman wrote to Temple the day the bank was dissolved, "As a matter of convenience to us both and to aid you in your designs as to future buildings in this city I propose to anticipate the payment of two of the promissory notes which I gave to you & Mr. Workman as part consideration for the purchase of your interests in the partnership assets of the late firm of Hellman, Temple & Co."[135]

Hellman did not wait long to form another bank. Two weeks after the closure of Hellman, Temple, and Company, Hellman, John Downey (whose Hayward and Company bank was absorbed in the new institution), and more than twenty other men formed Farmers and Merchants Bank, which thrived as one of the most stable and conservative banking institutions in southern California and which was guided by Hellman's firm hand until his death in 1920.

---

132 Cleland and Putnam, *Isaias W. Hellman and the Farmers and Merchants Bank*, 18.
133 *Agreement on the Dissolution of Hellman, Temple, and Company* and *Memoranda Regarding Promissory Notes in the Dissolution of Hellman, Temple, and Company*, 31 January 1871. Copies provided courtesy of Charles and Margaret Coker.
134 Quoted in Remi Nadeau, *City Makers* (Corona Del Mar: Trans-Anglo Books, 1965), p. 38.
135 Isaias W. Hellman to F.P.F. Temple, 31 January 1871. Copy provided courtesy of Charles and Margaret Coker.

Undaunted, F.P.F. Temple continued in his aim to be a successful banker and to participate in the continuing development in southern California. Convincing his seventy-one-year-old father-in-law to move on with him, the two announced the formation of their own private bank, simply known as Temple and Workman, to join Farmers and Merchants as the only banks in town. Given his increasing involvement in other projects, however, Temple, although holding the office of president, probably had little to do with much of the day-to-day management of the bank which fell to managing cashier, Henry S. Ledyard. Arthur Bullock and F.P.F.'s son and protege, Thomas W. Temple, were also cashiers for the institution.[136]

The earliest announcement for the new enterprise was on 24 March 1871, seven weeks after Hellman, Temple, and Company closed. In September a lengthy description appeared of the new three-story building Temple was building at the triple intersection of Main, Spring, and Temple streets to house the bank. After delays, the bank opened on 23 November with the *Star* noting that the debut occurred "under the most favorable auspices" due to the Temple Block's central location and imposing appearance and the fact that "the two proprietors rank among our oldest, very best, and wealthiest citizens." At the opening ceremonies, competitor Downey (Hellman was conspicuously absent) toasted the new enterprise by magnanimously stating, "There is plenty of room for two Banks in Los Angeles—and indeed two seem necessary in order to accomodate the public and meet the requirements demanded...there should never be anything between the two Banks, but a generous and gentlemanly rivalry." Among the well-wishers were men of prominence like Harris Newmark, Pío Pico, Phineas Banning, Henry D. Barrows, David Alexander, and Prudent Beaudry.[137]

The opening of Temple and Workman's bank was probably the pinnacle of F.P.F. Temple's career. Unfortunately, the bank's records have not survived and very little direct evidence is available on the day-to-day activities of the

---

136 Thomas Temple was clearly groomed to succeed his father in banking and other business enterprises. Known to friends as "Lord Chesterfield" because his manners were as elegant as those espoused by the eighteenth-century master of British manners and etiquette, Thomas first entered the Los Angeles business world as a partner in the J.D. Hicks iron works in 1868. After joining the Temple and Workman bank, he built an impressive home on Third Street near Main Street in Los Angeles, was a member of social clubs and fraternal organizations, such as the Los Angeles Social Club and Masonic Lodge and was a founding trustee, in 1872, of the Los Angeles Public Library, serving as treasurer for a time, and ending his tenure as trustee in 1877.
137 Los Angeles *Star*, 24 November 1871. A description of the bank's quarters, by J.J. Ayers, is in Spalding's *History and Reminiscences*, p. 199.

institution, except for information that was later made public through the press during its assignment in 1876 and the occasional mention in newspapers previously.[138] One of the few available pieces of information came in the New Year's Day 1875 issue of the *Herald*, which, calling the institution "one of the most substantial banks on the coast", noted that "deposits for the year [1874] have averaged $125,000 daily—$38,750,000 for the year." By contrast, rival Farmers and Merchants was said to have taken in $30 million in deposits during 1874.[139] In early 1875, the bank was selected to be the depository for the funds of the city of Los Angeles, which had previously kept funds at city hall, but was attracted by an offer of 13% interest put forth by the institution. Curiously, city treasurer James J. Mellus delayed in transferring the funds, which the Los Angeles *Herald* decried because, "Messrs. Temple & Workman stand ready to fulfill their contract with the city." Just a month later, however, after Mellus had deposited the funds, the *Herald* claimed , "it is generally understood...that they [the bank] are using it, they have never paid a cent of interest and do not intend to." Given that these remarks were made in a heated election mood, in which the *Herald* was a strong opponent of Temple, it is questionable as to whether the paper's assertion is true.[140]

Aside from these isolated reported examples of the bank's operation, there is no question that the institution was intended to be a booster for the city's increasing growth. With the paucity of available information about the enterprise, it can only be assumed that the many business projects of F.P.F. Temple involved the use of the bank's funds. Contemporary and later accounts almost universally mention Temple's liberality, charity, and, as a corollary, his naivete in regard to financial matters. One example of this, which was given a fair amount of attention in the local press, occurred in the fall of 1874. The account was that a poor family from Oregon entered the town in a rickety wagon. According to the *Star* the family "was jokingly referred to Mr. F.P.F. Temple, of "The Bank" when they asked where they could receive some assistance. Accordingly, Temple gave the family $150, this being verified by both the *Express* and the *Herald*. An amusing poem, titled *God's Temples* appeared in the *Star* from the fall of 1874 and seemed to read simultaneously as com-

---

138 Scattered records, such as some property tax assessments do survive. See *1873–1875 Tax Assessments*, Seaver Center for Western History Research.
139 Los Angeles *Herald*, 1 January 1875.
140 Ibid., 29 August 1875.

mendatory to Temple's generosity and a thinly veiled lampoon of his banking sense.[141] In part, the verse reads:

"One day in the Year of One Thousand
Eight hundred and seventy-four
('Twas that much I'm toler'bly certain
And couldn't been very much more)
A old fel' kem from up in the kentry
Way up cross the Oregon line,
And was busted as flat as a flounder
Tellin' facts now—he had'nt a dime

They came laborin into the city
A town with a angelic name
And they paused in front of a buildin,
And a bank it was into the same...

Then there kem to the front a white heart that's
As big as the biggest of stars;
A great soul, one of God's noblest Temples,
Leanin over says, "Joe—the cigars,"...

Then he turned, with that good face of his'n
To a feller whats countin a pile
Of gold notes, bout as high as a saw-horse
And says he, "Jest hold on there a while,
Draw a check for one hundred and fifty,
And charge to my private account,
Then pass the coin here to this weary
Good heart—I can spare that amount.

Then I saw great big tears slowly startin
Through the dust on that travel stained face,
And I saw up in Heaven the Angels
Fixin up for that Temple a place...

---

141 Los Angeles *Star*, 13 October 1874.

All praise to the noblest of Temples
Whose towering example uprears
To all hearts that are open to teaching
And should for the next thousand years.
T'was an act which a stranger here honors,
Best he can, in the poorest of rhyme,
For I don't know that Temple, nor he me,
But I desperately hope to some time."

"On Rather Hard Terms"—The Fall of Temple and Workman

Within less than a year of this incident, the bank was faced with the worst economic crisis to hit southern California since the drought of the 1860s. The state had initially seemed immune from the effects of the national depression starting in 1873, due to the state's isolation from the East, its rapid growth, and the boon of silver mining speculation in Virginia City and surrounding boom towns in Nevada. The years 1874 and 1875 were the most active business periods Los Angeles had ever experienced. Booster pamphlets, such as Benjamin Truman's *Semi-Tropical California* (1874), William McPherson's *Homes in Los Angeles* (1873) and the Los Angeles *Herald*'s *Ten Thousand Questions Answered* (1874), as well as and the city's newspapers were constant in their reporting of the favorable circumstances present in the emerging metropolis. A typical instance of this kind, from the *Express* in February 1875, waxed eloquently about how "[t]he very air is redolent of the march of progress, and a feeling prevails everywhere which is in unison with the glow of a new and prosperous epoch."[142] The "new prosperity", the title of this article, however, was soon overshadowed by events in the economic barometer of the state, San Francisco. There, speculation of the kind which made those of Los Angeles seem rather insignificant in comparison had reached a fevered pitch in the form of the Comstock Lode silver mines of Nevada.

On 26 August 1875, the telegraph relayed the news from San Francisco that, earlier in the day, the Bank of California had suspended business. As reported, "The cause of the suspension is the locking up of coin by Flood and O'Brien, the great rivals of Ralston and the Bank of California." The news

---

142 Los Angeles *Express*, 24 February 1875.

TEMPLE & WORKMAN BANK, CIRCA 1872
COURTESY OF THE SEAVER CENTER FOR WESTERN HISTORY RESEARCH,
LOS ANGELES COUNTY MUSEUM OF NATURAL HISTORY

was vividly described as spreading through San Francisco "like wildfire in a high wind" with California Street "literally black with human heads."[143] What was not reported was the collapse of a Bank of California speculation in Nevada silver mines. Matters intensified when bank president William C. Ralston was found dead, floating in San Francisco Bay the morning after the institution closed its doors. It must have felt like a wildfire in Los Angeles, where the thermometer registered a scorching 108 degrees that day, though there were the expected assurances from the newspapers that matters were not serious. The *Herald* noted that "the banks of this city have lost nothing by the suspension" that "the utmost confidence exists amongst the people of Los Angeles." Further reassurances stated that "patrons should sleep easy" because "the stability of our banks is assured by the private fortunes of their owners."[144] The *Express* concurred in asserting that "the panic is...an artificial one and will have no lasting consequences" that "there is the utmost harmony

---

143 Los Angeles *Herald*, 27 August 1875.
144 Ibid., 27 August and 2 September 1875.

amongst our banks."[145] Finally, the *Star* followed its colleagues, in an unusual, though understandable, show of solidarity by stating, "The absolute safety of our banking institutions is a potent fact and it is unnecessary to dilate upon that branch of the subject."[146] In the 27 August edition of the *Express*, Temple and Workman's head cashier and manager Henry Ledyard was interviewed and stated that, though the suspension of the Bank of California "will have a bad effect for a time in disturbing general confidence, and stagnating business," the local institutions would be affected, "[n]ot at all...The Los Angeles banks are all sound." Asked again for his opinion of the status of the city's banks and whether they were in good shape, as if to reinforce the point that there was nothing to worry about, Ledyard responded, "Undoubtedly, it could not be better."[147]

Isaias Hellman was on a European vacation and, in his stead, the Farmers and Merchants Bank was being run by John Downey . When Downey and Temple met to discuss the crisis, it was decided that both banks would suspend business for thirty days and try to ride out the panic.[148] Hellman, apprised of the state of affairs in Los Angeles and informed of his partner's actions while on his way to his native Bavaria, hurried back to Los Angeles, furious at Downey for closing the bank and betraying the trust of its clientele. Engineering Downey's dismissal as President, Hellman then went to San Francisco to seek out financial support for his bank. His reputation was high and he had little trouble getting the funds he needed to reopen. Consequently, Farmers and Merchants was back in business on 1 October.

The situation with Temple and Workman was entirely different. Initially it was publicly said that, "Temple and Workman have always been recognized as the two richest men in the county," and that, "The inconvenience resulting from temporary suspension can soon be relieved."[149] Temple, along with John Downey, was praised by the *Herald* for his actions in suspending the bank and averting a destructive run on the city's banks.[150] Privately, though, his reputation as a liberal dispenser of loans was evidently well-known. Managing cashier Ledyard was as enthusiastic as his employer in applying depositors' money to a variety of investment projects that the bank pursued. Because the bank

145 Los Angeles *Express*, 28 and 30 August 1875.
146 Los Angeles *Star*, 31 August 1875.
147 Los Angeles *Express*, 27 August 1875.
148 Los Angeles *Star* and Los Angeles *Express*, 29 August 1875 and 2 September 1875.
149 Los Angeles *Herald*, 2 September 1875.
150 Ibid., 9 September 1875.

records did not survive, though, it is difficult to pinpoint precisely the bank's problems. The fact that the bank remained closed for three months, however, is testimony enough that no one in the state seemed willing to loan substantial sums of money to float the bank.[151] On 4 September just three days after the suspension of the bank and Temple's election as county treasurer, he went to San Francisco.[152] After three weeks it was reported that Temple was returning to Los Angeles and was "assisted in his negotiations in San Francisco by Mr. Ledyard, and their result is favorable," with Temple, "having succeeded in his financial negotiations."[153] Favorable reports about the bank's situation appeared at the end of September when it was stated that, "we have yet to learn of a single draft of our banks having been dishonored" and that, "the private fortunes of the owners of our banks is ample to satisfy the most timid...Messrs. Temple and Workman are gentlemen of great wealth, owning vast quantitites of the choicest properties in this section, both city and county."[154]

Despite the reports of an agreement being reached to save the bank in September and with Farmers and Merchants being reopened on 1 October soon to bounce back under the capable leadership of Isaias Hellman, Temple and Workman remained closed. No news emerged until 9 November when it was reported that Henry Ledyard "has gone to San Francisco to complete the negotiations for opening the bank."[155] By this time, the *Herald* and the *Express* were again wrangling, this time over the issue of suits filed to nullify land patents, including that of La Puente. In this connection, the *Herald* of 13 November reported an *Express* accusation that the *Herald* had published articles on the 7th and 12th "for the purpose of compassing the defeat of negotiations under way in San Francisco to relive the financial stress in Los Angeles."[156] Although this issue soon passed away, a report from San Francisco on the 18th stated that the bank would reopen the following week.[157] This was followed by the notice that Ledyard "was at his place at the counter" of the bank on the 23rd and announced "that the bank would be opened in the return of Mr. Temple from San Francisco."[158] Temple and his son, William,

151 F.P.F. Temple evidently spent that greater part of September, October and November in San Francisco negotiating for a loan.
152 Los Angeles *Herald*, 4 September 1875.
153 Ibid., 25 and 30 September 1875.
154 Ibid., 29 and 30 September 1875.
155 Ibid., 9 November 1875.
156 Ibid., 13 November 1875.
157 Ibid., 18 November 1875.
158 Ibid., 23 November 1875.

who had been recalled from his legal studies at the Inns of Court in London to assist with the bank, arrived in Los Angeles on the 27th.[159] William's immediate roles seem to have been doing research at the county clerk's office on the family's voluminous landholdings and compiling a list of life insurance policy information.[160]

It had taken nearly three months, but finally something had been arranged in late November of 1875. F.P.F. Temple wrote from San Francisco to his aging father-in-law at Puente on the 20th. In handwriting that appeared agitated and hurriedly scrawled, Temple reported,

> You will please pardon me for not writing you before, my business here has been of a disagreeable nature, and have had nothing very encouraging to write until now. I have made arrangements to get money so that we can go on with our business, although on rather hard terms—of the two evils we must Choose the least,—we shall come out all right in the end, the idea will be to collect in fast as possible the amounts owing us, and pay our depositors.

> It has been very unpleasant for me to be away from home so long a time but under the circumstances I could not avoid it, Mr. Baldwin lets us have the money, we have to secure him—we will probably start down the coming week.[161]

"Mr. Baldwin" was one of California's most notorious and famous figures. Elias J. ("Lucky") Baldwin had been an investor in Nevada mining, most prominently the Comstock at Virginia City, and had come away with an immense fortune by a stroke of fortune (hence his nickname) in selling stock in 1875 just before the bubble burst. He was a major stockholder in the Bank of California, as well, but had already begun to look to southern California real estate for investments before the suspension of that institution. His first purchase of property was the Gold Mountain Mine in Bear Valley, situated in the

159 Ibid., 27 November 1875.
160 A ledger, dated 19 December 1875, kept by William Temple contains transcriptions of deeds is in the Homestead Museum collection and his notes on life insurance policies is owned by Josette Temple.
161 F.P.F. Temple to William Workman, 20 November 1875, [James] Perry Worden Papers, Huntington Library.

ELIAS J. 'LUCKY' BALDWIN, CIRCA 1875
COURTESY OF THE ARCADIA PUBLIC LIBRARY,
ARCADIA, CALIFORNIA

mountains near San Bernardino, where today's Lake Baldwin is a reminder of his early foray into local land acquisition. Next, in March 1875, came the purchase of the Rancho Santa Anita from Harris Newmark and Company for the unheard of sum of $200,000.[162] East of Santa Anita was the Rancho San Francisquito, then part-owned by Temple and Workman. Undoubtedly as a means of providing funds to the bank without a secured loan, Baldwin

---

162 Los Angeles *Express*, 25 March 1875. This article spotlighted Baldwin's activities, both actual and supposed. Among these were mentions of the Gold Mountain mine, a rumor that Baldwin had some $1.6 million ready to spend on southern California land, a tour with F.P.F. Temple's Centinela partner Daniel Freeman of the lands that Baldwin eventually took possession of as part of his assistance to the Temple and Workman Bank (Freeman also became an agent of Baldwin's, notable given Freeman's status as bank assignee in 1876), Baldwin's interest in purchasing the Rancho San Franciscquito, his plans for Santa Anita, and the possibility of his taking a large amount of the stock in the Los Angeles and Independence Railroad, if the line were to build a depot on the Santa Anita.

purchased the western two-thirds of the rancho in October.[163] Adjacent to this latest purchase sat the ranchos Potrero Grande, Potrero de Felipe Lugo, La Merced, and La Puente—all part-owned by William Workman, F.P.F. Temple and their *compadre* Juan Matías Sanchez.

It was undoubtedly the idea of over 25,000 acres of land held by desperate men that made Baldwin willing to sit at the negotiating table. If there was ever a clear-cut representation of the crux of change that was enveloping Los Angeles in this period, this may have been it. Baldwin was the prototypical businessman—tough, ruthless, acquisitive, and assured—one more example of how San Francisco's capitalists, such as the Southern Pacific's Big Four and Senator John P. Jones, among others, were wielding their influence in Los Angeles. Temple was a vestige of southern California's pastoral era who had gotten in over his head because he lacked Baldwin's business qualities and still kept to many of the archaic, at least from a business-like perspective, formalities of the ranchero culture.

The terms of the mortgage agreement that were drawn up on 2 December 1875 indeed reflected the "hard terms" referred to by Temple in his letter to William Workman. The conditions were precise and highly specific:

> Two years after date...we promise to pay to Elias J. Baldwin...$310,225 in gold coin of the United States with interest thereon at the rate of 1% per month from date, until paid with interest payable monthly at the end of each and every month, and if not so paid then the interest for the month so unpaid shall be computed at the rate of 2% and shall be added to the principal sum, become part of, and thereafter bear like interest.

In addition, Temple and Workman were "to have the privilege of paying $113,685 in one year from date, if we fail so to pay then said sum shall bear interest at 2% per month & compounded monthly." As with the larger amount, similar arrangements were made regarding non-payment when due.

The key condition was in Temple's comment that "we have to secure him." Baldwin required a blanket mortgage on Temple and Workman's interests in

---

163 F.P.F. Temple, William Workman, and Lewis Wolfskill to Elias J. Baldwin, *Deed for a Portion of the Rancho San Francisquito*, 13 October 1875, Book 39: 404, Los Angeles County Archives.

the ranchos Portrero Chico, Potrero Grande, La Puente, Potrero de Felipe Lugo, and La Merced; their interests in the Centinela subdivision (hence, to-day's Baldwin Hills); three parcels in Los Angeles—block one between Spring, Main, First, and Second streets, a section at Spring, Hamilton, and New High streets, and the Temple Block.[164]   Another provision was that Temple and

JUAN MATIAS SANCHEZ

COURTESY OF THE
JUAN MATIAS SANCHEZ ADOBE MUSEUM,
MONTEBELLO, CALIFORNIA

Workman had to prevail upon Juan Matías Sanchez to yield his holdings in La Merced and Potrero Grande as part of the arrangement. Here was another gesture laden with symbolism; this was the classic noble act of an old ranchero assisting his friends. Harris Newmark wrote in his autobiography:

> Sanchez, who transacted a good deal of business with H. Newmark & Company, came to me for advice. I felt con-vinced that Temple & Workman's relief could be at best but temporary, although I am sure that they themselves believed

---

164 F.P.F. Temple, William Workman, and Juan Matías Sanchez with Elias J. Baldwin, *Mortgage Agreement*, 2 December 1875, Book 17: 50, Los Angeles County Archives.

it would be permanent, and so I strenuously urged Sanchez to refuse; which he finally promised me to do. So impressive was our interview that I still vividly recall the scene when he dramatically said: *"No quiero morir de hambre!"*—"I do not wish to die of hunger![165]

Newmark wrote of his disappointment in learning that Sanchez had decided, after all, to put up his holdings to assist his old friends.

A great show was put up to convince Angelenos that the bank would use the funds from Baldwin to regain its prosperity. The institution reopened on 6 December with the *Herald* reporting that,

> An immense crowd besieged Temple & Workman's doors. ...At ten o'clock the doors opened and, when the crowd saw Mr. Temple standing behind his counter, smiling pleasantly as he stood flanked by piles of gold, a hearty cheer went up which meant encouragement to the bank and confidence in Los Angeles.[166]

According to the *Star*, the closing receipts showed a healthy net exchange of deposits over withdrawals. At the Pico House that evening, a banquet was held to honor F.P.F. Temple and "the banker's friend," Baldwin. The *Star* described the scene with enthusiastic partiality, asserting that the reopening was "one of the most interesting, as well as of the most auspicious, events that has ever occurred in Calfornia." The *Express* concurred in claiming that the reopening signalized the approbation of "the friends of Mr. Temple, who really compose the whole population of Los Angeles" and that the event "was really a personal ovation" to the bank's beleaguered president.[167]   Although more sanguine in its sentiments, the *Herald* echoed the hope implicit in the idea that the reopening "restores our financial matters to their old basis." Forty of Temple's friends and associates were present including Mayor Prudent Beaudry, who presided over the event. There were a number of speeches given, including one by the *Star*'s editor, Ben Truman, praising Temple and Baldwin and the

---

165 Harris Newmark, *Sixty Years in Southern California*, pp. 478–79.
166 Los Angeles *Herald*, 7 December 1875.
167 Los Angeles *Express*, 7 December 1875.

reopening of the bank. Others in attendance included Temple's sons, Thomas and William; Colonel James U. Crawford, superintendent of the Los Angeles and Independence Railroad; City Treasurer J.J. Mellus; bank employee Arthur Bullock and bank manager Henry Ledyard. [168]

There was no doubt a common vested interest for the city's business leaders and the press to put on at least a pretense of, if not a genuine feeling of, unity to promote the prospects of the reopened bank. If the papers were to be believed, the impressive showing of the first day's business and the sum of money involved seemed to augur well for the recovery of the bank and, by extension, the city. Little was reported in the city's newspapers, however, about how the bank fared as December wore on. On the 10th, the *Star* commented that with the reopening of Temple and Workman and the recent grand opening of the Los Angeles Commercial Bank, "Money is a great deal easier than it was a week ago, and our hard times are about passing away."[169] This was followed by the paper's year-end note that, "We may console ourselves with the fact that no man in this county has lost a cent through any of our banking institutions. We now have three flourishing banks in the city, all in splendid condition."[170] The *Herald* in its New Year's, 1876, sheet seemed to agree. In reviewing the status of the city's banks, it had this cheering note about Temple and Workman's prospects for survival:

> The firm hold which this institution has upon the confidence of the community was fully illustrated during the late panic. Several weeks elapsed, owing to the severe monetary stringency, ere Mr. Temple was enabled to obtain the necessary coin to open his doors. During this period there was no clamor on the part of the depositors, and when the coin was forthcoming and the doors opened, not only was there no rush for it, but several capitalists testified their faith by making large deposits. The institution is now in a prosperous condition, increasing its business from day to day.[171]

168 Los Angeles *Star*, 7 December 1875.
169 Ibid., 10 December 1875.
170 Ibid., 31 December 1875, the third bank was the new Los Angeles Commercial Bank. There was also a Los Angeles Savings Bank, which did not conduct commercial business.
171 Los Angeles *Herald*, 1 January 1876.

Given the above testimonial, it is unlikely that the following applied directly to Temple and Workman, but could, in light of subsequent events, be construed as applicable. The reference is from a rather oblique article from the *Herald*, appearing on 9 December 1875 with the title, "Safe and Unsafe Banking." Comparing the ostentatiousness of American banks with the relative reserve characterizing those of England, the article made the observation that,

> When we look around now as the year 1875 is coming to a close, and take a view of the disasters that have befallen these [unnamed] custodians of the earnings of the widow, the orphan, the confiding servant man and woman, we invariably find this hollow display, and the criminal rascality of those at their head arises from the use of other people's money in their private speculations. While we are for protecting legitimate businesses, private or corporate, the legislature must be invoked to throw some degree of security around institutions that open their doors for the reception of the earnings of the people.[172]

If there was no clamor or rush to withdraw funds, there was certainly a quiet steady stream that was not noticeable to the papers or just not reported. Despite the expressions of hope, it was a matter of five weeks before the funds had dwindled to the extent that Baldwin's additional $30,000 loan failed to keep the bank afloat. On 13 January 1876, a card was placed on the door to the bank announcing that the institution had again been suspended, this time permanently.

---

172 Ibid., 9 December 1875.

❧   C H A P T E R   F I V E   ❧

Failure and Ascendancy

❧ 1876–1914 ❧

"An Interesting Ethnological Study"

For the families of F.P.F. Temple and William Workman, the period following the failure of their bank was one of difficult economic times, frequent lawsuits, and an absence in the public life of southern California. Meanwhile, for the David Workman family, it was an era of ascendancy into the public arena when William Henry Workman, his son, Boyle, and daughter, Mary Julia, became prominent in business, politics, and social activism. All of these activities occurred when southern California grew at a rate rivaled by few cities in American history. Los Angeles, a town of some 15,000 in the mid-1870s, mushroomed to a city of nearly a half million by the beginning of the First World War. Technological changes emerging during this period also ended the isolation of the region from the rest of the United States. The first such improvement was the connection of the Southern Pacific railroad line from San Francisco in 1876. Later transportation advancements, such as improved harbor facilities, the introduction of the automobile and the development of the airplane, facilitated this change. Communications, too, bridged the gap, as the use of the telephone joined the telegraph wire as an agent of transmitting information. Los Angeles, instead of lagging behind eastern cities in improvements, began to be an innovator. It was one of the first American cities to employ street lights. Later, its public works projects, such as the Los Angeles Harbor and Los Angeles Aqueduct projects, though controversial, set examples for other regions of the country to follow. Still, though the era from 1876 to 1914 was one of general economic prosperity, the benefits were largely enjoyed by Americans and Europeans, while people of color were often excluded from participation in the "achievements of progress" touted during the period.

For F.P.F. Temple, William Workman, and their families, the struggle alluded to above began in earnest with the closure of the Temple and Workman bank. The assignment of the bank extended into the 1880s and was an agonizing mire of court proceedings in the form of lawsuits, bankruptcy filings, and foreclosures.

At first, there was little publicly expressed concern about the effect of the failure on the bank's creditors. The *Star*, for example, noted early on in the assignment process that, "[t]he private fortunes of Messrs. Temple & Workman will be more than ample to cover all liabilities."[1] The *Herald*, meanwhile, reported that the closing "will not seriously affect financial affairs in the vicinity", claiming, "Since the bank resumed business it has paid a large amount of money to its depositors, and this money is now in circulation. . .There is an abundance of money to be had."[2] Soon amending this position, the *Herald* was the most vigilant of the press in its reporting about the financial calamity.

The bank's assignment was placed in the hands of Daniel Freeman, partner of F.P.F. Temple in the Centinela subdivision, and Edward F. Spence, cashier of the newly opened Commercial Bank.[3] The two appointed a committee to assist them with the preparation of the inventory, which may indicate the difficulty they were finding in compiling the bank report. Among the committee members were future Los Angeles mayor James Toberman, who had worked in Hellman, Temple, and Company and Farmers and Merchants; Henry D. Barrows, later known for his writings on Los Angeles history; and chairman George E. Long, who would soon replace Freeman and Spence as the assignee.

A main issue in reference to the assignment had to do with the question of whether the bank should be thrown into bankruptcy or if the settling of debts owed to the bank was to be prosecuted. The *Star* noted, "If the concern is forced into bankruptcy, Temple and Workman and all their creditors, except Mr. Baldwin, will lose everything, for the law is plain that Mr. Baldwin is perfectly safe in any emergency."[4]

As the month wore on and the inventory results were eagerly awaited, the press began to allude to some of the rumor and innuendo that was swirling through Los Angeles. One of the earliest of these increasingly questioning editorials came on the 16th from the *Herald*, which professed not to "under-

---

1   Los Angeles *Star*, 14 January 1876.
2   Los Angeles *Herald*, 14 January 1876.
3   F.P.F. Temple and William Workman to Daniel Freeman and Edward F. Spence, *Assignment of Property*, 13 January 1876, Book 42: 78, Los Angeles County Archives.
4   Los Angeles *Star*, 29 January 1876.

stand how the managers of a banking institution could persuade themselves to continue receiving deposits up to the moment of closing their doors forever." While taking pains to praise Temple's "kind, generous heart and honorable nature" and assuring readers that the bank president "did not and could not permit a transaction of this kind over the counter of his bank," it noted that transactions were made at the bank "up to the last hour" of its existence. The editorial concluded with the following admonition, "It is a wrong, a cruel wrong, on the part of a man standing behind the counter of a collapsing bank, to take the deposits of the trusting poor." The insinuation seemed to be that, if Temple did not countenance such activity, it must have been managing cashier Henry S. Ledyard who permitted the receipt of deposits so late in the bank's existence.

A few days later, an editorial in the *Star* expanded more significantly than the *Herald* in respect to wrongdoing by the bank's managers and made reference to a rumor that, "depositors' moneys have been recklessly squandered, to the tune of a hundred thousand dollars by two attaches [Henry Ledyard and Thomas W. Temple]." It was asserted that this was done "with the permission of Mr. Temple." If this claim were true, declaimed the writer, "then Mr. Temple is not entitled to the sympathy which prevails." The *Star* then upped the ante in terms of identifying the nature of the bank's operations and the placing of accountability at the feet of Temple and his associates, stating that "from all accounts" the bank had misused the trust of its depositors in a way that was "extremely shocking in all its proportions." The paper employed the archetypal declamation that "the rich, the poor, the widow and the orphan alike have all been tearfully besought during the past months to leave their moneys in [the bank]," so that the bank's managers could engage in reckless speculation. It accused the institution of outright illegalities, noting, "In England and the East these things are called embezzlements."[5]

Yet, despite these dour pronouncements about the management of the institution, it is curious to note that the same article on 29 January offered a rather antithetical testimony to the bank's president stating, "We cannot conclude this article without paying a high tribute to the general character of Mr. Temple, outside of his experience as a banker." Old platitudes followed about Temple's charity, public spirit, liberality, and kindness. The article asserted that "to-day, in his ruin, he has more friends than some of the loftiest men in

5   Los Angeles *Star*, 29 January 1876.

our midst," taking care to add rather disingenuously that some of these unnamed men of prominence in the community "have contributed no little in
reducing him to the dire extremity in which he is placed, by their persistent
slanders and misrepresentations."[6]

The *Herald* also continued to juxtapose its critical probing of the bank
with a defensive posture for the benefit of Temple, writing on 28 January as
the bank's inventory neared completion, "We have maintained from the first
that he [Temple] has not intentionally wronged any one out of a cent. He is a
victim of circumstances that he could not foresee or control."[7] The next day,
the tribute continued as the writer expressed "profound regret...that through
false friendship and misplaced confidence, a man of such sterling worth, unimpeachable character and generous nature as Mr. F.P.F. TEMPLE, should
be deprived of the reward of a life of honest industry and careful economy."
Correctly noting the dramatic effect the failure of Temple and Workman had
on the economic situation and implying that this extended into a more person-
ally related nature, the article stated, "The misfortunes of Mr. TEMPLE are
the misfortunes of the whole community, and his losses are to a certain extent
the losses of all." The piece concluded with another round of tributes including the statement that "there are none who question his honesty of purpose
or the purity of his intention. Few have fallen from so great a financial height
and yet retained so universally the esteem of his fellow men."[8]

As the inventory neared completion, there was still some publicly expressed hope that the affair would work out reasonably well. One of the inventory committee members, as late as 27 January told the *Star* that Temple
and Workman would "pay nearly, if not quite, even, dollar for dollar" but "that
two of the attaches of the Bank—he called no names and we asked for none
[again, probably Ledyard and Thomas Temple]—were behind nearly $100,000."
Finally, this unnamed source believed that "the Bank could be put on its feet
in two years, pay all its creditors, with interest, and leave Messrs. Temple and
Workman in a better condition than they were in two years ago." Another
member told the paper that "there is no doubt about the Bank paying dollar
for dollar. He adds, however, that a full statement will show a pretty general

---

6   Ibid., 29 January 1876.
7   Los Angeles *Herald*, 28 January 1876.
8   Ibid., 29 January 1876.

piece of mismanagement and lack of ordinary business capacity on the part of Mr. Temple or some one else."[9]

The *Herald*, however, reflected a different mode of thought by noting that, whatever the declared assets of the bank and its owners might be, "a considerable portion of the assets cannot be collected, and . . . a large share of the indebtedness is secured by mortgages."[10] Later, the paper proclaimed that "perhaps the history of banking will not show a parallel case of mismanagement or total disregard of all business precaution." Finally, it declared that Temple and Workman really had no assets with the various mortgages held against their estates and that the liabilities were said to be at $1.1 million.[11] When the inventory release date neared, the *Herald* reported,

> It is undoubtedly true that Messrs. Spence and Freeman find Temple & Workman's books in terrible confusion. The General Ledger has not been written up for three years. We understand that the assignees are getting heartily sick of their work as the secret history of the bank is being exposed, and the prospect of a very unsatisfactory statement becomes apparent.[12]

Still, on 2 February when the assignees statement was filed, the *Star* continued to express the public sentiment, if not private belief, that "So far as we can judge the statement of the condition is far from being an unsatisfactory one." In printing some figures regarding the owners' assets and liabilities, though, the paper admitted "The following figures are not complete enough for us to present an opinion satisfactory to ourselves, even."[13]

It is interesting to see, then, the *Star's* florid account just two days later when the complete inventory was released. The headline blared: "The Inventory. A Document That Shocks A Community. Mismanagement, Wild Speculations, And A Betrayal Of Trust. An Unparalleled Array Of Dead Beats. An Interesting Ethnological Study." This was followed by the assertion that "In all the annals of collapsed moneyed institutions, no state-

---

9   Los Angeles *Star*, 28 January 1876.
10   Los Angeles *Herald*, 26 January 1876.
11   Ibid., 27 January 1876.
12   Ibid., 29 January 1876.
13   Los Angeles *Star*, 2 January 1876.

ment, or inventory...has ever elicited such general and pronounced expressions of disgust and disappointment." There had clearly been "great mismanagement all round, combined with a perfect recklessness of trust imposed." The managers of Temple and Workman had engaged in "the manipulations of depositors' moneys for purposes of the wildest speculation and an utter absence of the commonest kinds of business qualifications." In reviewing the list of overdrafts, while noting some "honorable exceptions", the paper called the remaining individuals "the most stupendous array of dead beats ever seen outside of the penitentiary," while those who composed the general list of bills receivable consisted of "a full regiment of professional bilks." In concluding, the *Star*'s account stated:

> We are not prepared to [in]criminate anyone, but we really do think it a pity that Messrs. Temple and Workman had not had guardians appointed to take care of them and their property. For, admitting that the creditors will get dollar for dollar, which we very much doubt after perusing the inventory, these two old gentlemen are ruined, unless this proves to be an unparalleled case."[14]

The *Herald*, while more probing in its coverage before and after the publishing of the document, was considerably less strident in its account. Titling its article "The Gordian Knot: A Synopsis of the Interesting Document Which Would Form a Valuable Treatise on the Science of Debits and Credits," the paper noted that "a comprehensive idea of the affairs of the bank may be had from the following figures," but refrained from the dramatic outcry that marked its rival's account.[15]

The bank inventory was published in both the *Star* and the *Herald*, though the latter provided a more comprehensive listing of creditors and debtors. The estates of William Workman and F.P.F Temple were together valued at $1.5 million dollars, except that all but some $150,000 were held in the mortgage with Baldwin, including the Temple Block, the post office building, and interests in the ranchos La Puente, La Merced, Potrero de Felipe Lugo and Potrero Grande. The two men had tried to file for homesteads at La Puente and La Merced on 12 January the day before the bank officially closed, but

14 Ibid., 4 February 1876.
15 Los Angeles *Herald*, 4 February 1876.

neither claim was allowed to stand because of the proximity of the filings to the imminent collapse of the concern. Workman claimed a personal property exemption of $800, as well as "all that part of the Rancho La Puente, in said county, occupied by my dwelling house and houses, orchards and vineyards, the surroundings of said dwelling, enclosed with fence, containing one hundred acres, more or less, and valued at $5,000." Temple claimed $1,145 in personal property and "all that portion of the Rancho La Merced, inclosed and occupied as a vineyard and orchard, and the dwelling house thereon, heretofore occupied by his family as a house, the land enclosed, being fifty acres, and valued at $5,000."

Other bank assets were a pittance in comparison to the mortgaged land holdings and there was the matter of the bills receivable, mortgages and overdrafts which totaled almost $650,000 yet to be collected. The amount of cash given was only a little over $5,000. Although total assets were listed as $2.2 million, they were either held in mortgage to Baldwin or were in the doubtful status of collection procedures to be instituted against the "unparalleled array of dead beats."

Liabilities amounted to nearly $800,000 in deposits, deposit certificates, bills payable, and F.P.F. Temple's personal liabilities, which were almost a quarter of the total, consisting mainly of mortgages to such capitalists as Senator John P. Jones (Temple's partner in the Los Angeles and Independence Railroad), Harris Newmark, Alexander Weill and the London and San Francisco Bank (from which Temple and Workman drew). Finally, there was "Lucky" Baldwin's mortgage of $340,225. The total, with unpaid drafts in San Francisco (referred to above) and unpaid salaries was $1.1 million.

As insinuated in press accounts before the release of the inventory, bank officials and their projects figured highly in the debit category. Thomas W. Temple was in arrears of nearly $60,000, Henry Ledyard was indebted for another $58,000 and cashier Arthur Bullock owed $12,000. Overdraft listing included a small amount from a "Campaign Fund," probably for F.P.F. Temple's successful run for county treasurer, a large amount for the San Jacinto Wagon Road, of which Temple and Ledyard were the principals as part of a lumber mill project, the Cerro Gordo Water and Mining Company, the Lake Vineyard Land and Water Company, the Los Angeles Petroleum Refining Company and the Alden Fruit Drying Works, a property owned by Thomas Temple.

It is noteworthy that among the major cash depositors was the City of Los Angeles, through its treasurer J.J. Mellus, for $23,000. Needless to say, Mellus was taken to task for deciding to make Temple and Workman the depository for city funds in January 1875, and resigned his office shortly after the bank's failure. It appears that all of the city's money was lost when the bank collapsed.[16]

The gloom expressed upon the release of the inventory report was justified by the resulting actions of assignment. F.P.F Temple declared bankruptcy in a federal court in San Francisco in July 1876, and a judge there created separate assignments for Temple, Workman, and the two as partners in the bank. Freeman and Spence, who were often criticized for their work, were replaced in October as assignees for the bank by George Long, while William Temple assumed the duty of administrator over the William Workman assignment and Los Angeles attorney Volney E. Howard dealt with F.P.F. Temple's estate.[17] As these assignees filed suits to recover money owed the fallen bank, these were countered with suits by creditors. By 1878, Long reported that, while judgments had been secured for $150,000 against debtors to the bank, less than 20% of that sum had actually been collected and only $13,000 disbursed to creditors.[18] Auctions and sales hardly made a dent in the immense debt piled up, especially as Baldwin's large mortgage incurred interest. The sale in September 1877 of the Temple Block to Newmark and Company, for example, yielded little more than one-half of its assigned value. Applying the funds to mortgages held by Newmark and San Francisco capitalist Alexander Weill left only $8,000 of the $131,000 purchase price to advance in payment of Baldwin's mortgage.[19] An auction of notes and judgments a year later yield-

---

16 Los Angeles *Star* and Los Angeles *Herald*, 4 February 1876.

17 Los Angeles *Star*, 13 October 1876; Daniel Freeman and Edward F. Spence to George E. Long, *Transfer of Property of Temple and Workman and F.P.F. Temple*, 19 April 1877, Book 54: 78, Los Angeles County Archives; *Probate for the Estate of William Workman*, No. 781, Superior Court, Los Angeles County Archives. William Temple's ledger book, dated 19 December 1875, survives as an artifact of the bank's failure, Homestead Museum Collection. It will be recalled that Howard and Temple's relationship extended back at least twenty years when the attorney, practicing then in San Francisco, was enlisted to put forward Temple's claim to Alcatraz Island (see Chapter Two.)

18 Los Angeles *Star*, 5 October 1878.

19 Ibid., 21 September 1877. Harris Newmark, purchaser of the Temple Block, recalled that his only competitor in the auction was Daniel Freeman, who was then acting as an agent for "Lucky" Baldwin. One wonders how Freeman's association with Baldwin affected his role as bank assignee. Newmark, *Sixty Years in Southern California*, p. 510. Another document that shows the range of Temple's business interests was a court decree in the summer of 1877 for the sale of property in the Bunker Hill tract of Prudent Beaudry, lots in several other city and county subdivisions, sections and parcels, property in Santa Monica, Compton, San Fernando, San Diego, Centinela, two

ed these results: "One note for $2,167 was sold for $6; another for $705.80 brought $1.72; other accounts went at a still greater sacrifice. The proceeds of the sale will hardly average a cent on the dollar."[20]

A desperate measure by Temple was a lawsuit filed against Henry Ledyard in April 1876, for embezzlement based upon events of three years earlier. The case, however, was thrown out of court because the statute of limitations had expired just two weeks before the case was heard. Symptomatic of the change in attitude towards Temple and of the frustration felt over the magnitude of the financial disaster, the *Star* wrote that Ledyard was not guilty of the accusation "because he was permitted by Mr. Temple to manipulate the funds on deposit in his own peculiar way for the space of years." The paper then asked the rhetorical question: "If, however, Mr. Ledyard can be convicted of embezzlement, will not Mr. F.P.F. Temple and Mr. T[homas] Temple soon be found guilty of the same charge?" The reporter reminded the reader that Thomas Temple "admits that he put in a few thousands of dollars and took out some hundred odd thousands." The article further asserted, "We know that between the three men named above money was so recklessly abstracted that the bank closed." Countering, at this date, the sympathy once so easily extended to F.P.F. Temple, if not to Ledyard and Thomas Temple, the paper reiterated the management, speculation and "profligacy on the part of the three above-named that brought a once excellent house into bad repute and subsequently to grief, and no gloss can make it otherwise." The paper, in what will be used here as a coda to the strange, sad circumstances attendant to the worst financial failure Los Angeles had experienced and would yet see for some time, concluded, "We know of no greater criminal than the private banker, who, by any means, permits himself to secure public confidence, and then closes the doors of his institution owing hundreds of thousands of dollars to men and women and children of all kinds."[21]

For all of the mention about F.P.F. Temple and the others associated with the bank in the press after the failure, little was said about the "silent part-

---

mining claims in Arizona, San Jacinto, stock in the Los Angeles Homestead Association, the Main Street and Agricultural Park Railway Company, the Southern District Agricultural Association, the Boushey Silver Mining Company (see Chapter Four for Temple and Boushey's mining associations), the Cerro Gordo Water and Mining Company; the San Jacinto Wagon Road Company and an assortment of wagons, tools, machines, and farm animals, including Temple's pedigree horses and bull, as well as sheep and a cow. United States District Court, *In the Matter of F.P.F. Temple, Bankrupt*, 8 August 1877, Book 56: 316-320, Los Angeles County Archives.

20 Los Angeles *Star*, 15 October 1878.
21 Ibid., 12 April 1876.

ner," William Workman, who may justly be considered the victim of the poor judgment and abilities of those who managed the institution. Little is known about Workman's activities in the immediate aftermath of the demise of the institution. On 12 February he assigned all interest in any property and his power of attorney to his grandson Francis W. Temple, hoping, in vain, to pass on something to his family and perhaps showing his disillusionment with his son-in-law, who had held Workman's power of attorney from 1868.[22] Francis, who had returned to Los Angeles in 1874 after a year or so of study at the Massachusetts Institute of Technology, supervised the wine-making operations at the Workman ranch and, thus, became a favorite of his grandfather. Five months following the failure of the bank, the *Herald* reported that, on the morning of 17 May 1876, "it appears that a receiver went out to take possession of his property." The receiver was Richard Garvey, also an agent of Lucky Baldwin. That evening at the Workman House, the paper continued, "Between five and six o'clock it appears that Mr. Workman arose, went to the parlor, took the pistol [that he had placed there some days before] and the next that was known he was found lying upon the floor of the middle room with a bullet hole under his right ear and he dead."[23]

A powerful surviving artifact from this tragedy is the note written by Francis W. Temple to his mother, addressed to Francis' brother, William, informing of her father's death:

> *La Puente*
> > *May 17, 1876*
>
> Dear Mother,
> > *Grandfather has shot himself this afternoon.*
> *Come at once,*
> > > *F. W. Temple*[24]

---

22 William Workman to Francis W. Temple, *Deed to All Right, Title, and Interest to the Property of William Workman*, 12 February 1876, Book 42: 233, Los Angeles County Archives; Workman's copy of the power of attorney document, dated 19 February is in possession of Josette Temple. See Footnote 97, p. 125 for Workman's previous power of attorney, assigned to Francis' father, F. P. F.

23 In 1879, after Baldwin foreclosed on his Temple and Workman mortgage, he sold Garvey land on the ranchos Potrero Grande and Potrero de Felipe Lugo that had belonged to Workman, Temple, and Sanchez. Garvey became a prosperous, well-known citizen of today's Monterey Park area.

24 Francis W. Temple to Antonia Margarita Workman de Temple, 17 May 1876, courtesy of Josette Temple.

WILLIAM WORKMAN, CIRCA 1870
COURTESY OF THE HOMESTEAD MUSEUM,
CITY OF INDUSTRY, CALIFORNIA

The report of Workman's death, carried at a late hour to Los Angeles, caused a stir in the city. On the day of Workman's funeral at his cemetery at *El Campo Santo* at La Puente, the *Star* wrote that the news of his death had "elicited general and spontaneous grief." Workman, it was said, was in good health and might have lived another decade if the bank disaster had not "worried the good old gentleman into his grave." In a pointed reference to F.P.F. Temple and his bank associates, the article declared that "[u]nless they are very stony, there are hearts that must have nearly broken yesterday upon the realization of the dreadful fact that their acts had driven this honorable old man to a violent death." Driving the point home further, it was noted that Workman's "honest, hard-earned possessions constituted in reality, a great reserve fund, from which the manager or managers drew, until, vampyre-like,

187

they sucked the last drop, leaving the old man a wreck financially and otherwise." The finale to this dramatic account was this florid recapitulation of Workman's last hours: "He saw, when too late, ruin, irremediable ruin, on all sides, and in a moment of great despair, he sent the messenger of death crashing through his brain."[25]

Although again more restrained in its expressions, the *Herald* published similar sentiments in its report, explaining that the realization that all of Workman's possessions "would be swallowed in the vortex and himself thrown upon the world without means, drove the old gentleman to desperation, and in a moment of wild despair he sent the bullet crushing through his brain. It is a deplorable circumstance, and has cast a gloom of sorrow over the entire valley."[26] Describing his funeral, the *Herald* grandiloquently ended by noting, "The weeping willows will wave and the wind will moan a sad requiem until the last trump shall sound."[27]

Workman's death has sometimes been employed as a symbol of the difficult economic period that ensued in southern California after the demise of the bank. One recent historian, for example, wrote, "That pistol shot sounded the death knell of El Pueblo's first boom years."[28] He also gave an indication of the effects of the bank's collapse upon southern California's economy during the last half of the 1870s. Land was sold for half or less of its value during the boom; the county's assessed valuation declined in 1876 for the first time in nearly ten years; and a number of new subdivisions failed. By 1880, the population of Los Angeles, which may have numbered 15,000 or more a few years earlier, had fallen to 11,000, and this remains the only instance in the city's history where the population actually dropped.

By decade's end, the bank assignment had essentially come to a close, although as late as 1882 actions were still being taken by George Long against debtors. In February 1879, Baldwin, acting through an intermediary named Camilo Martin, obtained court judgments that finalized, by sheriff's sale the following September his foreclosure on the Ranchos La Merced, La Puente, Potrero de Felipe Lugo, and Potrero Grande.[29] In 1880 and 1881, he arranged,

25 Los Angeles *Star*, 19 May 1876.
26 Los Angeles *Herald*, 19 May 1876.
27 Ibid., 20 May 1876.
28 Nadeau, *City Makers*, p. 139. Nadeau presents one of the better existing summaries of the suspension, reopening, and final closure of the Temple and Workman bank.
29 L.S.B. Sawyer to Camilo Martin, *Decree on the Estate of William Workman*, 20 March 1880, Book 73: 179, Los Angeles County Archives.

TEMPLE ADOBE AND BRICK HOUSE
RANCHO LA MERCED, CIRCA 1905
COURTESY OF THE HOMESTEAD MUSEUM
CITY OF INDUSTRY, CALIFORNIA

through another agent, William Alvord, former mayor of San Francisco and president of the Bank of California (of which Baldwin was a director and major investor in its resumption) to sell the Workman and Temple homesteads back to the families. The former, including the Workman House and seventy-five acres, was sold for $5,000 to Francis Workman Temple, Workman's grandson, and the latter for $3,000 to Antonia Margarita Workman de Temple, F.P.F. Temple's widow.

It is interesting to note that the administration of Workman's estate, as with that of the bank, not only provided little satisfaction to creditors, but great stress on young William Temple, called upon at age 25 to return from his studies at the Inns of Court in London, after graduating from Harvard Law School, to assume the responsibility of handling an estate that was in a massive tangle. After three years, he abandoned his position as administrator in 1879 to join the army. Still, he occasionally was called upon to intervene in family affairs. For example, in November 1880 from the U. S. Army base at San Francisco's Presidio, William wrote a letter to Lucky Baldwin concerning arrangements made to settle matters with the Temple family regarding the Workman and Temple family homes. In the letter he outlines his position with a not-so-veiled insinuation should Baldwin not keep his end of a bargain that had been agreed upon:

> Concerning those Homesteads, I am certain considering the assurances you have given and our agreement on the subject, that you will carry out your promises faithfully and honorably. Know you would not be the means of driving Frank away from his home or Mrs. Temple and the children from the Merced, I disclaim any pecuniary interest in any of them, and I hope we will not be disturbed in the peaceful and continuous possession of a few acres of land dear and sacred to us by the most endearing associations.

Specifically, William was most concerned about the Temple property at Rancho La Merced, but in a way that well illustrates what can happen when tragedy and loss divides families:

> Mrs. Temple's conduct to herself, her children, and her friends has in no way been creditable, but at the same time, while I hope never to see or speak to her again, I sincerely and heartily forgive her her faults and wish and earnestly hope that she may peaceably and quietly end her days in her old home. I care for no interest in the Merced and I would suggest that a deed be made to her of the Homestead for life, with [the] remainder in fee simple to her sons and daughters, Maggie, Lucinda, Charles, and Walter. John, Tom, Frank, and myself can take care of ourselves.

William's point was that three of his siblings (Margarita, Walter, and Charles) were minors living with their mother at home, and they and Lucinda needed to be provided for. As for William and his three brothers, John, Thomas, and Francis, they were not in such need. It is unknown if Baldwin responded to this letter, but he did sell the Temple and Workman homesteads to Antonia Margarita Workman de Temple and Francis W. Temple, respectively, in the fall of 1880 and spring of 1881 and seems to have made good on the bargain referred to in the letter.[30]

Later, when contacted by a family friend in California about the estate, Temple had these bitter words:

> I do not desire to have anything to do with the affair one way or the other. I Consider that I have stepped out of the damned Controversy long ago, am in the army now in a different line of business, and do not desire in the future to be written to or interviewed with regard to any such matters—I have given the folks in my day the best advice I could give them...have lost my time, my money and health and received no thanks. I have given this up and if there be one reason among others why I joined the army it was to avoid and get away from this cursed catagory [sic] of complicating troubles, law suits, fights, etc. You must fight your own battles and let me alone.[31]

While the failure of Temple and Workman had great significance to the larger southern California community, which stagnated economically until the great Boom of the Eighties from 1885 to 1888, it had more enduring repercussions to the families who lived on with the memory of the distress and humiliation as well as the economic hardships that followed.

Memories of the bank's collapse were, from time-to-time, revived by those who were present or very familiar with the event.[32] Fifty years later, Jackson Graves, president of Isaias Hellman's Farmers and Merchants Bank, devoted a chapter in his 1927 memoirs to a letter he wrote to Marco Newmark, son of Harris Newmark, regarding the rumor "that it was said that the Jews caused the failure of the Temple & Workman Bank." Graves replied, with no small measure of dramatic effect and exaggeration, "There never was a more villainous slander of the Jews circulated at any time or place since the world began."

---

30 William W. Temple to Elias J. Baldwin, 12 November 1880, courtesy of Josette Temple. This was a copy made by William and forwarded to his brother Francis, with a note that the original had been mailed that day.
31 William W. Temple to William W. Jenkins, 14 September 1881, *Probate for the Estate of William Workman*, No. 781, Superior Court, Los Angeles County Archives
32 A rather typical summary, by J.J. Ayres, may be found in Spalding, *History and Reminiscences*, pp. 218–219.

Because he was a partner in the law firm of Brunson, Eastman, and Graves, which served as counsel to initial bank assignees Freeman and Spence, Graves asserted, "No other man alive today is in as good a position to know its [the accusation] falsity as I am." In outlining his recollection of the bank's history and collapse, he noted, "The bank was headquarters for the speculators who built up a little real estate boom" and that "[t]here was located here [Los Angeles] quite a colony of Englishmen known as 'remittance men,' all without assets, and every one of whom owed the Temple & Workman Bank, and none of whom paid a cent of the indebtedness." Further, the bank "virtually had no commercial business, nearly all of which was in the hands of Jewish firms." Graves recollected "the bank never had an adequate cash reserve, but led a hand-to-mouth existence." Graves listed forty-one suits filed by his firm on behalf of Freeman and Spence, noting , "Of those actions which went to judgment, I think very little money was ever collected." Of these, only two, Matthew Kremer and Samuel Hellman, were Jews and both paid their debts.[33]

Another fascinating, though undocumented, later testament regarding the bank collapse was provided by the often hyperbolic Horace Bell. In his book, *On The Old West Coast*, Bell remembered the demise of the institution. Praising Workman as "a most excellent gentleman of rural manners" and Temple as "a well-educated man of great industry, indomitable energy, and a good generous heart," Bell repeated Graves' accusation that "they became the victims of sharpers" and that "it was claimed on behalf of the bankers that the sharpers on the outside conspired with the bank manager on the inside." Bell erred in recalling Baldwin's mortgage for $85,000 ("a mere bagatelle compared to the exigency of the situation"), and he claimed that bank assignee George Long approached him, saying,

---

33 Jackson A. Graves, *My Seventy Years in California* (Los Angeles: Times-Mirror Press, 1927), pp. 424–430. The inspiration for Graves' commentary came from [James] Perry Worden, editor of Newmark's *Sixty Years in Southern California* (in fact, J. Gregg Layne credited Worden with having essentially written the work) and intended biographer of the Temple and Workman families. In a dispute with the Newmark family over a negative portrayal (at least in Worden's mind) of Jonathan Temple in the Newmark book, Worden asserted that he had proof that the Jews had brought about the failure of the Temple and Workman bank. Marco Newmark's letter to Graves asked for clarification on this point. Perry Worden to Thomas W. Temple, 12 May 1929, Homestead Museum Collection. After a failed attempt by attorney Johnstone Jones and Luther Ingersoll, of the Los Angeles Public Library, to write a biography of the Workman and Temple families, Worden was hired in late 1921 to finish the project. Abandoning the format devised by Jones and Ingersoll, Worden engaged in the kind of minutely detailed research that marks Newmark's memoirs and worked from 1921 to 1929 without, evidently, putting together anything more than notes and sketched narratives. When the Temple family fortune was exhausted by decade's end, Worden ceased work. His papers were donated to the Huntington Library after his death in 1945.

Major, I have been thinking over this Workman and Temple
misfortune, and because you are prone to expose wrong-doing
and rascality I want you to see the Temple and Workman
books. I assure you that the books of that bank show more
rascality than it is possible to imagine. If you will accept
these books I will make a present of them to you for public
use. You can do with them as you will.

Meanwhile, Hubert Howe Bancroft traveled to Los Angeles in search
of material for his famed *History of California* and visited Bell for assistance,
upon which, Bell claimed, "Believing then that Bancroft was preparing a history that would be an honor to California and that the truth of the Temple-
Workman affair could find the widest publicity in his annals of Los Angeles
County, I gave the Temple and Workman Bank books into the possession
of Mr. Bancroft." Still, said Bell, when Bancroft's *magnum opus* appeared in
1885, "there was not a mention of the truth as contained in the bank's books."
Employing his rather dubious talent for untainted slander, Bell concluded
with a flourish, claiming that, "Somehow it seemed that about...every ras-
cal of prominence participating in the ruin of Temple and Workman, every
sharper whose hands were stained with their blood, became a subscriber to
the absurd Bancroft history at two hundred and eighty-four dollars the set of
volumes."[34] Whatever happened, the bank books have disappeared and the
Bancroft Library at the University of California, Berkeley does not know of
any such transaction made to Bancroft.[35]

After The Assignment

William Temple's aforementioned letter aptly testifies to the personal, as
well as financial, straits that affected the families of William Workman and
F.P.F. Temple in the years after 1876. For the next forty years, their descendants
receded from public life and lived quietly, though not necessarily peacefully.
F.P.F. Temple remained largely a recluse, despite finishing his term as coun-

---

34 Horace Bell, *On the Old West Coast* (New York: Grosset and Dunlap, 1930), pp. 289–292.
35 Bonnie Hardwick, Curator, Bancroft Library, to Don Rowland, 14 March 1995. Copy provided to
the author by Mr. Rowland.

ty treasurer in the spring of 1878, and maintaining some fraternal activities, including the Masons and the Coeur de Lion Commandery of the Knights Templar. He was beset by a series of strokes beginning soon after the collapse of his bank, some of which left him partially paralyzed and culminating, on 27 April 1880, with an attack of apoplexy that ended his life.[36]

The Temple homestead, reduced to fifty acres, was sold nine months later to his widow, Margarita, who, as was noted above, maintained land on the ranchos Potrero de Felipe Lugo and Potrero Grande, as well as several hundred acres around the Workman Mill on La Puente.[37] Though land was once considered a sure sign of prosperity, there was a lack of ready cash to pay the taxes imposed on those properties. Mrs. Temple, in the years after the bank failure and into the mid-1880s, distributed many of these holdings to her children, no doubt hoping that they, growing by then into adulthood, could, by their industry, hold onto these tracts. There were, however, several further difficulties that beset Mrs. Temple and her children in matters of land.

These problems dealt with three issues: the administration of the estates of F.P.F. Temple, the administration of the Temple minor children (Margarita, Walter and Charles), and court battles with "Lucky" Baldwin and others.[38] In January 1881, Mrs. Temple borrowed money from Baldwin to buy the family homestead with the property as collateral.[39] Four years later, Baldwin filed a

---

36 A letter to Francis W. Temple from a Massachusetts cousin notes "our hearts are saddened by the thought of Uncle's sickness." Ellen M. Bancroft to Francis W. Temple, 2 August 1877, courtesy of Josette Temple. Ellen Bancroft, daughter of Abraham Temple, brother of F.P.F. Temple, was reunited with the family when Walter Temple and his children visited in 1926. Temple's sons, Thomas, Walter, Jr. and Edgar spent many weekends and holidays with Ellen Bancroft and her family. There is also a surviving draft announcing Temple's death and funeral tellingly omits Thomas W. Temple, who had been in great debt to the Temple and Workman bank, and William W. Temple, who had fled the state after taking on the Herculean task of trying to sort out the family's affairs in the aftermath of the bank's failure, from the signature list of the Temple children. Strangely, Antonia Margarita Temple, the widow, is also not a signatory. Draft to "Mrs. R. C. P.", 28 April 1880, courtesy of Josette Temple.
37 The Temple Homestead was deeded by William Alvord to Margarita Temple on 26 January 1881, Lot Book P-49: 1143, Rancho La Merced, Title Records Incorporated, Sun Valley, CA.
38 Examples include complex agreements in 1880 and 1881 between William W. Jenkins, former administrator of F.P.F. Temple's estate, "Lucky" Baldwin, and Richard Garvey, the court-appointed receiver in the Baldwin foreclosure of the Temple and Workman properties and himself a claimant to some of that land. The widow of Jenkins' great-grandson, Charles Coker, is the owner of F.P.F. Temple's tin deed box, containing these records. Copies are housed in the Homestead Museum Research Archives.
39 Antonia Margarita Workman de Temple to Elias J. Baldwin, *Mortgage to the Temple Homestead, Rancho La Merced*, 26 January 1881, Book of Mortgages, 40: 395, Los Angeles County Archives. Occasionally, it appears, portions of the fifty-acre Homestead were leased, as evidenced by a lease executed by Francis W. and John H. Temple, as guardians for their minor siblings, with Simon Ortega for three acres at $2,000 for one year, 16 December 1882. Courtesy of Josette Temple.

foreclosure action against the unpaid note.[40] According to notes written in later years by Walter Temple, in 1887 his brother Francis, as administrator of their father's estate, paid $5,000 to Baldwin to free the interests of the Temple children from foreclosure.[41] Four years later, the entire fifty-acre homestead was back unencumbered in the hands of the Temple family.[42] In January 1892, during a two-week period that also included the deaths of her mother, Nicolasa Workman and her eldest child, Thomas W. Temple, Margarita Temple died at age sixty-one.[43]

After her death, the Temple Homestead was owned by her youngest children Walter and Charles, who shared it until they agreed to a partition in 1900. By 1907, Walter had acquired the entire parcel from his brother and had established a walnut and apple ranch.[44] In the meantime, he married Laura Gonzalez, who was born and raised near the Temple homestead and was descended from Gabrieliño and Californio families, such as the Lugos and Alvarados and the Alvitres. Living in a small wood frame house south of the old Temple adobe and brick house site, which had been destroyed after the turn of the century, the two raised four children and struggled with their ranch.[45]

Regarding the other Temple children, there were two daughters, Lucinda and Margarita, who were educated at the Sisters of Charity school in Los Angeles and Sacred Heart Academy (now Holy Names College) in Oakland. The former married twice, first to Jose Arnaz, of a prominent Ventura County family, and, after his early death, to Manuel Zuniga, a native of the Old Mission area where the Temples lived. Childless, Lucinda lived in later years with her brother,

---

40 Lot Book P-49: 1143, Rancho La Merced, Title Records Incorporated.
41 Unpublished manuscript by Walter P. Temple, circa 1910. Copy in the Homestead Museum Research Archives.
42 See title transaction listings, Lot Book P-49: 1143, Rancho La Merced, Title Records Incorporated.
43 Little is known about Nicolasa Workman, aside from a reference in an 1888 letter that she enjoyed a little wine once in a while and a few other tidbits. There is a surviving 1881 letter from Mrs. Workman to Richard Garvey, agent for Lucky Baldwin, who was given a substantial ranch on former Workman and Temple property by Baldwin, in which she asks Garvey to deliver some corn to her grandson, John H. Temple, from a tenant farmer using land that Mrs. Workman owned, probably on the Rancho Potrero Grande in the vicinity of South El Monte or Monterey Park. Nicolasa Workman to Richard Garvey, 21 November 1881, courtesy of Josette Temple. Nicolasa Workman's certificate of death stated that she was treated for over three weeks from flu and pneumonia. Similarly, her daughter died from pneumonia after six days' illness in the same period.
44 See tax assessments for Rancho La Merced, 1902–1910, Book 115: 53, Los Angeles County Archives. James Guinn, *A History of California and an Extended History of the Southern Coast Counties*, (Los Angeles: Historic Record Company, 1907), p. 860.
45 The Temples took out several mortgages prior to 1917, see title transaction listings, Lot Book P-49: 1143, Rancho La Merced, Title Records Incorporated.

Walter, in Alhambra and at the La Puente homestead of William Workman, dying in January 1928. Margarita married Samuel P. Rowland, a grandson of John Rowland, and had nine children. She also lived with her brother at the Workman Homestead and was allowed to remain there after he lost the property until 1941. She moved to Temple City and died in December 1953. After his stint in the army, William Temple lived for a time in Albuquerque, New Mexico and practiced law in Mexico City. He lived in Los Angeles in his last years and, in 1910, wrote a tract on the recent Mexican Revolution and an address on major issues of the late Progressive era in the United States, including anti-Asian immigration (reflecting the exclusionist views especially espoused on the West Coast); relations with Mexico, Central America, and Canada; education; temperance; and the role of women.[46] Temple died at the County Hospital in Los Angeles in 1917 in the care of his brother, Walter.

Thomas W. Temple, the cashier in the Temple and Workman bank, had been his father's protégé, but the bank failure and his significant debts to the institution ruined his rising prospects. In May 1876, less than two weeks after the suicide of his grandfather Workman, Thomas was married in San Mateo, near San Francisco, to Nettie Friend. He was previously married to Maria Refugia Martinez, whose family lived on Rancho La Puente, but after three years of marriage Refugia died in 1869. Thomas also had, with Petra Bermudez of the Old Mission area near the Temple Homestead, a daughter named Zoraida (later Perez). After Thomas married Nettie, he settled as a farmer on 100 acres of the Rancho Potrero de Felipe Lugo that had been held in his mother's name and, therefore, was excluded from the Baldwin mortgage.

In the mid 1880s, Temple lived in Hermosillo, Mexico, where he operated a tavern for a brief time.[47] Returning to Los Angeles, he was co-owner of the Los Angeles and Mexican Land Company and, then, proprietor of *La Cronica*, Los Angeles' only Spanish-language newspaper.[48] Thomas died in 1892 at the Workman Homestead, owned by his brother John, at age forty-

---

46 William Workman Temple, "The Mexican Revolution, and American Public Opinion" (San Diego: A.H. Heath, 1911) and "An Address to the American People" (Modesto: J.C. Cavell, 1910). Copies in the Homestead Museum Research Archives. Although Temple espoused the position that "if a woman does a man's work she should receive a man's pay", he also wrote, "we decry the mannish, blatant, rakish and selfish woman who seeks to live in an atmosphere not her own."
47 Los Angeles *Times*, 22 June 1883.
48 Los Angeles *Times*, 23 February 1887; Wallace E. Smith, *This Land Was Ours: The Del Valles and Camulos* (Ventura: Ventura County Historical Society, 1977), pp. 214–225.; *Los Angeles City and County Directory, 1886–87* (Los Angeles: A.A. Bynon, 1886), pp. 148, 223; see also subsequent listings in the Los Angeles city directories.

five of consumption, which also had claimed the lives of his mother and grand-mother in the preceding two weeks.[49] His wanderings and his varied pursuits well characterized the nature of his family members, as exemplified both by his father before and his brother Walter after.

The Workman Homestead, meanwhile, was owned successively by two other Temple boys. Francis W., after attending a college in San Francisco and the Massachusetts Institute of Technology in the early 1870s, returned to La Puente and ran his grandfather Workman's wine-making operations. Francis evidently took occupancy of the Workman House after his grandfather's sui-cide and purchased the home and seventy-five acres from Baldwin's agent.[50] He continued to make wine, raised fruits and walnuts and may have added a pump house and water tower that survive today.[51] His brother, John, described the winemaking operation as it existed in 1889, a short time after Francis' death: "The property...is fitted with press and storage facilities for the manufacture of 50,000 to 60,000 gallons of wine per annum, also with a still for the manufac-ture of brandy. At present the annual out-put does not exceed 10,000 gallons of wine."[52] The twenty-five acre vineyard, along with two acres of citrus and three acres of deciduous fruits, were irrigated by the ditch William Workman had dug through the Homestead years before.[53] Evidently achieving some fi-nancial success, Francis Temple died of influenza in August 1888, a few days short of his fortieth birthday.

After Francis' death, the Workman Homestead passed to his brothers William and John H., although the former was then in Mexico City and sold his interest to the latter.[54] John, who was finishing a commercial school course at the Bryant and Stratton Institute in Boston when the bank failure occurred, returned to southern California shortly after graduating in the summer of

49 Los Angeles *Times*, 26 January 1892, 5 February 1892, 12 February 1892; Los Angeles *La Cronica*, 12 February 1892.
50 William Alvord to Francis W. Temple, *Deed to a Portion of the Rancho La Puente*, 19 October 1880, Book 76: 304, Los Angeles County Archives.
51 From an 1880 survey by Los Angeles County surveyor E.T. Wright of the "La Puente Homestead" commissioned by Francis Temple, Huntington Library; Wilson, *Thompson and West's History of Los Angeles County*, pp. 72, 133, 186; *Los Angeles City and County Directory, 1881–82* (Los Angeles: Southern California Directory Company, 1881), p. 230; *Los Angeles City and County Directory, 1886–87*, p. 177; Francis Workman Temple, "How To Make Wine," unpublished manuscript, no date, copy courtesy of Betty Temple Miner in the Homestead Museum Research Archives.
52 Biographical sketch of John Harrison Temple, *An Illustrated History of Los Angeles County, California* (Chicago: Lewis Publishing Company, 1889), p. 655.
53 Hall, *Irrigation in (Southern) California*, p. 485.
54 William W. Temple to John H. Temple, *Deed to One-Half Interest in the Workman Homestead*, Book 574: 86; *Decree of the Estate of Francis Workman Temple*, 30 June 1892, Book 805: 156–159, Los Angeles County Archives.

JOHN H. TEMPLE FAMILY, WORKMAN HOUSE, CIRCA 1890
COURTESY OF THE HOMESTEAD MUSEUM, CITY OF INDUSTRY, CALIFORNIA

1876, and took up residence on land in the Rancho Potrero de Felipe Lugo that was also owned by his mother, and there he raised walnuts.[55] In 1886, he married Anita Davoust, whose mother was a member of the Dominguez family, and, two years later, the couple moved to La Puente. John was the first of his siblings to raise a family, which consisted of seven children. Despite the presence of the large wine producing facilities he described above, John struggled to maintain the ranch and, probably hampered by the strictures imposed by the Depression of 1893, the worst in American history to date, and a prolonged period of drought in southern California, mortgaged his holdings to make improvements to the property. This failing, he was foreclosed upon by the end of the decade and, for the second time, the Workman Homestead was lost by the family.[56] Temple, who then moved his family to Los Angeles, later

---

55 Wilson, *Thompson and West's History of Los Angeles County*, p.186; *An Illustrated History of Los Angeles County*, p. 655. There is a copy of a mortgage between John H. Temple and his mother, Antonia Margarita Workman de Temple, for forty-four acres of Rancho Potrero de Felipe Lugo and 150 acres of the Workman Mill tract, dated 13 September 1880 as well as the indenture of 23 April 1883 to cancel the promissory note on this mortgage, and a description of the forty-four acres, as surveyed by a H. J. Stevenson, dated 3 February 1881, in the possession of Josette Temple.
56 *Foreclosure Action Against John H. Temple, et. al., for the Workman Homestead*, 2 September 1899, Book 1307: 290, Los Angeles County Archives. The property was sold to Fred J. and Louise C. Smith for $12,109.50.

ran a gas station for some years for his brother Walter at the Temple oil lease in Montebello. For a time, he also assisted his brother in running the ranching enterprise at the Workman Homestead and died in 1926.[57] Fortunately, it was through John H. Temple that much of the family history, in the form of collected artifacts, letters and documents, and his own notes on family history, was preserved.

Struggles were not limited to the Temple family. William Workman's only son Joseph, and his family continued to own their 814 acres of La Puente, which was excluded from the Baldwin mortgage. They operated a sheep ranch there until 1881, when they moved to Boyle Heights and built a home on an acre deeded to them by Joseph's cousin, William Henry Workman, and leased out their La Puente property. Due perhaps to the same difficulties that affected his cousin John H. Temple at the Workman Homestead, namely the depression and drought of the 1890s, as well as because of providing money to some of his children, Joseph mortgaged his La Puente ranch to a bank for two loans. When the notes expired in the spring of 1895, the bank foreclosed, and the Workmans resorted to deeding the parcel to O.T. Bassett of El Paso. Bassett, in return, paid off the mortgage, gave the Workmans some property in El Paso, and began subdividing the Workman tract. After his death, his son continued the development of the subdivision that bears the family name today.[58] Meanwhile, the Workmans separated, Joseph living at several addresses until his death in 1901, and his ex-wife, Josephine operating a number of boarding houses in Los Angeles until she remarried in the 1910s.[59] She died in Los Angeles in 1937.

It was from this little known branch of the Workman family that an interesting public aspect of the family history developed. In 1909, Joseph and Josephine's youngest surviving child, Josephine, began a career in Hollywood's budding motion picture industry as an actress with Bison Studios. Carrying some of the features of her Latina heritage, Josephine, using the stage name Princess Mona Darkfeather, starred in some seventy films, mostly shorts, for companies such as Nestor, Kalem, Centaur and Universal until her retirement

---

57 Los Angeles *Times*, 12 April 1926.
58 See Josephine Akley, *et al.* v. Charles Bassett, *et al.*, Case 7625, Los Angeles Superior Court, V.1: 5–398. This case sought ownership of part of Bassett's property by Joseph's children, claiming that the youngest Workman child, Josephine, was not properly served Bassett's notice to quiet title. Although she won at the Superior Court, Josephine's victory was overturned on appeal to the state Supreme Court in 1924.
59 Los Angeles *Times*, 14 March 1901; see Los Angeles City Directories from 1894 until 1915.

in 1917. Few prints of her work have survived, but the titles of her films, including *The Fate of the Squaw, The Vengeance of Winona, An Indian Maid's Strategy*, and her last film, *The Red Goddess* imply that she played the kind of stereotyped native American characters that proliferated in surviving early Westerns. After leaving the film industry, she led a quiet life in Los Angeles as the wife of a film director and technician, until her death in 1977 at the age of ninety-five.[60]

The Workmans of Los Angeles

Amidst the struggles in one branch of the Workman and Temple family, another was on the rise in the public affairs of Los Angeles and southern California. Ironically, the head of this branch, David Workman, brother of William Workman, had brought his wife, Nancy, and their three sons, Thomas, Elijah, and William Henry to southern California only to lose his life within a year. His widow and sons remained at La Puente for a brief time before moving into Los Angeles to begin their lives anew. Elijah and particularly William Henry entered into careers that made them among the most prominent of a new generation of Angelenos. Unlike their uncle William, Elijah and William Henry arrived in the American period and did not have the identification and affinity with the Californio and Mexican influences that had been prevalent when William Workman and F.P.F. Temple rose to prosperity. Young adults during the boom of the late sixties and early seventies, the two participated in the transformation of Los Angeles that supplanted Californio predominance and replaced it with American and European practices.

As noted in Chapter Three, the eldest of the Workman brothers, Thomas, was head clerk for Phineas Banning and appeared to be headed for a public career before he was one of those fatally injured in the explosion of the steamer *Ada Hancock* at San Pedro in April 1863.[61] Elijah and William Henry also worked early in their careers for the Banning Transportation Company. The former later worked for the government at Fort Tejon and as a salesman before engaging as a saddler in 1857. William H., meanwhile, worked as a "printer's devil" for the early regional newspapers, the *Southern Californian* and the

60 Billy H. Doyle, "Lost Players—Princess Mona Darkfeather," *Classic Images*, 219 (September 1993): 54–55, from research by Donald Lee Nelson and this author.
61 Los Angeles *Star*, 7 June 1856; Los Angeles *Semi-Weekly Southern News*, 7 August and 6 September 1861.

JOSEPHINE WORKMAN,
A.K.A. PRINCESS MONA DARKFEATHER, CIRCA 1914
COURTESY OF DOUGLAS NEILSON

Star. A remarkable anecdote from his employ in the media business was related by Harris Newmark regarding the lynching of a convicted Los Angeles
murderer, David Brown, in January 1855. According to Newmark, Workman,
then working for the *Southern Californian* "planned to print a full account of
the execution in time to reach the steamer [for San Francisco]." Although the
lynching was slated to take place *after* the departure of the ship, "Billy sat down
and wrote out every detail...and several hours before the tragic event actually

took place, the wet news-sheet was aboard the vessel and on its way north." In the dry humor that makes much of Newmark's narrative so engaging, it was noted that "[a] few surplus copies gave the lynchers the unique opportunity... of comparing the written story with the affair as it actually occurred."[62] By contrast, William's son, Boyle, whose semi-autobiographical account of Los Angeles, *The City That Grew*, published in the 1930s, mentioned the incident without specifically identifying his father's role in the affair.[63]

Another anecdote of William H.'s early years was related by both Newmark and Boyle Workman and regarded his role as campaign manager for his brother's candidacy for county clerk in 1861. Intended to be amusing when such racially-tinged accounts were commonplace and notwithstanding the accuracy of the two accounts, the episode reveals something of the unfortunate, darker side not only of politics, but of the ethnic and racial relations in the city. Newmark remembered: "On the evening before the election, he rented a corral...and there, with the assistance of friends, he herded together about one hundred docile though illegal voters, most of whom were Indians, kept them all night and, by supplying fire-water liberally, at length led them into the state of bewilderment necessary for such an occasion."[64] According to Newmark, the opposition intercepted this rather pathetic parade and "stampeded the whole band" into reversing their position. The author attempted to explain the incident off as "a perfectly legitimate transaction to buy votes." Boyle Workman's book reported events differently, "Father collected a lot of Indians and bedded them for the night" and that the opposition, "those conscienceless rascals", foiled the scheme by "an efficacious and deadly weapon— the potent grape brandy, aguardiente."[65]

In 1864, Elijah and William H., who had joined his brother not long after Elijah entered the business seven years before, purchased a saddlery in Los Angeles and opened it as the Workman Brothers. The partnership folded three years later when Elijah left for a brief period of residency in Missouri. Meanwhile, William continued in the trade as Workman and Company. Elijah's return in the fall of 1868, however, led to the resumption of the business that was a highly successful enterprise for the next nine years.[66] Aside

62 Newmark, *Sixty Years in Southern California*, p. 141.
63 Boyle Workman, *The City That Grew* (Los Angeles: Southland Publishing Company, 1935), pp. 62–63.
64 Newmark, *Sixty Years in Southern California*, pp. 42–43.
65 Workman, *The City That Grew*, pp. 42–43.
66 Los Angeles *Star*, 14 January and 9 July 1870; Los Angeles *Herald*, 30 October 1873.

ELIJAH WORKMAN, CIRCA 1870

COURTESY OF THE

WORKMAN FAMILY COLLECTION

from the work in the saddlery, the brothers dabbled, before the devastating drought of 1862–64, in sheep raising and sales of wool. One newspaper article, from 1862, showed the brothers to be the ninth largest wool producers in Los Angeles County.[67]

Increasingly, the brothers engaged in the public life of the city. Elijah served four terms on the city council between 1866 and 1876 and sat on the Board of Education in 1864 and from 1880–1882. He was also a founding member of the 38s Volunteer Fire Company in 1873, the second organized fire fighting squad in Los Angeles.[68] Among his most lasting legacies were the planting of shade trees in Central Park (now Pershing Square) and in the Plaza, where some of the trees still stand. He maintained his trade as a saddler even after his brother left the business and retired in the early 1880s to spend

67   Los Angeles *Semi-Weekly Southern News*, 16 May 1860 and 26 September 1862
68   Boyle Workman, *The City That Grew*, p. 116.

WILLIAM H. WORKMAN
CIRCA 1887

COURTESY OF THE
WORKMAN FAMILY COLLECTION

his remaining years at his ranch just south of the downtown district. There he raised on seven acres an impressive array of fruits as well as a flower garden and walnut orchard.[69] He died in July 1906, having survived three wives and three of his five children.

William H. had a notable career in the public sector, especially after he left the saddlery business in 1877. A major change in his fortunes was his marriage in 1867 to Maria E. Boyle, whose father, Andrew, was the owner of an extensive ranch on the bluffs and bottom lands along the east bank of the Los Angeles River. Boyle was a native of Ireland who survived the defeat of an Irish brigade fighting for the American rebels in Texas in 1836, and over-came a shipwreck while transporting goods from New Orleans to Mexico.

---

69 See the extensive description of the Elijah Workman ranch by Benjamin C. Truman in the Los Angeles *Star*, 5 June 1874 and his book, *Semi-Tropical California* (San Francisco: A.L. Bancroft and Company, 1874), pp. 56–57.

When the news of the latter reached his wife in New Orleans, she, believing that Boyle had perished, succumbed to an attack of brain fever, leaving him to raise their only child. He moved to California and established a thriving mercantile house in San Francisco before settling with his daughter in Los Angeles in 1858, where he operated a successful viticulture and wine-making operation. Upon Boyle's death in April 1871, his daughter and son-in-law assumed ownership of his impressive ranch, which was extensively developed. In 1880, the 330 acres featured 40,000 vines on the bluffs with the intention of doubling their number, as well as 30,000 vines on the flatlands next to the river that were said to date to the 1810s or 1820s, 2,000 budded orange trees on both the bluffs and bottom lands, 400 lemon trees, 250 limes trees, 200 walnut trees, and a smaller number of "a great variety of temperate and semi-tropical fruits."[70]

In 1876, Workman, at the tail-end of the boom of the late sixties and early seventies and only months after the failure of the Temple and Workman bank, began the subdivision of part of Andrew Boyle's ranch, named Boyle Heights in his honor. Although the community grew slowly in the depressed economic conditions of the late seventies, it gradually assumed importance as one of the residential districts of the city. By 1880, Boyle Heights was described as a "village...which contains some fifty or sixty families." The Aliso Street Railway was developed by Workman in 1876 and was followed two years later by the opening of a water supply and irrigation system into the community. Continuing to provide for park and school sites and another street car line in late 1886 along First Street, Workman's involvement in the development led to an estimated population, on the eve of the great land boom that would break out the following spring, of some 2,500 persons.[71]

Meanwhile, Workman's involvement in public life began in the late 1860s with nine years of service on the Board of Education.[72] While on the board in 1872, he was one of a three-person building committee (the others being Matthew Kremer and Henry D. Barrows) involved in overseeing the construction of the first city high school.[73] The same year, he was one of the many public leaders in Los Angeles who took part in the railroad conferences that culminated in the agreement to bring the Southern Pacific's railroad line

70 Wilson, *Thompson and West's History of Los Angeles County, California*, p. 184.
71 Los Angeles *Herald*, 6 December 1886.
72 Spalding, *History and Reminiscences*, p. 170.
73 Ibid., p. 176.

CUMMINGS BLOCK, BOYLE HEIGHTS, CIRCA 1889
COURTESY OF THE WORKMAN FAMILY COLLECTION

from San Francisco to San Diego through the city. Like Thomas W. Temple, he was a founding trustee of the Los Angeles Public Library. Active in the Democratic Party since his early twenties, Workman served six terms on the city council between 1873 and 1880 and was sent by the party's local commit-tee to Baltimore as the alternate delegate to the national party convention in

1872.[74] He also ran unsuccessfully for City Treasurer in 1870 and the state Assembly in 1873, when he was described as

> ...a self-made man, having built up for himself a handsome fortune in Los Angeles, and [a] most honorable reputation in this part of California. His course in the [City] Council seems to be marked by a conscientious disposition to do right and guard the people's welfare. Although a generous friend and forebearing, he sometimes gets 'warm' when in debate.[75]

He may have been even more prosperous in his real estate dealings during the fabulous boom of 1886 to 1888, except that his election as mayor forced him to pull back on his speculative enterprises. The boom was so extensive that the earlier boom of the late sixties and early seventies paled in comparison. The preemiment fact was the completion of the Atchison, Topeka and Santa Fe rail line in 1885, which gave Los Angeles a direct transcontinental railroad link and broke the local railroad monopoly held for a decade by Southern Pacific. This brought fierce railroad competition and cheap fares that lured many to the region. Shrewd marketing by southern California promoters encouraging emigration to southern California was also a major impetus. New towns, such as Puente, just a short distance northeast of the Workman Homestead, popped up throughout the region and somewhat established subdivisions like Boyle Heights flourished anew during the boom. Although the excesses of the growth spurt led to a depressed market in the late 1880s and early 1890s, followed by depression and drought, and many of the townsites languished, Los Angeles could acknowledge its maturity as a city and southern California began to take on the charateristics of a true metropolitan region, continuing thereafter to grow at fantastic rates.

The fact that Workman won election as mayor was somewhat remarkable because he was a Democrat, albeit a conservative one, in an era when Republicans dominated Los Angeles politics. His ability to swing some Republican votes testified to his general popularity among the voting public, although he faced

---

74 Wilson, *Thompson and West's History of Los Angeles County*, p. 115; Los Angeles *Star*, 15 July 1872.
75 Los Angeles *Star*, 6 December 1870, 17 March 17 June and 1 July 1873.

a fair share of criticism. One such jab dealt with one of the touchiest issues of the period, the presence of Chinese in southern California. Despite the lessening of violence after the horrid Chinese Massacre of 1871, agitation against them loomed again in the eighties. One attack on Workman was over the hiring of Chinese labor at his Boyle Heights orchards. In response, Workman wrote an open letter in which he stated,

> To save my crops from perishing I have sometimes been compelled to employ Chinamen, but I have never done so when white help was available. I am opposed to the employment of Chinese, but there are cases where persons in my situation are absolutely forced by the necessities of the situation to accept their work. The assertion that I am the steadfast friend of the Chinese is false, as is also the declaration that I never give employment to white men.

Workman even had his ranch foreman, Walter Drown, who, as noted earlier was the ward of William Workman, then lived and worked on the Workman Homestead with Francis W. Temple at Rancho La Puente as late as the early 1880s, gave a statement verifying his account. Drown noted,

> Mr. Workman has uniformly instructed me to get all the white men I could...and I have only employed Chinamen upon the place when it has been absolutely necessary to do so. Had I not done so Mr. Workman's crops would have perished. I have found from personal experience that a white man who endeavors to irrigate vines and trees to any great extent runs the risk of becoming seriously ill...Mr. Workman has two Chinamen employed, who do this kind of work.[76]

Workman's views were those of the vast majority of Americans and Europeans in Los Angeles; nonetheless, after his election as mayor, Workman was invited by a representative of the Chinese Buddhist temple to attend the

---

76 Los Angeles *Times*, 5 December 1886.

Ah Dieu ceremony, a remembrance of the 1871 massacre against nineteen Chinese, although it is unknown if Workman actually attended.[77]

Some of the major issues of Workman's mayoral term included the creation of a new city charter that set out new systems for government. Another was the abolishment of the onerous duty of the Mayor's Court, which presided over the lowest misdameanor crimes and violations of city ordinances. After ten weeks in that capacity, Workman was freed from that responsibility and a new judgeship was created. In 1888, a new city hall was completed, although Workman never occupied the new mayoral office, since his term had expired.[78] Another notable issue involved the health of the city, after a few smallpox cases in the spring of 1887 led to a panic. Workman responded by creating a temporary commission of health officers, who canvassed the town, encouraging citizens to contribute to a general cleansing of streets and property.[79] Additionally, the problem of badly flooded Los Angeles streets during the rainy season was addressed, when for the first time street paving was provided in the city during the Workman administration. Finally, Workman played a significant role in rail developments, including the construction of a new depot by the Southern Pacific, and the completion of the terminal railroad at San Pedro.

After his mayoral term expired, Workman returned to private business, serving as a director of the University Bank of Los Angeles and operating a real estate firm called the Workman Company. Later, in 1903, he was a founder and President of the American Savings Bank. [80] In the 1890s, however, Workman reentered public service when he served on the Los Angeles Parks Commission. This had been a favorite enterprise of the former mayor, who had helped to establish Hollenbeck Park in Boyle Heights, one of the most beautiful parks in the city.[81] During his mayoral administration, a number of parks were established to meet the increasing need for recreational spots. Westlake Park (now MacArthur), South Park, Sunset (now Lafayette), Echo, and Eastlake (Lincoln) opened during the years 1887 and 1888. One of the major actions taken during Workman's service on the commission in the nineties was the

---

77 Ah Foy to William H. Workman, 23 October 1887, Workman Family Papers, Center for the Study of Los Angeles, Loyola Marymount University.
78 Workman, *The City That Grew*, p. 106.
79 Los Angeles *Times*, 4 April 1887.
80 *Los Angeles City and County Directory, 1887–88* (Los Angeles: George A. Maxwell and Company, 1886), p. v, and other city directories for the 1890s.
81 Spalding, *History and Reminiscences*, p. 300. Workman donated two-thirds of the land, while the widow of his friend and business partner, John E. Hollenbeck, donated the rest for the creation of the park.

assumption of the gift of Griffith J. Griffith's property north of downtown that became Griffith Park, one of the city's most notable public spaces. After a few more years in the business world, Workman was called back to politics in 1900 to run for city treasurer. He was elected to three successive terms, from 1901 to 1907, during which he was involved in a number of controversial, but pivotal, projects for the continued expansion of Los Angeles and the southern California region.

One of the initial undertakings of Workman's first term was the transfer of management of city water from a private lease arrangement to municipal control. This was subject to the city's purchase of the private water company with a price fixed by arbitration after the expiration of the lease. In February 1902, four years after the thirty-year lease arrangement lapsed, Workman's suggested price of $2 million, a million lower than the owners of the company had previously asked, was agreed upon. A voter-approved bond issue was then followed by the dilemma of how to market the bonds in order to pick up a franchise operator. Workman and city attorney William B. Matthews journeyed to New York and, after a month of fruitless negotiations, were able to find investors who offered $5 million to the city for franchise rights. Fearing that opposition in Los Angeles would bring legal proceedings to halt the arrangement, Workman and Matthews decided to turn the bonds over to the franchise holders and to receive payment in New York. This required, however, that Workman sign each of the 2,000 bonds valued at $1,000 each. Boyle Workman recalled, "It seems that every time Father dipped his pen in the ink-well, he absently shook it...to rid it of any spare ink that might cause a blot. By the time he had finished the two thousandth signature...the president's office, including a brand new carpet, presented a general poker [sic] dot effect."[82] Acting as treasurer while his father was in the East, Boyle Workman presented the check, the largest ever drawn by the city, for $2 million to the owners of the old water company, and presided over the transfer of control of water to the city.

Regarding the monumental Los Angeles Aqueduct project, William H. Workman played a significant role in the early financing stage. He supervised the appropriation of $150,000 in city funds in the summer of 1905 to pay for the purchase of the Owens Trough. This strip of land was to be used for the aqueduct channel that, being outside of the boundaries of Los Angeles city,

---

82 Workman, *The City That Grew*, pp. 294–297.

was not legally available for purchase by the city. A proposed bond issue of $1.5 million for surveys and land purchases was to be up for voter approval in September. Noting sententiously that "such crises in the life of a city require extra-legal action," Boyle Workman asserted, "[M]y father knew if he honored the demand for $150,000, and the bond issue failed, the diversion of funds would have to be made good by himself. He consulted the men who were on his indemnity bond of $300,000. They sanctioned his going ahead, regardless of the liability they might incur."[83]

Perhaps the risk was not as dangerous as it may have appeared to Boyle Workman, given the "extra-legal" determination city leaders had to see water brought to the city. The bond issue passed by a seven to one margin, giving Workman the justification he needed for his proactive decision. The following summer, Congress passed a right-of-way bill that gave legal authority for the city's purchases of land for the aqueduct outside city limits. Another bond issue in 1907 authorized a staggering $23 million towards the project, which was considered a marvel of engineering, both scientifically and politically, when it opened in November 1913.[84] The way was then cleared to even greater levels of development, especially in the enormous San Fernando Valley, where a syndicate of landowners who had been instrumental in getting the Aqueduct built, stood poised to make fortunes in subdividing the newly-watered plains.

Another development during Workman's tenure as treasurer was the provision for depositing city funds in a bank to develop returns on interest. This practice had first been developed in 1875 when City Treasurer J.J. Mellus invested the city's funds in the Temple and Workman bank, only to see it disappear in the failure of the bank. The fact that it was a full generation until the city felt confident enough to resume the practice is another testament to the impact of the bank failure. At this late date, though, Workman was successful in his attempt to reintroduce the concept. An amusing anecdote passed along by his son reminds of the simplicity of office procedures in the era. Cash for the payroll was picked up by the treasurer himself, occasionally without a guard, who would then hoist the sack of $20 gold pieces over his shoulder and cross the busy street back to his office. On this occasion the string broke sending coins rolling in every direction. Boyle Workman then related that

---

83 Ibid., p. 307.
84 Joseph O'Flaherty, *Those Powerful Years: The South Coast and Los Angeles, 1887–1917* (Hicksville, N.Y.: Exposition Press, 1978), pp. 229–230; Workman, *The City That Grew*, pp. 307–08, 310, 315.

"Father summoned an officer and then rushed into the treasurer's office, with his characteristic: 'My God, Boyle, I'm ruined. There are $20 gold pieces all over Broadway. Some of you boys come out and help.' A big crowd had gathered. Father selected various men out of the crowd to assist in picking up the gold. When we finished not one single gold piece was missing!"[85] Although Los Angeles had grown into a metropolis, incidents like this remind one of the archaic practices still employed by city leaders!

Despite the occasional roving gold piece, Workman was widely respected and liked by his contemporaries and colleagues. It was noted by the *Los Angeles Times* that, despite Workman's Democratic Party affiliation, his alignment with Republican principles made him one of Los Angeles' most popular political personages during his years as city treasurer.[86] His example in the field of public service would be carried on by his children Boyle and Mary Julia, as southern California grew from a city to a metropolis during the boom of the 1920s.

---

85 Workman, *The City That Grew*, p. 299.
86 Los Angeles *Times*, 6 and 7 December 1904.

CHAPTER SIX

Modern Times

ᔕ 1914–1930 ᔕ

Mary Julia Workman: Social Activist

From the 1870s until 1930, Los Angeles experienced one developmental boom after another, each much larger than its predecessor. In the case of the era between 1914 and 1930, when the city's population jumped from below 500,000 to nearly 1.5 million, the pattern was extended to tremendous suburban growth in all directions. The increasingly common use of the automobile contributed to the uniqueness of the basin's development, where rather than building up, as in New York and Chicago during the pre-auto age, building out was made possible by the spread of the car among southern California's households. The Pacific Electric Railway system was also a major component of the suburban sprawl that developed during this period.

At the same time, as the pace of life quickened, through the impetus of urban expansion; the growth of industry; faster modes of transportation; high-speed communications, such as the telephone and radio; and other factors, southern Californians also longed for the slower paced simplicity, real or imagined, of the past. This desire did not necessarily reflect a need for a thorough reevaluation of the history of the past, but rather revealed a deep-seated need to find some repose from the hurried life of an urban metropolis. Residents developed a romantic fascination regarding the lifestyle of Spanish and Mexican California that was so decisively uprooted and replaced in the latter half of the nineteenth century. Although Hollywood has received more than its fair share of recognition for contributing to this process, the film industry is only one example of the dynamic that makes this period one of fascination. While the period of 1914-1930 was a period of expansion in the region, it was, for the Workman and Temple families, another period of prominence in the public life of the southern California region.

MARY JULIA WORKMAN, CIRCA 1900
COURTESY OF THE WORKMAN FAMILY COLLECTION

Although the nineteenth century has left a great paucity of information about the women of the Workman and Temple families, it was during the early twentieth that the first woman in these families played a prominent public role in southern California. A movement that was largely spearheaded by women provided this opportunity. Progressivism, an engine for social reform beginning in the mid-nineteenth century, created an arena of public life that was one of the few in which women participated in great numbers. Mary Julia Workman, daughter of William Henry and Maria Boyle Workman, was a leader in progressive causes in Los Angeles after the turn of the century.

Mary Julia was born in January 1871, when her father was gradually becoming more prosperous and involved in civic affairs in Los Angeles. Her grandfather, Andrew Boyle, died in April leaving William H. Workman his valuable property east of the Los Angeles River. Additionally, the Workman Brothers saddlery and livery stable had made William and his brother Elijah quite wealthy. By her school age years, Mary Julia Workman's surroundings were comfortable and she received an education to which few of her peers of either gender had access. Her mother's Catholicism was a dominant influence in the young girl's life and Mary Julia received her primary instruction from the Sisters of Charity at their school on Alameda Street across the Los Angeles river from the Workman home. While her father served as mayor, she was sent with her sister, Elizabeth, to the Sacred Heart Academy (now Holy Names College) in Oakland, a convent that educated some of California's most elite young women. Although an education such as this was as much a finishing school as a conduit to higher learning, Mary Julia did not follow the usual path of marriage and pursued teaching as a career.

In 1899, Mary Julia entered a training program for kindergarten instructors at the State Normal School, later to become the University of California, Los Angeles. Concepts of universal education, especially for the very young, were still fairly new and she demonstrated her ability to master a wide variety of issues in her three years in the program. In 1905, she received her lifetime credential to teach kindergarten. Meanwhile, she was hired by the Los Angeles School District after graduating from the State Normal School program and she began her twenty-year teaching career at the Utah Street School. This was the first of several assignments in underprivileged areas of the city. In graceful and stately prose, Mary Julia wrote of the optimism and opportunity of working with an ethnically diverse group of young children and "to evolve the rudiments of order, to establish the calm majesty of law" and instill other notions of respect and dignity.[1]

Even before she began her teaching career, however, Mary Julia had demonstrated an interest in working with the underserved. After attending a lecture in early 1901 by Reverend John Clifford, assistant pastor of St. Vibiana's Cathedral, she joined a group of women in founding the Brownson House Settlement Association. Located in a small home on Aliso Street, the association provided catechism instruction, organized clubs, and visited homes with

---

1   Undated letter to Mary Leopold, as quoted in Michael E. Engh, "Mary Julia Workman: The Catholic Conscience of Los Angeles," *California History*, 72 (Spring 1993), 7.

the aim of improving the lives of youngsters in the surrounding neighborhood. The organization moved to larger quarters after a few years, and by 1916 more than sixty women and a few men were making the Brownson House a success story with few peers in the southern California social service arena.

John J. Cantwell, who assumed the position of the bishop of the Diocese of Monterey and Los Angeles in 1917, established a more centralized system of controlling church charitable functions, resulting in the formation of the Associated Catholic Charities. Mary Julia, who had conflicting ideas with Reverend William Corr, the new director of the organization, promoted the management of Brownson House through locally based workers in collaboration with the community it served. Corr's representation of a less personalized approach of bureaucratic management led Mary Julia to resign her position as president of the board of directors for the settlement in 1920, followed by a number of her colleagues. The settlement continued to operate under the Associated Catholic Charities, renamed the Bureau of Catholic Charities. The Brownson House, meanwhile, still operates in East Los Angeles.[2]

After leaving Brownson House and retiring three years later from teaching, Mary Julia embarked on a remarkable period of social activism during the 1920s. She was the secretary and treasurer for the Alliance of Social Agencies, an umbrella entity for over sixty privately operated welfare organizations in the region. In 1923, she became a member of the Municipal League in which prominent citizens served as monitors of civic activity. She had also developed an interest in Native American issues during the early years of the decade.

Meanwhile, Bishop Cantwell, recognizing the value of Mary Julia's work in the realm of social welfare and wishing to make amends for the uncomfortable situation arising out of the Brownson House affair, approached her in 1924 about being the diocesan representative of the National Conference of Catholic Women. During that year she organized the local Council of Catholic Women, serving for two years as its president. At the conclusion of her term in 1926, Mary Julia was sponsored by Cantwell in the awarding of the *Pro Ecclesia et Pontifice*, a commendation issued by the Pope. This honor was the first ever made to a lay person in the Los Angeles diocese and was perhaps the pinnacle of her career in early social activism.

All of this activity in the religious sphere soon led her to the political world. In 1925, while her brother Boyle served as president of the Los Angeles City

---

2   As with the rest of this section, a fuller examination of the Brownson House Settlement under Mary Julia Workman is in Engh's "Mary Julia Workman", pp. 8–13.

Council, Mary Julia was named by Mayor George Cryer to serve on the Civil Service Commission, making her the third woman to serve on the commission in the first quarter century of its existence. In 1927 and 1928, she served as the commission's president. Although the commission normally went through its coordination of civil service examinations without much publicity, her presidency was filled with notoriety when one of the commissioners, a labor activist, pushed pro-union candidates for the city council in an era where unions were anathema in southern California.

Her work continued after 1930 in an amazing range of activities, including international peace efforts, the treatment of Japanese-Americans during the painful years of the Second World War internment process, race relations, a film industry worker's dispute, and others. She was active in the 1938 recall of Mayor Frank Shaw, wielded an influential hand in the administration of Shaw's successor, reform-minded Fletcher Bowron, and actively promoted Democratic Party principles. She also was involved in the National Council of Christians and Jews. Mary Julia remained active in social issues until just shortly before her death, at age 93 in October 1964, from complications of a broken hip. As her biographer, Father Michael Engh, has written, "The breadth of her interests and the length of her commitment place her in the forefront of noted women reformers in Los Angeles in the first half of the twentieth century. . .few advances in social welfare in Los Angeles failed to attract her careful review and active support."[3]

Boyle Workman: Following His Father's Footsteps

Mary Julia's brother, Boyle, largely followed in the footsteps of his father, except for interludes such as his commercial enterprises during the 1890s. He was his father's secretary during William H. Workman's terms as mayor and city treasurer of Los Angeles. He also assisted his father in business enterprises such as the Workman Company, a real estate firm, and the American Savings Bank, founded in 1903. Boyle also served on the Public Service Commission from 1913 until 1917, when the city arranged for municipal ownership of electric power development. In the summer of 1914, a bond issue authorizing city control of distribution was passed, followed two years later by the construction

---

3 Engh, "Mary Julia Workman", p. 18.

BOYLE WORKMAN, CIRCA 1927

COURTESY OF THE WORKMAN FAMILY COLLECTION

of a system, now the Department of Water and Power (DWP) that generated its first current in November 1916.[4]

Upon his father's death on 21 August 1918, Workman became the administrator of the estate, incorporated as the Workman Properties. In 1919, he was a founder of the Gesel Plan Corporation, a company that offered a savings and life insurance investment plan, but was called upon to run for the city council, to which he was elected later that year. The respect he had earned through his more than thirty years in public life led to his becoming president of the council, a post he held until 1927. In his work, *The City That Grew*, Workman made mention of what he considered to be the most significant events during his eight years on the council, a period that saw incredible development in the

4 Shortly before Workman ended his service on the commission, the new Southern California Edison Company, Ltd, a combination of the old Edison Company and the Pacific Light and Power Company, was selected to be the seller of distribution on behalf of the city.

Los Angeles area. Workman was associated with major civic projects, such as the Los Angeles Memorial Coliseum (1923), Los Angeles City Hall (for which the Temple Block was demolished), which opened in 1928, the Central Public Library (1926), and Union Station, a project begun in the 1920s, though not completed until 1939.

One of the main boosters of the Coliseum project was William May Garland, Workman's real estate partner in the early 1890s. Garland and others formed the Community Development Association, Ltd. to build the structure, which was seen as a necessity for holding the 1932 summer Olympic Games. The Association submitted its plans to the City Council, which were approved, and the 73,000-seat stadium was completed in the fall of 1923. The Association paid for the cost of construction and was reimbursed through tax allotments, after which the city and county assumed ownership of the structure.[5]

In the long process of approval for Union Station, Workman claimed a crucial role. He noted that once, during a discussion on

> . . .a subject entirely apart from the union terminal. . .a councilman moved that the city abandon the union terminal project. I ruled him out of order, but he appealed from the decision of the chair. A vote on the appeal resulted in a tie. As president of the Council I was able to cast the deciding vote. Otherwise, the sudden vote might have resulted in dropping the project which means so much to this city.[6]

By the time the terminal was completed in 1939, however, the use of the railroad as a passenger conveyance in automobile-driven southern California was on a rapid decline.[7]

The move to build a new city hall was part of an ambitious and aggressive plan for a new civic center that began in the early 1910s. Workman wrote, "The Council was very popular when it became known that the city government was to have a new home. We were constantly invited to banquets for the purpose of viewing plans for the new Civic Center."[8] According to Workman,

---

5   Workman, *The City That Grew*, p. 364.
6   Ibid., p. 373.
7   The station has only recently seen a resurgence with recent rail developments, such as Metrolink.
8   Ibid., p. 376.

WALTER AND LAURA TEMPLE FAMILY, CIRCA 1919
COURTESY OF THE SEAVER CENTER FOR WESTERN HISTORY RESEARCH,
LOS ANGELES COUNTY MUSEUM OF NATURAL HISTORY

early proposals actually favored the Courthouse as the focus of the civic center, but the council opposed this leaning.[9]

Bertram Goodhue's landmark Central Public Library opened in 1926, and Workman claimed that he was responsible for the agreement for the new site. He wrote, "When the Library Board, through its president, Orra E. Monette, consulted with the Council, my proposal that we turn the "Normal Hill" site over to them met with favor. We also purchased the Flower Street frontage for $100,000 and added it to the Library property." When, upon completion, the actual transfer of ownership of the site was to be made to the city, Workman

---

9   It is interesting in this respect to peruse Kevin Starr's description of the City Hall, which "unambiguously bespoke civic power and ambition" and served, "to symbolize the collective identity and shared consciousness of the new metropolis. Raising the ancient ziggurat symbol of power and wealth above its skyline, Los Angeles declared its material dream." Kevin Starr, *Material Dreams: Southern California through the 1920s* (New York: Oxford University Press, 1990), p. 112. One of the victims of the construction of City Hall was the Temple Block, which was razed in 1925.

recalled, "Mayor George E. Cryer was ill when the building was completed, and as acting mayor it was my privilege to accept the property for the city."[10]

Just as his father had an important role in water development during his years as city treasurer, Workman also took part in city council meetings during 1924 regarding the proposal of William Mulholland for the development of the Colorado River Aqueduct, a project completed in the 1930s after Workman left the council. Another accomplishment was the council's vote to select the site for the University of California branch campus that opened in Westwood in 1929.[11] In the midst of the trumpeting of the accomplishments of these major public projects, it is refreshing to note that Workman thought it worthy to mention that it was also during his years on the city council that the fire department exchanged horse drawn fire trucks with automobiles.[12]

As president of the city council, Workman served as acting mayor whenever the mayor was out of town or ill. Although there was normally little to do in this capacity, on one such occasion he was taken to task by the Los Angeles *Times*, which reported on a golfing trip Workman took to Catalina "while $1,000,000 in water bonds lay on the Acting Mayor's desk awaiting his signature." One councilman called Workman's action "outrageous", and three others expressed their disapproval. A council telegram was sent to the acting mayor conveying their feelings, but it was noted that the total loss of interest that would have been earned on the bonds if Workman had been at his post amounted to a total of $200.[13]

Despite these occasional disruptions and the usual controversies attendant to such a position, Workman completed his eight years on the city council and, while president of that body, turned his attentions to the municipality's highest office. He ran for mayor in 1929, but lost to used-car salesman and expressive optimist John C. Porter by a narrow margin. Perhaps it was just as well, since Porter presided over the beginnings of the Depression and is best remembered for his off-the-cuff dismissal of the dismal economic picture of early 1930s Los Angeles. After the campaign, Workman stepped out of politics and into a gradually more retiring public life. His legacy today, however, is not necessarily his prominent role in political affairs for which he should be remembered, but in the publication of his semi-autobiographical narrative of Los Angeles, *The City That Grew*. Published in 1935, the work is filled with colorful re-

10 Workman, *The City That Grew*, 375.
11 Ibid., pp. 374–375, 380.
12 Ibid., pp. 373–374.
13 Los Angeles *Times*, 8 June 1924.

membrances and second-hand accounts of the city in the tradition of other local luminaries, such as Harris Newmark and Jackson Graves.

"Gold of a Different Color"

By 1920, Walter P. Temple, Boyle Workman's cousin and schoolmate during the 1880s at St. Vincent's College (now Loyola Marymount University), experienced a resurgence in fortune that enabled him to enter the public arena in southern California through oil, real estate and construction. His story mirrored in several ways that of his father, some fifty years before, leading to similarly grievous consequences.

Temple grew up during the years of difficult financial circumstances for his family following the failure of the Temple and Workman bank. After his mother's death in 1892, Temple and his younger brother Charles inherited the Temple Homestead. A decade later, Temple was the sole owner of the fifty-acre parcel and raised walnuts and apples. He, his wife Laura Gonzalez, and children Thomas, Agnes, Walter, Jr. and Edgar lived in a one-story frame house built just after the turn of the century and just southeast of the old Temple adobe and 1870s brick house. As was characteristic of the family since 1876, the Temples were in frequent economic trouble. But, in October 1912, Temple, acting upon the advice of an old friend, Milton Kauffman, made an arrangement to purchase sixty acres of land on the Rancho La Merced formerly owned by his father, but then owned by the Baldwin estate.[14] Kauffman evidently told Temple that Standard Oil of California, having discovered a major oil field recently in northern Orange County, was scouting for nearby locations, including Montebello, to test for crude. Ironically, to pay for the purchase, Temple borrowed money from the Baldwin Estate.[15] Selling the Temple Homestead,

---

14 Baldwin had died in 1909.
15 The deed from the estate of E.J. Baldwin was made to Walter Temple on 30 October 1912, and a mortgage on the same parcel executed from the Temples to H.A. Unruh, the Baldwin estate executor, for $3,875. In April 1916, the Temples were released from the mortgage, having conveyed the hillside acreage by trust deed to the Fidelity Savings and Loan and the Title Guaranty and Trust Company for a $5,000 consideration. From Lot Book P-49: 1143, Rancho La Merced, Title Records Incorporated. Also, see Johnstone Jones, "Montebello Oil Field Is Alluring Prospect", Los Angeles *Times*, 28 January 1918: "At the time of this lucky purchase, no one knew or even supposed that the land was oil territory though it appears that the first draft of the deed conveying the title from the Baldwins to Temple contained a clause reserving to the grantors all mineral rights. This restriction was cut on objection by the purchaser's agent, Milton Kauffman." Walter Temple's son, Walter Jr., recalled in a 1983 interview that, "this is where Kauffman comes in. I think he was the forerunner leasor for Standard Oil." In another interview five years later, he remembered, "I guess it was through Milt that Dad was able to make the lease with Standard Oil." Walter Temple, Jr., "Recollections of Family, Community, and Business Life.", *Workman and*

the family relocated west a mile or so across the Rio Hondo, or old San Gabriel River, and occupied the Basye Adobe, an 1869 structure, which once was owned by Temple's sister Lucinda and her husband, Manuel Zuñiga.

The Temple family's ownership of this property probably raised few eyebrows at the time, but in the spring of 1914, nine-year-old Thomas, the family's oldest child, and, later, a noted historian and genealogist, made a discovery which became something of a local legend, not a little embellished upon by the discoverer himself. Thomas elaborated upon his tale over the years, but perhaps the most fanciful is one penned in 1961, which employed the type of romantic mythology about earlier days in California that, by the 1910s, had fully permeated the southern California consciousness.

Thomas began his tale with a discussion of a poor family whose father and oldest sons worked for F.P.F. Temple. The youngest son of this unnamed family, José María, came upon two strangers camped out on the boy's favorite locale on what became known as the Montebello Hills. "From their fierce looks and bristling guns," Thomas wrote, the boy observed that "they must be Bandidos." One of them, though, was nursing a wound and the boy's naive pity aroused him to bring food to the two men. Nevertheless, "the long arm of the law closed in on the bandidos", who fled, but not before thanking young José María by revealing the obligatory hiding place of their ill-gotten gains. When the bandidos were captured and hung, José María was taken sick and passed away not long after, and so too disappeared knowledge of the secret gold. Invoking "the mysterious ways of God," Thomas related how the charity of José María was reincarnated to "another little boy, blood relative of the first, and perhaps as good and charitable, with gold of a different color."[16]

Painting a prototypical picture of a bright rain-washed spring day, Thomas told how, in April 1914, he roamed the hills "in search of wild flowers, johnny jump-ups, poppies, cacomite, and wild onions", as well as wild oat shoots useful for catching blue-bellied lizards. Seeing a gully with a pool of water, he was attracted to rainbow-like streaks, the odor of rotten eggs, and a gentle bubbling on the surface. Rushing home "down the steep trail he could see his father, Walter Temple, tending one of the horses in the barns to the rear of the[ir] adobe. Out of breath and excited, the boy told his father in a matter-of-fact manner: 'Daddy, I have found oil for you!'"

Temple Family Homestead Museum Oral History Program, 1983, p. 15.; Temple, "An Oral History Interview with Walter Temple, Jr.", ibid., 1988, p. 18.

16   It would appear that Josè Maria was a relative of Thomas' mother, Laura Gonzalez.

TEMPLE OIL LEASE, MONTEBELLO, CIRCA 1921
COURTESY OF THE HOMESTEAD MUSEUM, CITY OF INDUSTRY, CALIFORNIA

Rather foolishly lighting a match and holding it nervously over the bubbles, the two noted "a sputtering and a flash —natural gas! A good indication of oil pools beneath, and the future Montebello oil fields had been discovered." In this way, concluded Thomas, José María's kind deeds were "a gift of God that brought much happiness to the boy's family and prosperity to the valley."[17]

A more mundane explanation of how the oil was discovered was reported in the *Whittier News* in 1917:

> [W]orkmen who had been driving piles for a county bridge
> over the river at that point [the Rio Hondo] noticed a black
> scum of oil emerging from the hole made by the huge pile.
> It was not long before experts examined it, and the result
> has been that Montebello has become a great oil-producing
> center.[18]

---

17 Thomas Workman Temple II, "Legend of the Secret Gold Comes True With Black Gold", Temple City *Times*, 7 July 1973.
18 "Fortune Smiles on Pioneer Family," Whittier *News* (reprinted from the *La Puente Valley Journal*), 30 November 1917.

**TEMPLES AT BARBEQUE CELEBRATING FIRST OIL WELL,
BASYE ADOBE, JULY 1917**
COURTESY OF HOMESTEAD MUSEUM, CITY OF INDUSTRY, CALIFORNIA

However the discovery happened, the Temples executed in September 1915 a lease of the sixty-acre hillside property to a James M. Kent. After a modification the following April, Kent made an assignment of the lease to Standard Oil Company of California in November 1916, a month before the company began the first test well in the Montebello Hills parcel owned by Anita Baldwin, "Lucky" Baldwin's daughter.[19] A few months after Thomas Temple's discovery, Standard was first made aware of Montebello's potential and sent a geologist to the area. A judgment that surface inidications were as favorable as those in Orange County led to the lease agreements.[20] The Baldwin test well proved successful and led to the first producing well in Montebello in March 1917. A month later, Temple Number One was begun and was put on the pump about the first of June producing 500 barrels of oil per day. The family, recipients of a one-eighth royalty, celebrated the opening of the first

---

19 From Lot Book P-49: 1143 for the Rancho La Merced, Title Records Incorporated.
20 Gerald T. White, *Formative Years in the Far West: A History of Standard Oil Company of California and Predecessors Through 1919* (New York: Appleton-Century-Crofts, 1961), p. 416.

well with an "Old California Barbeque" in a willow grove behind the Basye Adobe, the Temple residence.[21]

Between the summer of 1917 and the end of 1921, sixteen wells were drilled on the Temple oil lease with several gushers. At a rate of two dollars per barrel and production running at some 10,000 barrels daily, the Temples were initially enjoying an income of $2,000 per day from the rich deposits along the riverbottom and hillside portion of the Montebello Hills.[22] Standard Oil, by 1919, was pumping out some 21,000 barrels of oil a day (30% of the company's entire output) from thirty-two wells on the Baldwin, Temple, and a few other small leases, totaling some $12,000,000 in value.[23] Montebello, along with the West Coyote Hills/Emery field in north Orange County, helped the company, which had contributed less than four percent of the oil production in the state in 1911, to seize a nearly 26% share within eight years.[24]

Meanwhile, Temple began his own oil company that drilled wells in northwest Whittier, and invested in fields in Ventura, Huntington Beach, Texas, and Mexico. None of these ventures, however, could compete with the power and wealth of the big concerns or measured up to the fantastic results of the lease at Montebello, though even this fertile field yielded its oil at shallow depths for only a fairly short period of time.[25] For example, surviving financial statements from 1921, when the Montebello fields began to decline in production, showed that the Temples were receiving between $23,000 and $28,000 per month. Five years later, that amount had dropped to just over $11,000.[26] By then, Walter Temple had moved into the highly volatile world of real estate and construction and away from the steady flow of revenue from the Montebello lease, on which he had depended for his speculative capital.

---

21 The Basye Adobe was built in 1869 by Rafael Basye. His wife, Maria Alvitre, was a relative of Walter Temple's wife, Laura. The adobe had housed a store and tavern, which were run by Walter Temple's brother-in-law, Manuel M. Zuniga. The adobe later became the headquarters of the Temple Oil Lease site. For the barbeque, which was "attended by about 1000 persons", see the Alhambra *News*, 24 July 1917.

22 Los Angeles *Times*, 25 June 1917 and 28 January 1918.

23 White, *Formative Years in the Far West*, pp. 416–17.

24 Ibid., pp. 406–07. Monthly field reports in *The Oil Age* and weekly updates in the Whittier *News* documented the progress of the Temple lease wells beginning in February 1917.

25 Regarding the resources at Montebello, a 1921 report published by the California State Mining Bureau noted that, "This field has been one of the most prolific in southern California, but it can be considered as having passed the day of flush production." Lawrence Vander Leck, *Petroleum Resources of California*, Bulletin 89 (San Francisco: California State Mining Bureau, 1921), p. 135. The bulletin contained a panoramic photograph of the Temple Lease.

26 Monthly Report: Receipts and Expenditures for Walter P. Temple, 18 June-17 July 1921, 18 November-17 December 1921, 18 December 1921–20 January 1922; Financial Statement of Temple Estate Company as of 31 December 1926, Thomas W. Temple II Collection, Homestead Museum Research Archives, courtesy of Ruth Ann Michaelis.

A Monument to the Temple Family

As soon as the first royalty checks arrived in the mail, the Temples acted on their revitalized fortunes. In late November 1917, they made two important real estate purchases. The first was a residence in Alhambra, a city that in the early 1920s, like so many other communities, was the beneficiary of still another southern California land boom. For a family of former farmers who had frequently struggled financially, the expansive Craftsman-style home in a fashionable neighborhood of the town was a world away from the plain one-story frame house and the fifty-year old Basye Adobe at La Merced.[27] Alhambra gave the Temples access to better schools for their children and another field of activity for Walter Temple to apply his oil income, that of development. The other transaction was the acquisition of the seventy-five acre Workman homestead at La Puente, which had been lost by Temple's brother, John H., at the turn of the century. In the intervening years there had been three owners. One of them, Lawrence F. Lewis, had allowed the old Workman cemetery to fall to near-ruin, demolished the St. Nicholas chapel, removed three of the perimeter walls, and allowed cattle to graze in the burying ground and trample the gravestones. Temple galvanized the support of others, including members of the Rowland family, and filed a successful lawsuit, restraining Lewis from further desecrating the cemetery.[28] The judgment also called for Lewis to pay for the reconstruction of the three walls he had removed, but Lewis sold the Homestead a few months later, in December 1907, to Thomas Pratt and Eugene Bassett.[29] Pratt and Bassett leased the Homestead and, at one time, a family operated the Puente Packing Company on the grounds. Pratt and Bassett were the owners when Walter Temple purchased the parcel from them for $40,000, an exorbitant sum for the period, well over $500 an acre.[30]

Because the Homestead had been leased to a family of farmers, the Temples did not actually take full possession of the property until 1919.[31] Their first

27 See "Temple Is Making Beautiful Home", Alhambra *Advocate*, 13 June 1919 and the Progress Edition supplement of the *Advocate*, 30 January 1920. The Temples moved from the home in 1923 and the lot was purchased by a Methodist church. The home, heavily remodeled and indistinguishable from the rest of the church buildings complex, survives as the rectory.

28 "Is Plowing Graves His Right?," Los Angeles *Times*, 6 February 1907; Walter Temple to Josiah W. Hudson, 23 July 1907, courtesy of the La Puente Valley Historical Society.

29 L.F. Lewis to T.H. Pratt and Eugene Bassett, *Deed to the Workman Homestead*, 11 December 1907, Deed Book 3168: 197, Los Angeles County Archives.

30 T.H. Pratt and Eugene Bassett to Walter Temple, *Deed to the Workman Homestead*, 28 November 1917, Deed Book 6587: 119, Los Angeles County Archives.

31 A July 1918 newspaper article, however, noted that Walter Temple's brother, John, was the superintendent of the ranch. "Some Side Lights on the History of Puente Valley and Rancho La Puente," *La Puente Valley Daily Journal*, 5 July 1918.

project in restoring and renovating the Homestead was to work on the cemetery. Their plans initially included "the rebuilding of the Catholic church which William Workman erected within the walls of a cemetery...and [which] was accidentally destroyed by fire in 1903."[32] Instead, the Temples built a steel pole fence to replace the three destroyed brick perimeter walls, and then hired the Whittier contracting firm of E.M. Wheatland to construct a Greek Revival mausoleum designed by the architectural firm of Garstang and Rea.[33] The "temple" configuration was no doubt an intentional play on the family name and contained the curious inscription "Walter P. Temple Memorial." The cast concrete structure, with twenty-four marble-faced crypts, was completed in the spring of 1921 and inaugurated with a ceremony conducted by Roman Catholic Bishop John J. Cantwell. Within its walls were reinterred members of the Workman and Temple families, including William and Nicolasa Workman, David Workman, and F.P.F. and Margarita Temple, as well as Pío Pico and his wife, María Ygnacia Alvarado. The Picos had been buried at the old Calvary Cemetery in Los Angeles, which had been closed in preparation for the construction of Cathedral High School. Today, the remains of these friends and neighbors, the Picos, Temples, and Workmans, lie side-by-side in the mausoleum.[34]

Further plans for the site included the renovation of the old Workman wineries, one of which was converted into an auditorium, containing a stage with a curtain featuring a painted backdrop of Mount Baldy by noted artist Boris Deutsch, as well as billiard and ping-pong tables. Here, the family showed motion pictures to guests, presented music recitals by the children, and held other entertainments. A smaller, adjacent structure was remodeled into a kitchen and dining hall, with a capacity to serve 150 persons. The third building, the smallest of the trio, was converted into a nine-car garage. The Temples were lavish entertainers, hosting, for example, annual barbeques for the southern California Elks lodges, with as many as 1,500 guests as well as the entire senior class of St. Mary's Academy in Los Angeles, where daughter Agnes graduated.[35] Other improvements made during the early 1920s included

32 Jones, "Montebello Oil Field Is Alluring Prospect," Los Angeles *Times*, 28 January 1918.
33 A copy of the original drawings are in the Homestead Museum Research Archives. Charles Garstang and Alfred Rea began practicing architecture in 1913 and completed many projects, largely for civic, religious, and educational structures in southern California. Rea was a board member and treasurer of the southern California chapter of the American Institute of Architects during the 1920s. See the California Biographical File, Los Angeles Central Public Library.
34 Rose Ellerbee, "Honor for Ashes of Pío Pico," Los Angeles Times, 6 March 1921
35 Alhambra *Advocate*, 30 July 1920; *Alhambra News*, 2 August 1921, 30 August 1921, 7 February 1922, and 1 August 1922; *Lightning*, St. Mary's Academy Yearbook (1925), pp. 31, 67.

the addition of a laundry room; servants' quarters; homes for the ranch fore-man and his family; houses for Walter Temple's sisters, Lucinda and her hus-band Manuel Zuniga, and Margarita Rowland and some of her family; barns and stables; a reservoir, doubling as a swimming pool, complete with dress-ing rooms, diving board, and a grandstand; and a tennis court. The Temples added seventeen acres to the parcel, totaling ninety-two, and planted much

EL CAMPO SANTO CEMETERY CIRCA 1925

COURTESY OF THE HOMESTEAD MUSEUM, CITY OF INDUSTRY, CALIFORNIA

of it with walnuts, the occupation Walter Temple had held before becoming an oil magnate and capitalist. Further, the Temples extensively remodeled the seventy-five year old Workman House, adding electricity, heating and closets, and used the old adobe on weekend visits to the ranch.

The most impressive improvement on the Homestead, though, was the construction of *La Casa Nueva*, a twenty-six room, 11,000 square foot Spanish Colonial Revival mansion built adjacent to the Workman House. Originally conceived by the Temples with contractor Sylvester Cook, the blueprints were drawn up by the well-known Los Angeles architectural firm of Walker and Eisen.[36] The home was built with a wealth of finely crafted architectural de-

36 Original drawings for the house from Walker and Eisen, known mainly for their commercial struc-tures in Los Angeles, are in the Homestead Museum Collection. Walker and Eisen also designed many of Walter Temple's commercial structures in the San Gabriel Valley. See also Donald J.

tails, including stained and enameled glasswork and handmade and painted tile. Examples of some of the glass work include an enormous triptych window in the main hall providing a romantic depiction of early California; irises and wisteria in a sun-drenched breakfast room; composers, such as Bach, Beethoven, Mozart, and Chopin in the Music Room; scenes from *Don Quixote*, as well as portraits of Cervantes, Shakespeare, Milton, and Longfellow, in the Library; portraits of the two oldest Temple children, Thomas and Agnes, modeled from photographs, dressed in Mexican costume; and French doors in the master bedroom that pay tribute to the Temple and Workman families. Laden with tile, the house features three panels by an artist from Puebla, Mexico, including peacocks feasting on watermelon in the breakfast room and a 1920s stylized portrait of the Madonna (modernized with bobbed hair, lipstick, and eye shadow) and the infant Jesus in Thomas Temple's bedroom. Carved plaster corbels in the main hall reveal eagles from the Mexican seal holding lamp chains from their beaks, while wooden corbels in the living and dining rooms include carvings of Indians, Spanish *conquistadores*, and even a couple of canines attired in jacket and tie. Other historically-inspired items include a tepee-shaped retreat used as a home office by Walter Temple and a walkway spanning three sides of the house with the names of the California missions inscribed in cement floor panels. For many years, the Temples had lived near the original Mission San Gabriel site, near today's Whittier Narrows dam, and then resided in Alhambra a short distance from the current mission, of which they were enthusiastic patrons and boosters. Adding to the mission influence, grape vines cut from the mother vine at San Gabriel were planted on the trellis work of the Mission Walkway and a large palm tree, said to have been planted by the padres at San Gabriel in 1775, was moved to the ranch in 1925 and set between the walkway and the house.

The house is best described, however, as a monument to the Temple and Workman families. In addition to the family-themed windows in the master bedroom, the family's English coat of arms is displayed prominently throughout the house; cattle heads, grape vines, and stalks of wheat, remembrances of William Workman's ranching and agricultural pursuits, grace doors and corbels; the courtyard fountain features two millstones, believed to have been salvaged from the old Workman Mill; and the basement contains the vault taken from the cellar of the former quarters of the Temple and Workman bank

Schippers, "Walker & Eisen: Twenty Years of Los Angeles Architecture, 1920–1940", *Southern California Quarterly*, XLVI (December 1964): 371–394 for a summary of the careers of these prolific architects.

in the Temple Block.[37] Even the flagstone walkways that surround the house are marked with broken pieces of tableware thought to have been buried by Workman, whose trash pit may have been on the site of *La Casa Nueva*.

The project had hardly begun, however, when, at the end of 1922, Laura Temple died from complications of colon cancer and an intestinal blockage.[38] Her son, Walter Temple, Jr., recalled, "[W]hen mother passed away, there was a period there when they didn't know whether they were going to finish it or not. Of course, Ines and Tomas [Walter's sister and brother, Agnes and Thomas] and Dad got together and said, 'Well, we are going to finish it and dedicate it in her memory.'"[39] The first step in the family's resolve to honor Mrs. Temple through the construction of the house came in 1923 on the first anniversary of her death, when Bishop John J. Cantwell officiated at a dedication ceremony during which a plaque was placed on the house in Mrs. Temple's memory. Although Walker and Eisen were listed on the plaque as the home's architects, a new architect, Roy Seldon Price, was brought in to supervise the completion of the building.[40] Price incorporated a number of changes into the original design, and the house was not completed until 1927, by which time Walter Temple was already experiencing financial difficulties and had mortgaged *La Casa Nueva* and the Workman Homestead.

Walter Temple: Coming Full Circle

These problems were centered around Walter Temple's avid participation in real estate and construction, the largest industry of 1920s southern California. By 1919, during the heady years of the oil boom at Montebello, Walter Temple had begun to use his oil income as a springboard for investments in both the San Gabriel Valley and Los Angeles. Many of his projects

---

37 Although Walter Temple believed he was salvaging the vault from the Temple and Workman bank, the vault was probably an addition made by the Los Angeles County Savings Bank, which occupied the bank quarters after 1878. Los Angeles *Star*, 28 April 1878. Copies of letters between Temple and attorney Will D. Gould, who maintained his offices in the Temple Block from 1873 until it closed in 1925, detailing Gould's efforts to salvage elements of the Block for Temple are in the Homestead Museum Research Archives. Brick and wood from the Block were used in the construction of a Tepee-shaped office next to the Temple's home, *La Casa Nueva*.

38 "Impressive Services Mark Funeral of Mrs. W. Temple", Monterey Park *Progress*, 5 January 1923; Laura Gonzales Temple's obituary, "Life Linked With Local History", Pasadena *Star-News* (Alhambra edition), 28 December 1922.

39 Walter P. Temple, Jr., "Recollections of Family, Community, and Business Life", pp. 45–46.

40 Price is best known for designing the Spanish colonial revival home of motion picture director Thomas Ince, now destroyed, but appears to have been relatively inactive before his early death in 1940. Many photographs of the construction of La Casa Nueva and other elements at the Homestead site are in the Homestead Museum Research Archives.

La Casa Nueva, circa 1928

COURTESY OF THE HOMESTEAD MUSEUM, CITY OF INDUSTRY, CALIFORNIA

were timely and well-conceived; the crux, however, lay in the execution of his plans and in the pace which he was setting when embarking on these projects. In the hurried atmosphere of another of southern California's boom periods, Temple was one of many drawn in by the rush to partake of the promise of profit. He formed a partnership with Milton Kauffman and attorney George Woodruff to launch his career in real estate. This alliance was formalized in May 1923, with the creation of the Temple Estate Company.[41] Initially, there were only the three men as directors and officers: Temple as President, Woodruff as Vice-President and Kauffman as Secretary. Later, the company added two directors, who at various times included Temple's eldest children, Thomas and Agnes, and the company's auditor, Charles W. Tandy. Kauffman, an old friend of Temple's, was from El Monte, where his father, Isaac, owned a large mercantile establishment and a hotel. Kauffman had some real estate experience in Baldwin Park, a new town on former Workman land taken by Baldwin in the aftermath of the Temple and Workman bank failure. He had acted as Temple's agent in arranging the purchase of the Montebello Hills property that yielded the fabulous oil lease and became Temple's manager, supervising

---

41 Temple Estate Company, *Articles of Incorporation*, 31 May 1923, California State Archives, copy courtesy of Dr. Kaye Briegel.

the investment projects Temple financed. Woodruff, the legal member of the team, was a native of Connecticut who had settled in Whittier at the turn of the century, serving as the city attorney. Later, he moved to Pasadena and conducted a private law practice in Los Angeles. Generally, Kauffman selected the projects that Temple invested in and Woodruff oversaw the execution of contracts. As Walter Temple, Jr., remembered, "[T]here were decisions to be made and Dad wasn't any businessman. He would say, 'Well, if that's the way it's got to be, why, that's the way it's got to be.' You had some things that would come up and so naturally they would go ahead and sign it off. He'd give his okay to do that."[42]

Temple's first commercial property investment came in the summer of 1919 with the purchase of a lot in the downtown business district of Alhambra.[43] His entrance into the world of southern California real estate, primarily focused on the San Gabriel Valley, was part of the larger movement that made the 1920s a period of unparalleled growth in the region. While the population of Los Angeles nearly tripled, the suburbs boomed as well. Established towns, such as Glendale and Alhambra, were among the fastest-growing cities in the United States, and subdivisions and townsites were springing up throughout southern California. From upscale projects, such as Rancho Palos Verdes, Bel-Air, and Beverly Hills, to more modest enterprises like Walter Temple's Town of Temple, the enthusiasm for development was rampant in the first half of the twenties. Temple's participation was characteristic of the story of many other like-minded capitalists.

Although it was two years before Temple built on his first purchase, it was a timely venture. The advent of motion pictures made the industry a force in southern California. As towns like Alhambra grew, motion picture theaters became hallmarks of town development, along with a library, a post office, and business blocks. Walter Temple's first building was a movie theater, of which its manager claimed, "Mr. Temple will build a structure that will be a credit to the town and a credit to him and there we will be able to offer entertainment on a par with the finest cinema palaces in the country."[44]

The Temple Theater, designed by Walker and Eisen, was built in the popular Egyptian revival style, cost $100,000, seated 1,000 persons, and featured murals by nationally known artist Julian Garnsey. Garnsey's work, often with his

42 Walter P. Temple, Jr., "An Oral History Interview with Walter P. Temple, Jr.", Workman and Temple Family Homestead Museum Oral History Program, 1988, p. 6.
43 "Temple Purchases Business Corner," Alhambra *Advocate*, 18 July 1919.
44 "$100,000 Building Deal Is Completed," Ibid., 3 June 1921.

father Elmer, included the New York House of Customs, the St. Louis Public Library, and the state capitols of Minnesota and Wisconsin. The theater was his first California project, but five years later, Garnsey also created murals for the Los Angeles Central Public Library that are extant.[45] Expected to be opened in the fall, the theater did not premiere until just before Christmas 1921. It was explained, as it so often would be with Temple-financed projects, that "Mr. Temple was determined to carry out some very high ideas, from an artistic standpoint, in its construction and decoration, so that all the time was taken to carry out the elaborate scheme that was planned."[46] The grand opening was a spectacle for the growing city with all of the theater's seats filled and hundreds turned away.[47] Temple's first project as a capitalist could not have been more successful.[48]

The theater was followed in the summer of 1923 by two buildings: an adjacent Spanish colonial revival building, another Walker and Eisen design, constructed for a mortuary, and a post office and hotel purchased soon after construction started.[49] Two additional lots on the city's Main Street gave Temple ownership of a block and a half of the choicest downtown property in Alhambra. On these two latter parcels, Temple completed his last projects in the city. The first, another Spanish colonial revival production by Roy Seldon Price, was known as the Temple Building. With a second floor iron grille, featuring the Temple family coat of arms and a distinctive tower, the building, finished in April 1926, featured the local branch of the Security Trust and Savings Bank as the anchor tenant.[50]

Temple's most impressive edifice in Alhambra was announced in 1925 as the Temple Estate Company Building.[51] Intended initially to be six stories, the structure was a Walker and Eisen design unlike the Spanish Colonial Revival

45 "Noted Artist Doing Temple Theatre Work," Ibid., 18 November 1921. See Garnsey's work in the children's room at the Los Angeles Central Public Library. Glenn B. Opitz, ed., *Mantle Fielding's Dictionary of American Painters, Sculptors & Engravers* (2nd ed., New York: Apollo Publishing, 1986), p. 314.
46 "Temple Theatre To Open Thursday, 23," Alhambra News, 20 December 1921.
47 "New Theater at Alhambra Has Opening", Los Angeles *Times*, 25 December 1921.
48 The theater, however, which thrived as a Paramount Pictures associate during the 1920s and often showed premieres, changed to the El Rey in the early 1930s, when it was one of the first theaters purchased by James Edwards, whose company owned the site when it was torn down in 1990.
49 "Fine New Business Building To Be Erected At Fourth and Main," 10 January 1923 and "Alhambra Postoffice In New Location On North Fourth St.," Pasadena *Evening-Post* (Alhambra edition), 6 August 1923.
50 The Utter and Sons mortuary building and the Temple Building were razed in February 1997 as part of a redevelopment project. This leaves the Edison Building, the former post office and Temple Hotel, and an adjacent retail structure as surviving buildings owned or erected by Temple in the city. Temple Building Section, Alhambra *Post-Advocate*, 21 April 1926.
51 "Announce Plans for Temple Building", Ibid., 27 June 1925.

buildings they usually designed for Temple, but more akin to their many commercial projects in Los Angeles. At $250,000, this was one of Temple's most extravagant outlays. It was also highly ambitious to expect a town of 35,000 people to support an office structure of that size. By the time construction began in 1926, it had been scaled back from six stories to four, a possible reflection of the economic difficulties Temple was experiencing.

When the building was finished in April 1927, the opening was marked with an eight-page supplement to the city's *Post-Advocate* newspaper. The Temple Estate Company took out a full-page ad, featuring a medieval herald blowing the trumpet announcing the edifice as "The Pride of Alhambra."[52] Because the anchor tenant was the Southern California Edison Company, it was renamed the Edison Building, which remains the largest structure in Alhambra's business district. A few months later, George Woodruff noted that the Edison Building's success would be a gauge for the increasing growth of the community's business area.[53] The building was heavily advertised in the local paper, but was completed at a time of declining fortune for Walter Temple and his estate company.

In addition to Alhambra, Temple expanded his development plans into the nearby towns of San Gabriel, El Monte, and Monterey Park, although his proposal to build an office building in the latter was thwarted by strict ordinances, as well as a dispute over the quality of a just-completed building that he bought, so he sold his holdings there by early 1923.[54] In El Monte, still a small town of a few thousand residents, he constructed a one-story building that housed the city's post office and the Rialto Theater, a small movie house.[55]

Historic San Gabriel, dating to the relocation of the mission there in 1775, was important to the Temple family, who had baptisms, weddings, and other important events at the old church. Like El Monte, it was a small town of a couple of thousand residents during the early 1920s. Temple's activity in the town began in 1922 with the donation of a lot for the city hall, another Walker

52 Edison Building Section, Alhambra *Post-Advocate*, 8 April 1927.
53 "Office Building is Barometer of City's Progress", Ibid., 10 August 1927.
54 "Berry Block Contractor Advised By Trustees to Follow Building Law", Ramona Acres [Monterey Park] *Progress*, 2 June 1922; "Temple Plans $40,000 Building", Monterey Park *Progress*, 15 December 1922; "Store and Lodge Building", Los Angeles *Times*, 17 December 1922; "Temple Building Delay Disappoints Citizen", Monterery Park *Progress*, 9 March 1923. Temple sold his Monterey Park property to George Pethybridge, likely in exchange for the Alhambra post-office building and adjacent lot during the spring of 1923.
55 "El Monte Theater," Los Angeles *Times*, 10 September 1922; "Post Office Will Have New Home", 24 January 1923 and "Big Building Arising In El Monte", Pasadena *Evening-Post*, 22 March 1923. The building survives, although with only the shell intact. The Rialto was purchased by the Sanborn family, whose SoCal Theatre chain still operates.

and Eisen design, which was completed in March 1924. In July the town honored Temple by placing a plaque on the building recognizing his donation and

TEMPLE THEATRE, ALHAMBRA, CIRCA 1927

SECURITY PACIFIC COLLECTION/ LOS ANGELES PUBLIC LIBRARY

hanging an oil painting of their benefactor in the lobby.[56] Temple also built a two-story Temple Block, completed in September 1922, which housed the library and a real estate office for Temple and Thomas Berry, an associate from Monterey Park. Adjacent to the Temple Block, a post office was completed soon afterward. Lastly, in late 1923, an arcade of shops was finished between the Temple Block and City Hall, marking the end of Temple's remaking of the downtown business area.[57]

Temple also purchased a number of lots in the unincorporated townsite of Puente, near the Workman Homestead, including the historic Rowland Hotel, built during the real estate boom of the 1880s; although he never did improve any of his holdings in the townsite.[58]

56 "Build City Hall Near Old Church", Los Angeles *Times*, 14 January 1923; "Mission City Renders Temple High Honor", 1 July 1924 and "Render Honor to Founder of Temple", Alhambra *Post-Advocate*, 3 July 1924.
57 "New Temple Block for San Gabriel", Alhambra *News*, 7 March 1922; "Temple Real Estate Office Is Opened", Ramona Acres [Monterey Park] *Progress*, 15 September 1922; Los Angeles *Times*, 2 September 1923. San Gabriel's awareness of its historic downtown has contributed to the preservation of these structures. Temple's portrait still hangs outside the council chambers.
58 See Tax Assessment books, *La Puente Township, 1919–1933*, Los Angeles County Archives.

Temple's activities were not solely restricted to the San Gabriel Valley, but included investments in Los Angeles and San Pedro. He was a major investor in the construction of two eleven-story business structures, the Great Republic Life and the National City Bank buildings located at opposite corners of Spring and Eighth streets. These were just a few blocks south of where his uncle and father had erected the famous Temple Block, the last of which was demolished in 1925 before the erection of Los Angeles City Hall. An office in the Great Republic Life building served as headquarters, from 1924 to 1927, for the corporations in which Temple was a partner or owner. These included the Talbert Oil Company, which had its operations in Huntington Beach wells, the Central Finance Building Company, owner of the building, the Walter P. Temple Oil Company, the Temple Estate Company, and the Temple Townsite Company.[59] With the completion of the Edison Building in Alhambra in 1927, the operations of the last three were moved there, while Temple had divested himself of involvement in the former two corporations.[60]

Temple also maintained offices in San Gabriel and El Monte during the 1920s.[61] In addition to the Spring Street holdings in Los Angeles, Temple owned a lot at the corner of Sixth and Hartford streets in the city.[62] In San Pedro, Temple purchased thirty-one vacant lots and three houses in two tracts and had an interest in ninety-eight acres of lands believed to be potential oil producers.[63]

Amidst all of these projects, Temple engaged in his most significant and elaborate project of all in the spring of 1923. This was the Town of Temple, on the previously proposed townsite of Sunnyslope Acres, a 640-acre tract on the Rancho San Francisquito. This portion of the rancho had formerly been part-owned by William Workman and F.P.F Temple, before they sold, during the suspension of their bank, the tract to Lucky Baldwin in late 1875. The townsite parcel was owned in 1921 by the Burkhard Investment Company, which intended to open its subdivision in March 1922, extend Las Tunas Drive east of San Gabriel and rename the street Main to link it with Alhambra and

59 See the *Los Angeles City Directory* for the years 1924–1927 (Los Angeles: Los Angeles Directory Company).
60 *Newton Directory, Alhambra Edition, 1927* (Los Angeles: Newton Directory Company, 1927), p. 268.
61 *San Gabriel City Directory, 1924* (Los Angeles: Los Angeles Directory Company, 1924), p. 486; Samples of Walter Temple's office stationery from El Monte and San Gabriel, Homestead Museum Archives, courtesy of the San Gabriel Historical Society.
62 *Statement of Property Owned by the Temple Estate Company*, 15 July 1930. Copy in the Homestead Museum Research Archives, courtesy of Gabriela Quiroz Temple Sutter.
63 Ibid. It is not known if any oil drilling was attempted at the San Pedro property.

petition the Pacific Electric Railway Company to add to its Alhambra line along this thoroughfare.[64] When the plans for the tract development failed, Walter Temple and his associates, Milton Kauffman, George Woodruff, and Sylvester Dupuy, the latter a longtime friend of Temple and a sheep rancher and Alhambra resident, stepped in with a smaller subdivision that "will be built as a memorial to the pioneer Temple family which came to Los Angeles a century ago and which has been prominently identified with the development of the Southwest."[65] At the same time the Temple Estate Company was incorporated, the five men organized the Temple Townsite Company to manage the growth of the new community.[66]

As reported in press accounts, the land for the Town of Temple consisted of a half-million dollar purchase of 285 acres of the Sunnyslope Acres tract. The minute book of the Temple Townsite Company shows that, on 29 May 1923, George Woodruff and unnamed associates sold parcels of land from four tracts (Bradbury Park, Lincoln-Garfield, Santa Anita Land Company, and East San Gabriel) for $500,000, payable in 5,000 shares of Townsite Company stock, and it may be that these parcels constituted additional land for the town.[67] An additional half million dollars was expended on the construction of a business district and the extension of the Pacific Electric Railway line and erection of a depot. With some 1,300 business and residential lots, the townsite's original configuration was designed to accommodate some 5,000 residents. As was common in most southern California subdivisions of the period, racially restrictive covenants were incorporated into the development of the town. One advertisement noted, "There will be building and racial restrictions and the entire enterprise will be designed to establish a model community. Potential buyers were assured that "property owners in the Town of Temple will be permanently protected through rigid enforcement of sensible race and building

---

64 "New Town of Temple to be Developed on Big Tract", Alhambra *Advocate*, 11 May 1923.

65 "New Town of Temple to be Developed on Big Tract", Ibid., 11 May 1923; "Site for New Town Acquired", 20 May 1923 and "Temple Plans New Block", Los Angeles *Times*, 30 September 1923. Dupuy's thirty-room house in Alhambra, completed in 1926, long-known as the "Pyrenees Castle," after the part of France were Dupuy's family hailed from, became notorious in 2003 when pop music producer Phil Spector, its owner, was arrested in the shooting death of a female companion inside the home.

66 Minute Book, Temple Townsite Company, May 1923-October 1931, courtesy of the Historical Society of Temple City. There was another director, Dolores Bingham, who was also elected Assistant Secretary at the inaugural election in May 1923. Bingham, however, did not attend meetings after the first two and was not reelected as a director at the next election in 1925. In January 1926, Bingham held one share of company stock, while the others each held 1,251 shares. It appears from census records that Bingham was a stenographer for George Woodruff. See also, *Walker's Manual of Pacific Coast Securities* (San Francisco: Walker's Manual, Inc., 1928), p. 796.

67 Minute Book, Temple Townsite Company, 29 May 1923, pp. 11–15.

restrictions."[68] A later sales brochure for the community noted, "Only white people reside here, white people of a desirable class who take pride in their homes and the upbuilding of the community." No small irony comes in the fact that the city's founder was one-third Latino on his mother's side. Indeed, Temple indulged himself, however romantically, in surrounding himself with reminders of this heritage in his home, while maintaining an "American" aspect in his business affairs.[69]

Temple and his associates promoted the townsite's proximity to Los Angeles, a mere forty-five minute drive from downtown, with its rural atmosphere, and its middle-class priced lots. An advertisement from August 1923 indicated that $350,000 worth of property had been sold in the three weeks since the townsite had opened and that forty homes were built.[70] A month and a half later, another ad promoted the community as "California's Newest, Prettiest, and Most Charming Home Community—a veritable paradise, lavishly favored by Nature with exceptionally fertile soil, ideal climactic conditions, wonderful scenic views and a bountiful supply of pure mountain water."[71]

Fifty-foot lots sold for $1,200, while half-acre "garden plots" were priced at $1,950, including such improvements as graded streets, cement walks and curbs, and electricity, gas, and water. By June 1924, it was advertised "The Spirit of Progress has transformed Temple" into "a well established prosperous community of handsome bungalows and busy stores." A hundred homes had been built, the Pacific Electric track had been laid, and fifteen stores opened, including a pharmacy and hardware store.[72] When the city celebrated its first anniversary at the end of September it made plans to accommodate 25,000 people with a barbeque, rodeo, and entertainment that the Alhambra *Post-Advocate* called, "the most gigantic birthday party ever staged in California," claiming, "It is doubtful if the history of the west can supply a parallel for the free anniversary celebration to be held at the Town of Temple." Although the community's Chamber of Commerce advertised that the event would feature no sales and, therefore, no taint of commercialism in the celebration, the methods employed in the town's promotion were typical of those used in similar real estate developments throughout southern California.[73]

68 Alhambra *Advocate*, 11 May 1923; Los Angeles *Times*, 20 May 1923.
69 Temple City Chamber of Commerce brochure, 1928, Homestead Museum Collection.
70 Advertisement, Alhambra *Advocate*, 4 August 1923.
71 Advertisement, Los Angeles *Times*, 30 September 1923.
72 Advertisements, Ibid., 18 May 1924 and 15 June 1924.
73 "Temple Town to Celebrate Birthday with Big Party", Alhambra *Advocate*, 27 September 1924; "Celebrate Birthday Today", Los Angeles *Times*, 28 September 1924.

TOWN OF TEMPLE, CIRCA 1924

SECURITY PACIFIC COLLECTION/LOS ANGELES PUBLIC LIBRARY

For the first three years, the town showed every indication, at least publicly, of a thriving community. The Pacific Electric line opened in the fall of 1924 and the Temple National Bank, Santa Anita School, and Temple Community Church were constructed. Water was contracted with the Sunnyslope Water Company, a privately managed concern, which catered exclusively to individual property owners. On the urging of company director, George Woodruff, vice-president of the Temple Townsite Company, the company made the Town of Temple its first community customer.[74] In addition to access from the west by Las Tunas Drive and the Pacific Electric line, the town was linked to the regional Arrow Highway, which was completed in 1928. By the end of 1926, 968 of the 1,285 business and residence lots had been sold, implying, by this indicator, that the town was one of the many successes in southern California's booming real estate industry.[75] Sales of lots, however, do not necessarily constitute a thriving community, particularly if the lots remained undeveloped and uninhabited, as most of the sold properties were, and heavily traded for speculative purposes. Additionally, the southern California real estate market, which had peaked in 1923, when the townsite was opened, cooled off afterward.

74 William A. Myers, *Ranches to Residences: The Story of Sunny Slope Water Company, 1895–1995* (Pasadena: Sunny Slope Water Company, 1994), pp. 43–48.
75 *Walker's Manual of Pacific Coast Securities*, p. 796.

> ## RESTRICTIONS—
>
> The restrictions placed on race and building have made Temple City, with its 3,500 population, the highly desirable place to reside that it is today. Only white people reside here—white people of a desirable class, who take pride in their homes and the upbuilding of the community. While the building restrictions do not require the erection of costly mansions, they are strict enough to prevent the construction of unsightly homes. There is not a shack in Temple City. Every home owner takes pride in the appearance of his property.

TEMPLE CITY CHAMBER OF COMMERCE BROCHURE, 1928,
COURTESY OF THE HOMESTEAD MUSEUM, CITY OF INDUSTRY, CALIFORNIA

Further, there were several other problems that were evident from the Townsite Company's minute book. For example, a contract was drawn up with contractors Thomas and James McAnulty for general building projects in the town, but the McAnultys got into debt and were unable to fulfill their obligations. Ultimately, the Townsite Company assumed this debt and the responsibility to complete the McAnultys' projects. From early on in the project, loans were taken out with Los Angeles banks, which appear to be indicators of a lack of ready capital from the Townsite Company partners for unforeseen expenses.

Another problem was that sales agents Byron Marsh and Douglas Coughran, who were hired when the project started, had not sold the townsite lots as required in their one year contract when it expired in June 1924. An extension of six months was given, but George Woodruff reported "no lots have been sold...and that they have done nothing in the way of advertising...and have no plans under way or in course of preparation at this time for putting on a campaign for selling out the balance of the lots in the tract."

When the Townsite Company hired the Barry Realty Company in January 1925 to assume the responsibility of selling lots in the tract, the enterprise must have immediately gone wrong, as the contract was terminated less than six months later.

While the aforementioned bank loans totaled some $335,000 by mid-1925, it became readily apparent that financial matters required a much bigger form of relief. A special directors' meeting of the Townsite Company was called in December to establish a bonded indebtedness of $550,000. First mortgage sinking fund gold bonds, 500 of them at $1,000 each and 100 at $500 each, bearing the date of 1 January 1926 and due on 1 January 1936, were issued by the California Trust Company in Los Angeles. These bonds, filed with the state of California in late January carried interest at 6.5% payable semi-annually with the collateral naturally being the property held by the Townsite Company in the Town of Temple.[76] Although the over half-million dollars would provide capital for continuing the development of the townsite, it also put the company into a position of amassing significant debt if matters did not improve.

In fact, matters did not improve in the later 1920s, as the seemingly unstoppable real estate market in the Los Angeles region began to falter. It was another boom period, much as the 1870s had lured Walter Temple's father F.P.F. Temple and grandfather William Workman into a similar rush to development that overextended their resources. In the matter of a few short years, between the summer of 1921 and the spring of 1927, Walter Temple had established his own town and entirely or partially paid for the construction of eleven buildings in Los Angeles, Alhambra, San Gabriel, and El Monte, including two eleven-story office towers, a four-story office building, two movie theaters, and three post office buildings. The amount of money expended to complete these projects would have to be matched by the profits realized by oil well royalties, building occupancy and rental income. Before much of these latter funds had been received, Temple and his associates, specifically Milton Kauffman, had moved on to other projects. Furthermore, Temple's investments in oil had expanded from the Montebello lease to projects in Huntington Beach, Ventura, Whittier, Texas, and Mexico, none of which came anywhere near the productivity of the former.

---

76 Minute Book, Temple Townsite Company. Unfortunately, records from fall 1926 to fall 1929 are missing from the book.

In fact, by the spring of 1926, before work began on the four-story Edison Building in Alhambra and as *La Casa Nueva* was still under construction, Walter Temple was mortgaging his land holdings to Farmers and Merchants Bank, presided over by fellow Alhambran Jackson Graves, and California Bank's California Trust Company.[77] A surviving personal financial statement at year-end 1926 revealed that, though Temple's listed assets were in excess of $2.3 million, only $4,468.51 was in cash. The remainder, including $1.5 million in real estate parcels, leaseholds, and improvements (much of which was subject to the abovementioned mortgages), over $350,000 in mortgages and notes receivable, and more than $275,000 in stocks and bonds, were subject to the fluctuations of the market and the ability of debtors to pay, if it came down to sale and foreclosure. Meanwhile, there were $729,000 in liabilities, including $235,000 in notes payable on the mortgages, nearly $100,000 in contract payments ($94,000 of which was to the contractors of the Edison Building), and $365,000 in bonds and interest payable.[78] Almost exactly fifty years after the failure of the Temple and Workman bank, the family was again experiencing financial difficulties and in eerily similar circumstances.

In addition to his business and personal expenses, Temple also poured large sums of money into philanthropic endeavors, the earliest of which was the commission of a monument to partner Milton Kauffman's brother, Joseph, who was killed in France in the First World War.[79] Said at the time to be the first privately funded memorial after the Great War, the cenotaph originally stood at the Temple oil lease in Montebello and was flanked by two cannons, evidently used at the Battle of Los Angeles fought nearby in 1847, at which Temple's grandfather Workman had such a key role.[80] Added to this site, in the summer of 1922, was a granite marker commemorating the sesquicentennial of the founding of the Mission San Gabriel, which was established in 1771 in the Whittier Narrows area.[81] Temple's donation of a flag pole to the La Puente School, which was established on an acre donated, in 1868, by his father, was followed by the naming of the school and district after the family.[82] In San

77 Walker's Manual of Pacific Coast Securities, 1926, p. 796 and 1930, p. 768. See also tax assessment listings for Temple's various properties, 1926-1933, copies from the Los Angeles County Archives in the Homestead Museum Research Archives.

78 *Financial Statement of Temple Estate Company as of 31 December 1926.*

79 "Shaft Dedicated to Local War Hero," Alhambra *News*, 15 July 1919.

80 The war memorial was moved to Temple City Park, where the cenotaph and one of the cannon still are located.

81 "Tablet Marks First Site of San Gabriel," Alhambra *Advocate*, 5 August 1921.

82 La Puente School District to Los Angeles County Board of Supervisors, *Petition for District Name Change to Temple School District*, 9 February 1921. Ralph and Carole Temple Collection. Copy in the Homestead Museum Research Archives.

Gabriel, Temple was an enthusiastic supporter of John Steven McGroarty's "The Mission Play" and was a generous contributor to the building of the Mission Playhouse, now the San Gabriel Civic Auditorium.[83]

Through such a variety of investment and charitable projects, Temple had

EDISON BUILDING, ALHAMBRA, CIRCA 1927
SECURITY PACIFIC COLLECTION/LOS ANGELES PUBLIC LIBRARY

committed himself to a long-term dependence on the boom to realize the potential for recouping the money he expended. Some of the attempts to deal with the mounting debt incurred by Temple and his companies are known. In May 1926, at the same time as was done for the Temple Townsite Company, the Temple Estate Company filed a certificate of bonded indebtedness, creating $350,000 worth of bonds to be paid off incrementally in larger amounts over fifteen years, with the final redemption of the bonds to come in 1941 with a $125,000 payment.[84]

Two years later, in April 1928, Temple's lawyer, George Woodruff, wrote him with a detailed outline of a plan recommended to attempt to save the Workman Homestead and half of the oil lease at Montebello. The agreement would provide Temple a monthly allowance of $1,000 until the sale of

83 "Oil Man Buys Mission Play House Stock," Los Angeles *Times*, 4 July 1926; "Walter Temple Invests $15,000 in Mission Play Stock", Alhambra *Post-Advocate*, 5 July 1926. Temple purchased $15,000 in stock in the summer of 1926, even though he had only recently begun mortgaging many of his holdings. He and capitalist Henry E. Huntington, also a donor of $15,000, were the largest invid/idual donors to the project. The playhouse is still in operation as the San Gabriel Civic Auditorium.
84 Temple Estate Company, *Certificate of Bonded Indebtedness*, 26 May 1926, California State Archives, copy courtesy of Dr. Kaye Briegel.

TEMPLE FAMILY, 1926

COURTESY OF THE TEMPLE FAMILY COLLECTION

the properties of the Temple Estate Company and Temple Townsite Company could be executed. Woodruff admonished Temple to remember that any sales of Temple's holdings as part of the plan "would only afford temporary relief and you would still have no assurance of being able to save the Montebello Oil Property or the Workman Homestead Ranch."[85] Two months earlier, the Temple Townsite Company assigned the management of the town to the Davis-Baker Company, a firm which managed a large subdivision in Pasadena.[86] Still matters continued to worsen as some of Woodruff's plan seems to have been followed. In early June 1929, the Temple Estate Company filed a certificate to increase its bonded indebtedness from the $350,000 created three years earlier to $550,000. These bonds were due and payable on 1 June 1934.[87] The sale, however, in early July of the Edison Building and Temple Theater in Alhambra for some $425,000 was not enough to bring relief.[88] Woodruff,

85 George H. Woodruff to Walter Temple, 5 April 1928. Ralph and Carole Temple Collection. Copy in the Homestead Museum Research Archives.
86 "Davis-Baker Co. Will Handle Local Tract", Temple *Times*, 12 January 1928.
87 Temple Estate Company, *Certificate of Increase of Bonded Indebtedness*, 8 June 1929, California State Archives, copy courtesy of Dr. Kaye Briegel.
88 "Alhambra Property Sale Made", Los Angeles *Times*, 7 July 1929.

writing to Temple in September 1929, described in blunt terms the situation: "The Temple Estate Company is struggling from day to day to take care of interest and other carrying charges and operating expenses. . .You will have to impress upon all of the members of the family that the financial affairs of the company are now in such shape that the strictest economy must be practiced by every one."[89] Six weeks later, on 29 October, the mortgage taken out with Farmers and Merchants Bank on the Homestead was due. This occured days after the crash of the stock market that signaled the beginning of the Great Depression.

MISSION PLAYHOUSE, NOW SAN GABRIEL CIVIC AUDITORIUM, CIRCA 1927
SECURITY PACIFIC COLLECTION/LOS ANGELES PUBLIC LIBRARY

By 1930, it was evident that matters were irreversible when it came to Temple City. At the 3 February 1930 stockholders' meeting, the distribution of stock showed a marked change from the earlier years of the townsite's development, when the four principals, Temple, Kauffman, Woodruff, and Dupuy, had equal shares. Now, the Temple Estate Company was the majority owner, at 3,750 shares, while Kauffman held 1,226. Clyde Shoemaker,

---

89 George H. Woodruff to Walter Temple, 12 September 1929. Ralph and Carole Temple Collection. Copy in the Homestead Museum Research Archives.

George Woodruff's law firm partner, had 25 shares, while Dolores Bingham, Dupuy, Temple, and Woodruff each had only one share.[90]

In late May 1930, the Temple Townsite Company sold off its remaining interests in Temple City to a new concern, the Temple City Company.[91] A month later, the Temple Estate Company made out its last mortgage on the year's walnut crop at the Workman Homestead.[92] A statement of the affairs of the Temple Estate Company was made in July giving an idea of the strained financial circumstances of the Temples.[93] In the spring of 1930 the Temples vacated the Workman Homestead property and Walter Temple moved to Ensenada in Baja California, Mexico.[94]

Temple spent several years in quiet retirement in Ensenada and Tijuana as well as in San Diego, occasionally writing letters to his children on old Workman Homestead stationery with the address crossed out. There was a lease arranged through the Temple Estate Company to a military academy for the use of the Workman Homestead, and the company maintained offices in Los Angeles until the middle part of the decade, while the Temple Townsite Company continued to hold meetings through at least October 1931.[95] But by 1932, as the Great Depression began in earnest with bank failures throughout the country, there was no relief for the fortunes of Temple and his drastically reduced holdings, and the Homestead lease to the military academy passed to California Bank. Again, the Workman and Temple families had lost their financial fortunes, and, for the third time, the Workman Homestead property slipped from their grasp. In the mid-1930s, suffering from cancer, Temple returned to southern California, living his last years in the Lincoln Heights home of family friends. Surrounded by his children, he died on 13 November 1938, only a few days before the marriage of his son Thomas, and was buried in a simply marked plot at the Mission San Gabriel cemetery.[96]

90 Minute Book, Temple Townsite Company, 3 February 1930 (p. 148)
91 "Temple Townsite Sells to Coughran and Others", Temple *Times,* 30 May 1930. Douglas D. Coughran had been a partner of the original firm to sell lots in the townsite. Curiously, there is no record of this in the Townsite Company minute book.
92 Temple Estate Company to California Bank, *Mortgage of Walnut Crop at the Workman Homestead*, 25 July 1930, Book 10148: 219, Los Angeles County Archives.
93 *Statement of Property Owned by the Temple Estate Company*, 15 July 1930. Copy in the Homestead Museum Research Archives
94 Thomas W. Temple II to Walter P. Temple, 4 May 1930, Ruth Ann Temple Michaelis Collection and George H. Woodruff to Walter P. Temple, 15 August 1930. Ralph and Carol Temple Collection. Copies in the Homestead Museum Research Archives.
95 *Statement of Property Owned by the Temple Estate Company*, 15 July 1930. See various Los Angeles city directories for the period 1930 through 1936 and the Minute Book, Temple Townsite Company.
96 Alhambra *Post-Advocate*, 14 November and 17 November 1938; Pasadena *Star-News*, 17 November 1938.

Walter Temple's story makes for an appropriate and fascinating study of 1920s southern California. Born at the beginning of Los Angeles' first sustained growth boom, during which his father served as a principal booster, Temple's childhood was one of financial uncertainty after the failure of the Temple and Workman bank. Catapulted into sudden wealth by the discovery of oil on land he bought that had once belonged to his father, Temple sought to reestablish his family to prominence through real estate and construction investments and philanthropic endeavors. His enthusiasm and eagerness were characteristic of the boom mentality that pervaded southern California in the Roaring 'Twenties, and he was but one of many whose ambitions fell short.

Temple's legacy remains even now, in attractive and well-designed office buildings, in the carefully planned and developed townsite, known today as Temple City, and in his home, *La Casa Nueva*, the beautifully realized tribute to his family now part of an historic site museum dedicated to interpreting the story of Temple and his grandfather William Workman as participants in many important events in the history of southern California.

Fittingly, on June 7, 2002, the 133rd anniversary of his birth and sixty-four years after the California Bank denied the Temples their request to bury him in the mausoleum Temple erected in *El Campo Santo*, he was reinterred in the family plot behind the mausoleum, just behind the gravemarker of his son, Walter Jr. and his wife Nellie Didier. In the 1920s, it was Temple's custom to welcome his guest with a short, but heartfelt "Welcome to the Homestead!" His return to the Homestead allowed his descendants to say to Temple, "Welcome back to the Homestead!

❧ BIBLIOGRAPHY ❧

❧ *Books* ❧

Alhambra City Directories (including El Monte, San Gabriel, and Temple City), 1920-1930, various publishers.

Bancroft, Hubert Howe. *History of California.* 7 vols. Santa Barbara: Wallace Hebberd, 1966.

-------. *California Pioneer Register and Index.* Baltimore: Regional Publishing Company, 1964.

Batman, Richard. *The Personal Narrative of James Ohio Pattie.* Reprint ed. Missoula, Mont.: Mountain Press Publishing Company, 1988.

Beard, Henry. *In the Matter of the Application of John Rowland and William Workman for the Patent to the Rancho La Puente.* Washington, D.C.: Gibson Brothers, 1866.

Bell, Horace. *Reminiscences of a Ranger.* Santa Barbara, Ca.: Wallace Hebberd, 1927.

-------. *On The Old West Coast.* New York: Grosset and Dunlap, 1930.

Bowman, Jacob N. *Index of the Spanish-Mexican Land Grant Records and Cases of California.* Berkeley: The Bancroft Library, 1941.

Boyd, William Harland. *A California Middle Border.* Richardson, Tx.: The Havilah Press, 1972.

Bryant, Edwin. *What I Saw in California.* Minneapolis: Ross and Haines, Inc., 1967.

Busch, Briton Cooper, ed. *Alta California, 1840-42: The Journal and Observations of William Dane Phelps.* Glendale, Ca.: The Arthur H. Clark Company, 1983.

Centennial History of Lexington Lodge No. 104 F & A.M. El Monte: Lexington Lodge No. 104 F & A.M., 1955.

Chavez, Thomas E. *Manuel Alvarez, 1794-1856: A Southwestern Biography.* Niwot, Co.: University Press of Colorado, 1990.

Cleland, Robert G. *Pathfinders.* Los Angeles: Powell Publishing Company, 1929. Appendix, "The Narrative of Benjamin D. Wilson" [1877].

-------. *Cattle on a Thousand Hills.* 5th ed. San Marino, Ca.: The Huntington Library, 1975.

Cleland, Robert G. and Frank E. Putnam. *Isaias W. Hellman and the Farmers and Merchants Bank.* San Marino, Ca.: The Huntington Library, 1965.

Colton, Walter. *Three Years in California.* Reprint ed. New York: Arno Press, 1976.

Craver, Rebecca McDowell. *The Impact of Intimacy: Mexican-Anglo Intermarriage in New Mexico, 1821-1846.* El Paso: Texas Western Press, 1982.

Crowe, Earle. *Men of El Tejon.* Los Angeles: The Ward Ritchie Press, 1957.

Dana, Richard Henry. *Two Years Before the Mast.* John H. Kemble, ed. 2 vols. Los Angeles: The Ward Ritchie Press 1964.

Eaton, Lilley. *Genealogical History of the Town of Reading, Massachusetts.* Reprint ed. Bowie, Md.: Heritage Books, Inc., 1994.

Englehardt, Zephyrin, O.F.M. *San Gabriel Mission and the Beginning of Los Angeles.* San Gabriel, Ca.: Mission San Gabriel, 1927.

Engstrand, Iris Higbie [Wilson]. *William Wolfskill, 1798-1866.* Glendale: The Arthur H. Clark Company, 1965.

Farnham, Thomas Jefferson. *Life, Adventures, and Travels in California.* New York: Nafis and Cornish, 1849.

The First Los Angeles City and County Directory, 1872. Los Angeles: Ward Ritchie Press, 1963.

Frost, John. *Frost's Pictorial History of California.* Auburn, N.Y.: Derby and Miller, 1850.

Grant, Blanche C. *Kit Carson's Own Story of His Life.* Taos, N.M.: Blanche C. Grant, 1926.

Graves, Jackson A. *My Seventy Years in California.* Los Angeles: Times-Mirror Press, 1927.

Guinn, James M. *A History of California and an Extended History of the Southern Coast Counties.* Los Angeles: Historic Record Company, 1907.

Gulick, Charles A., ed. *The Papers of Mirabeau Bonaparte Lamar.* 6 vols. Austin, Tx.: Texas State Library, 1968.

Hafen, LeRoy and Ann. *The Old Spanish Trail.* Lincoln, Neb.: University of Nebraska Press, 1993.

Hall, William H. *Irrigation in [Southern] California.* Sacramento: State Printing Office, 1888.

Hammond, George P., ed. *The Larkin Papers.* 9 vols. Berkeley: University of California Press, 1951.

Harlow, Neal. *California Conquered.* Paperback ed. Berkeley: University of California Press, 1989.

Historical Review of Los Angeles Lodge No. 42, F & A.M. Los Angeles: Los Angeles Lodge No. 42, F & A.M., 1929.

Hunt, Rockwell N., ed. *California and Californians.* Chicago: Lewis Publishing Company, 1926.

An Illustrated History of Los Angeles County. Chicago: Lewis Publishing Company, 1889.

King, William F. *The San Gabriel Valley: Chronicles of an Abundant Land.* Northridge, Ca.: Windsor Publications, 1990.

Krythe, Maymie. *Port Admiral: Phineas Banning, 1830-1885.* San Francisco: California Historical Society, 1957.

Kuykendall, Ralph S. *The Hawaiian Kingdom.* Vol. 1, *Foundation and Transformation, 1778-1854.* Fifth Ed. Honolulu: University of Hawaii, 1976.

Los Angeles City and County Directories, 1873-1942, various publishers.

McGroarty, John Steven. *Los Angeles: From the Mountains to the Sea.* Chicago: The American Historical Society, 1921.

Miller, Henry. *California Missions.* Santa Barbara, Ca.: Bellerophon Books, 1983.

Myers, William A. *Ranches to Residences: The Story of Sunny Slope Water Company.* Pasadena, Ca.: Sunny Slope Water Company, 1994.

Nadeau, Remi. *City Makers.* Corona Del Mar, Ca.: Trans-Anglo Books, 1965.

Newmark, Harris. *Sixty Years in Southern California.* Edited by Maurice H. Newmark and Marco R. Newmark. New York: Knickerbocker Press, 1926.

Nunis, Doyce B., Jr., ed. *The California Diary of Faxon Dean Atherton, 1836-1839.* San Francisco: California Historical Society, 1964.

-------. *The Bidwell-Bartleson Party: 1841 California Emigrant Adventure.* Santa Cruz, Ca.: Western Tanager Press, 1991.

O'Flaherty, Joseph. *Those Powerful Years: The South Coast and Los Angeles, 1887-1917.* Hickville, N.Y.: Exposition Press, 1978.

Opitz, Glenn B., ed. *Mantle Fielding's Directory of American Painters, Sculptors, and Engravers.* 2nd ed. Poughkeepsie, N.Y.: Apollo, 1986.

Penniou, Ernest P. and Sidney S. Greenleaf. *A Directory of California Wine Growers and Wine Makers in 1860.* Berkeley: Tamalpais Press, 1967.

Pico, Pio. *Historical Narrative.* Arthur Botello, trans. and Martin Cole and Henry Welcome, eds. Glendale, Ca.: The Arthur H. Clark Company, 1973.

Powell, Dan and Janet. *La Puente Valley--Past and Present.* La Puente, Ca.: La Puente Chamber of Commerce, 1958.

Robinson, W.W. *Land in California.* 2nd ed. Berkeley: University of California Press, 1979.

Rowland, Leonore. *The Romance of La Puente Rancho.* Covina, Ca.: Neilson Press, 1958.

Shunk, James F. *Photographic Exhibits in California Land Cases from the Mexican Archives.* San Francisco: n.p., 1861.

Smith, Wallace E. *This Land Was Ours: The Del Valles and Camulos.* Ventura, Ca.: Ventura County Historical Society, 1977.

Spalding, William A., comp. *History and Reminiscences: Los Angeles City and County, California.* 3 vols., Los Angeles: J.R. Finnell and Sons Publishing Company, n.d. [1931.]

Starr, Kevin. *Material Dreams: Southern California through the 1920s.* New York: Oxford University Press, 1990.

Temple, Levi Daniel. *Some Temple Pedigrees: A Genealogy of the Known Descendants of Abraham Temple.* Boston: David Clapp and Son, 1900.

Temple, William Workman. *An Address to the American People.* Modesto, Ca.: J.C. Cavell, 1910.

-------. *The Mexican Revolution and American Public Opinion.* San Diego: A.H. Heath, 1911.

Truman, Benjamin C. *Semi-Tropical California.* San Francisco: A.L. Bancroft and Company, 1874.

Turner, Rebecca. *My Story.* Los Angeles: Typecraft, Inc., 1960.

Vander Leck, Lawrence. *Petroleum Resources of California.* California State Mining Bureau, Bulletin 89. San Francisco: California State Mining Bureau, 1921.

Vickery, Joyce. *Defending Eden.* Riverside: History Department, University of California, Riverside, 1977.

Vorspan, Max and Lloyd P. Gartner. *History of the Jews of Los Angeles.* San Marino, Ca.: The Huntington Library, 1970.

Walker's Manual of Pacific Coast Securities. San Francisco: Walker's Manual, Inc., 1928, 1930, 1933, 1934.

Warren, John Quincy Adams. *California Ranchos and Farms, 1846-1862.* Edited by Paul W. Gates. Madison: The State Historical Society of Wisconsin, 1967.

Weber, David J. *The Mexican Frontier, 1821-1846: The American Southwest Under Mexico*. Albuquerque: University of New Mexico Press, 1982.

White, David A. *News of the Plains and Rockies, 1803-1865*. 9 vols. Spokane, Wa.: The Arthur H. Clark Company, 1996–2001.

White, Gerald T. *Formative Years in the Far West: A History of Standard Oil Company of California and Predecessors Through 1919*. New York: Appleton-Century-Crofts, 1961.

White, Michael. *California All The Way Back to '28*. Los Angeles: Glen Dawson, 1956.

Wilson, John A., ed. *Thompson and West's History of Los Angeles County, California, 1880*. Berkeley: Howell-North, 1959.

Workman, Boyle. *The City That Grew*. Los Angeles: The Southland Publishing Company, 1935.

Wright, Doris Marion. *A Yankee in Mexican California: Abel Stearns, 1798-1848*. Santa Barbara: Wallace Hebberd, 1977.

✌ *Articles* ✌

Alexander, Sol. "Juan Temple and the Mint of Mexico", *Plus Ultra*, no. 116, (May 1973), pp. 3-5.

Ames, George Walcott, ed. "A Doctor Comes to California--The Diary of John S. Griffin, 1846-47", *California Historical Society Quarterly*, 21 (December 1942), pp. 333-357.

Barrows, Henry D. "Recollections of the Old Court House and Its Builder", *Historical Society of Southern California Annual for the Year 1894*, pp. 40-46.

Doyle, Billy H. "Lost Players--Princess Mona Darkfeather", *Classic Images*, no. 219 (September 1993), pp. 54-55.

Engh, Michael E. "Mary Julia Workman: The Catholic Conscience of Los Angeles", *California History*, 72 (Spring 1993), pp. 2-19.

Lawrence, Eleanor. "Mexican Trade between Santa Fe and Los Angeles", *California Historical Society Quarterly*, 10 (March 1931), pp. 27-39.

Layne, J. Gregg. "Annals of Los Angeles", *California Historical Society Quarterly*, 13 (December 1934), pp. 301-354.

-------. "First Census of the Los Angeles District", *Historical Society of Southern California Quarterly*, 18 (September 1936), pp. 81-145.

Newmark, Marco R. "The Life of Jonathan (John) Temple", *Historical Society of Southern California Quarterly*, 36: 1 (March 1954), pp. 46-50.

Robinson, W.W. "The Story of Ord's Survey", *Historical Society of Southern California Quarterly*, 19 (September-December 1937), pp. 121-131.

Weber, David J. "William Workman", in *The Mountain Men and the Fur Trade of the Far West*, edited by LeRoy Hafen and Ann Hafen. Vol. 7. Glendale, Ca.: The Arthur H. Clark Company, 1969, pp. 381-392.

Workman, William. "A Letter from Taos, 1826", David J. Weber, ed., *New Mexico Historical Review*, 41 (April 1966), pp. 155-164.

Workman, William Henry, "Reminiscences of My Coming to California", *Annual Report of the Pioneers of Los Angeles County, 1908-09*, 1909, pp. 6-11.

Yaari, Moshe, "The Merced Theater", *Historical Society of Southern California Quarterly*, 37 (September 1955), pp. 195-210.

"The Journal of Captain John Paty, 1807-1868", *California Historical Society Quarterly*, 14 (December 1935), pp. 291-346.

✌ *Unpublished Manuscripts* ✌

Foster, Stephen C., "Los Angeles from 1847-1849", Bancroft Library, University of California, Berkeley, 1877.

Given, Isaac, "A Pioneer of '41", Bancroft Library, University of California, Berkeley, no date.

Middleton, John, "William Gamble, M.D.U. of Pa., 1848, Ornithologist", Historical Society of Pennsylvania, no date.

Temple, Francis Pliny Fisk, "Recollections of Francis Pliny Fisk Temple", Bancroft Library, University of California, Berkeley, 1877.

Temple, Francis Workman, "How to Make Wine", no date, Homestead Museum Research Archives.

Temple, Thomas Workman II, "Don Juan Matias Sanchez and Rancho La Merced", 1959, Montebello Historical Society.

Temple, Walter Temple, jr., "Recollections of Family, Community, and Business Life", The Workman and Temple Family Homestead Museum Oral History Program, 1983.

----------------------------------, "An Oral History Interview of Walter P. Temple, jr.", The Workman and Temple Family Homestead Museum Oral History Program, 1988.

White, Michael, "California All The Way Back to '28", Bancroft Library, University of California, Berkeley, 1877.

✌ *Newspapers and Periodicals* ✌

Alhambra *Advocate*, 1919-1924.

Alhambra *News*, 1917-1922.

Alhambra *Post-Advocate*, 1924-1929.

Los Angeles *Express*, 1874-1876.

Los Angeles *Herald*, 1873-1876, 1886.

Los Angeles *La Cronica*, 1892.

Los Angeles *News*, 1860-1870.

Los Angeles *Southern Californian,* 1854-1855.

Los Angeles *Star*, 1851-1879

Los Angeles *Times*, 1883-1887, 1892, 1901, 1903, 1905, 1907, 1917-1929

Monterey Park (Ramona Acres) *Progress*, 1922-1923.

Pasadena *Star-News*, 1922-1923.

San Francisco *Daily Alta California*, 2 July 1865.

San Francisco *California Star*, 1847.

San Francisco *Evening Bulletin*, 27 July 1868.

Temple [City] *Times*, 1926-1930, 1941, 1961, 1967

The Oil Age, 1917-1922.

Whittier *News*, 1917-1920.

❧ *Collections* ❧

Bancroft Library, University of California, Berkeley (California land claims papers, Jenkins family papers on Alcatraz Island.)

Krebs, Conrad, private, Collection, private (family letters.)

La Puente Valley Historical Society Collection, La Puente (family material.)

Los Angeles City Archives, Los Angeles (City land deeds.)

Los Angeles County Archives, Los Angeles (Court and probate records) and Norwalk (Real Estate Records--deeds, tax assessments, maps, mortgages.)

Michaelis, Ruth Ann Temple, private, (family material.)

National Archives, Western Regional Center, Laguna Niguel (census, land claims, agricultural and industrial schedules.)

New Mexico State Archives, Santa Fe (family material.)

Rancho Los Cerritos Historic Site, Long Beach (family letters.)

Seaver Center for Western History Research, Natural History Museum of Los Angeles County, Los Angeles (tax assessments, articles of incorporation, cattle brand books.)

Temple, Ralph and Carole Collection, private, (family material.)

Temple, Thomas Workman II Collection, Homestead Museum, City of Industry, (family material.)

Temple, Walter P., Jr. Collection, private, (family material.)

Title Records Incorporated, Sun Valley, private, (land transactions.)

Worden, Perry Collection, Huntington Library, San Marino (family material.)

Workman, David A. Collection, private, (Alcatraz and San Clemente islands material.)

Workman Family Papers, Loyola Marymount University Special Collections, Los Angeles.

Workman and Temple Family Homestead Museum Research Archives.

❧ *Photographs* ❧

See publisher's thank-you page

❧ I N D E X ❧

Index

Lake Vineyard Land and Water Company 144, 183
Lake Vineyard subdivision, 1875-76 144, 183
Lambourn, Frederick (b. 1837) 115, 137, 138, 161
Larkin, Thomas O. 14, 17, 18, 19
Ledyard, Henry S. 142, 150, 163, 168, 169, 175, 179, 180, 183, 185
Lewis, Lawrence F. (owner, Workman Homestead, 1899-1907) 227
Los Angeles (California)
  boom of the late 1860s and early 1870s 127
Los Angeles, California 11, 13, 14, 15, 16, 17, 19, 20, 21, 22, 23, 24, 31, 34,
    41, 46, 47, 48, 49, 50, 51, 52, 53, 54, 56, 57, 60, 64, 66, 67, 68, 69, 70,
    71, 72, 73, 74, 75, 76, 77, 78, 79, 80, 81, 82, 83, 84, 87, 88, 89, 90, 91,
    92, 93, 94, 96, 98, 101, 102, 103, 105, 106, 107, 108, 109, 110, 111,
    112, 115, 118, 119, 120, 121, 122, 123, 124, 125, 127, 129, 130, 131,
    133, 134, 135, 136, 137, 138, 139, 140, 141, 142, 143, 144, 145, 146,
    147, 148, 149, 150, 151, 152, 154, 155, 156, 158, 159, 160, 161, 163,
    164, 165, 166, 167, 168, 169, 170, 171, 172, 173, 174, 175, 177, 178,
    179, 180, 181, 182, 184, 185, 186, 187, 188, 191, 192, 193, 194, 195,
    196, 197, 198, 199, 200, 201, 202, 203, 204, 205, 206, 207, 208, 209,
    210, 211, 212, 213, 214, 215, 216, 217, 219, 220, 221, 222, 226, 227,
    228, 229, 230, 231, 234, 235, 236, 237, 238, 239, 242, 243, 244, 245,
    247, 248
Los Angeles and Independence Railroad Company 154, 155, 156, 157, 158,
    183
Los Angeles and Mexican Land Company 196
Los Angeles and Pacific Railroad Company 144, 154
Los Angeles Aqueduct 177, 210
Los Angeles Central Public Library (1926) 219, 234
Los Angeles City Hall (1928) 146, 219, 237
Los Angeles Memorial Coliseum 219

ᐉᔈ M ᐉᔈ

Mexican-American War, 1846-48 76
Mexican National Mint 96
Miller, Henry 112, 114, 116
  architect of St. Nicholas' Chapel 116

Index

❧ THE ❧
❧ PUBLISHER THANKS ❧

The publisher wishes to thank author Paul Spitzzeri for his well-researched contribution to southern California history, his signing on with Seligson Publishing and for the many long hours of editing he put in, in addition to his regular duties as the curator of the Homestead Museum. I also owe a debt of gratitude to editors Lisa Hall, Laura Coggins and Julia Begert and artist Chris Flynn for their invaluable editing and artistry skills. Additionally, I would like to thank the individuals and institutions listed below for allowing their photos to be used in this work.

Dara Jones
President, Seligson Publishing Inc.

Cover Photographs

Francisco Pliny Fisk Temple and
Antonia Margarita Workman de Temple
Courtesy of the Seaver Center for Western History Research,
Los Angeles County Museum of Natural History

Temple Block
Courtesy of the Seaver Center for Western History Research,
Los Angeles County Museum of Natural History

☙ *Chapter One* ☙

Jonathan Temple circa 1855—page 12
Security Pacific Collection/Los Angeles Public Library

William Workman & his daughter,
Antonia Margarita Workman de Temple, circa 1852—page 33

Courtesy of the Homestead Museum, City of Industry, California

ᕗ *Chapter Two* ᕗ

David Alexander & William Workman, 1851,
Photograph attributed to Mathew B. Brady—page 61
Courtesy of Thomas E. Temple

Manuel Micheltorena and Pio Pico—page 70
Courtesy of the Bancroft Library,
University of California, Berkeley, California

Robert Field Stockton—page 78
Courtesy of Bancroft Library,
University of California, Berkeley, California

ᕗ *Chapter Three* ᕗ

Market House, circa 1870—page 93
Security Pacific Collection/Los Angeles Public Library

Temple Adobe—page 98
Rancho La Merced, circa 1870
Courtesy of Philip Nathanson

Map of Rancho La Puente, 1867–68—page 99
Courtesy of the Homestead Museum, City of Industry, California

John Rowland, Charlotte Gray Rowland
and unidentified child, circa 1860—page 104
Courtesy of La Puente Valley Historical Society

✑ *Chapter Four* ✑

❧ *Chapter Five* ❧

❧ *Chapter Six* ❧

Walter and Laura Temple family circa 1919—page 220
Courtesy of the Seaver Center for Western History Research,
Los Angeles County Museum of Natural History

Temple Oil Lease, Montebello, California—page 224
Courtesy of the Homestead Museum, City of Industry, California

Temples at barbeque celebrating first oil well—page 225
Basye Adobe, July 1917,
Courtesy of the Homestead Museum, City of Industry, California

El Campo Santo Cemetery 1920's—page 229
Courtesy of the Homestead Museum, City of Industry, California

La Casa Nueva, circa 1928—page 232
Courtesy of the Homestead Museum, City of Industry, California

Temple Theatre, Alhambra, circa 1927—page 236
Security Pacific Collection/Los Angeles Public Library

Town of Temple, circa 1924—page 240
Security Pacific Collection/Los Angeles Public Library

Temple City Chamber of Commerce brochure, 1928—page 241
Courtesy of the Homestead Museum, City of Industry, California

Edison Building—page 244
Security Pacific Collection/Los Angeles Public Library

Temple Family 1926—page 245
Courtesy of The Temple Family Collection

Mission Playhouse,
now San Gabriel Civic Auditorium, circa 1927—page 246
Security Pacific Collection/Los Angeles Public Library

❧ NOTES ❧

1437231